TWENTY F
SCI

C000318711

GCSE Science
Foundation

Project Directors

Jenifer Burden   Andrew Hunt

John Holman   Robin Millar

Project Officers

Peter Campbell   John Lazonby

Angela Hall   Peter Nicolson

Course Editors

Jenifer Burden   Andrew Hunt

Peter Campbell   Robin Millar

Authors

David Brodie	Ann Fullick	John Lazonby	Cliff Porter
Jenifer Burden	Anna Grayson	Jean Martin	David Sang
Peter Campbell	John Holman	Robin Millar	Charles Tracy
Anne Daniels	Andrew Hunt	Peter Nicolson	Jane Wilson

RECOGNISING ACHIEVEMENT

Curriculum Centre

THE UNIVERSITY of York

OXFORD

Contents

Introduction

Welcome to *Twenty First Century Science*

Everyday life has many questions science can help to answer.
These may be questions about:

- who we are: for example, the history of planet Earth
- personal choices: for example, how healthy our lifestyles are
- how we use scientific knowledge: for example, controlling air pollution

TV, radio, newspapers, and the Internet are full of scientific information.
But it's not always reliable. Often, facts are mixed with opinions, and there are different points of view.

GCSE Science is a course for everyone. You will learn about some of the most important **Science explanations**. These can help you make sense of the world around you. You will also learn about how science works. In this course it is called **Ideas about science**. You will develop skills to help you:

- weigh up evidence on both sides of an argument
- make decisions about science issues that affect you

By the end of this course you will be more confident about dealing with the science you meet everyday.

How to use this book

Introduction Each Module has two introduction pages. They tell you the main ideas you will study.

Why study your genes?
Why it is useful to know about this topic.

The science
The scientific information you will learn about in this chapter.

Ideas about science
What you will learn from this chapter about how science works.

Find out about
Questions this chapter answers, and ideas it explores.

Why study genes?
What makes me the way that I am? Your ancestors probably asked the same question. How are features passed on from parents to children? You may look like your relatives, but you are unique. Only in the last few generations has science been able to answer questions like these.

The science
Your environment has a huge effect on you, for example, on your appearance, your body, and your health. But these features are also affected by your genes. In this Module you'll find out how. You'll discover the story of inheritance.

Ideas about science
In the future, science could help you to change your baby's genes before it is born. Cloned embryos could donate cells to cure diseases. But, as new technologies are developed we must decide how they should be used. These can be questions of ethics – decisions about what is right and wrong.

B1

You and your genes

Find out about:
- how do genes and your environment make you unique
- how and why do people find out about their genes
- how can we use our knowledge of genes
- should this be allowed

Nine Modules This book is divided into nine Modules. Each Module is about a different topic: three Modules look at Biology (B1 – B3), three at Chemistry (C1 – C3), and three at Physics (P1 – P3).

Each Module is split into Sections. Pages in a Section look like this:

Heading
Each section looks at a different part of the Module.

Find out about
The key points explored in the Section.

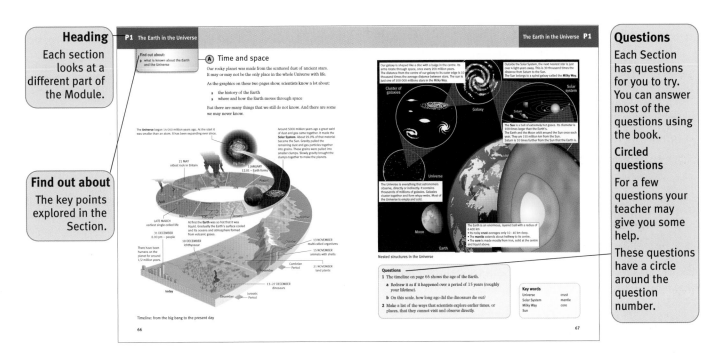

Questions
Each Section has questions for you to try. You can answer most of the questions using the book.

Circled questions
For a few questions your teacher may give you some help.

These questions have a circle around the question number.

Science explanations
A checklist of key points explained in this Module.

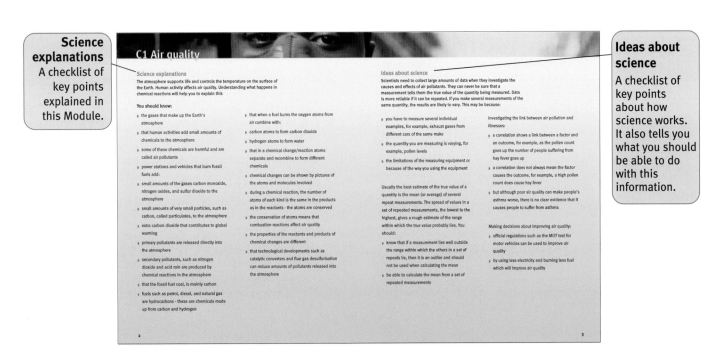

Ideas about science
A checklist of key points about how science works. It also tells you what you should be able to do with this information.

Contents/Index/Glossary If you want to find a particular area of science use the Contents and Index pages. You can also use the Glossary. This explains many of the scientific terms used in this book.

Internal assessment

Internal assessment: In *GCSE Science* your internal assessment counts for 33.3% of your total grade.

Marks are given for a Case Study and a Data Analysis task.

Your school or college may give you the marking schemes for this.
This will help you understand how to get the most credit for your work.

Internal assessment (33.3% of total marks)

Case Study (20%)

Everyday life has many questions science can help to answer. You may meet these in media reports, e.g. on television, radio, in newspapers, or magazines. A Case Study is a report which weighs up evidence about a scientific question.

You choose a topic from one of these categories:

- A question where the scientific knowledge is not certain. For example, 'Is there life in other parts of the Universe?', or 'Does using mobile phones cause brain damage?'

- A question about decision-making using scientific information. For example, 'Should cars be banned from a shopping street to reduce air pollution?', or 'Should the government stop research into human cloning?'

- A question about a personal issue involving science. For example, 'Should my child have the MMR vaccine?'

You should find out what different people have said about the issue. Then evaluate this information and make your own conclusion.

Selecting information:

- collect information from different places – books, the Internet, newspapers

- say where your information has come from

- choose only information that is relevant to the question you are studying

- decide how reliable each source of information is

Understanding the question:

- use scientific knowledge and understanding to explain the topic you are studying

- when you report what other people have said, say what scientific evidence they had (from experiments, surveys etc)

Making your own conclusion:

- compare different evidence and points of view

- consider the benefits and risks of different courses of action

- say what you think should be done, and link this to the evidence you have reported

Present your study:

- make sure your report is laid out clearly in a sensible order

- you may use different presentation styles, e.g. written report, newspaper article, PowerPoint presentation, poster, script for a radio programme or a play etc

- use pictures, tables, charts, graphs etc to present information

- take care with your spelling, grammar, punctuation, and use scientific terms where they are appropriate

Data Analysis (13.3%)

Scientists collect data from experiments and studies. They use this data to explain how something happens. You need to be able to assess the methods and data from scientific experiments,. This will help you can decide how reliable a scientific claim is.

A Data Analysis task is based on a practical experiment which you carry out. You may do this alone, or work in groups and pool all your data. Then you interpret and evaluate the data.

Interpreting data:

▶ present your data in tables, charts or graphs

▶ say what conclusions you can make from your data

▶ explain your conclusions using your science knowledge and understanding

Evaluation:

▶ look back at your experiment and say how you could improve the method

▶ explain how reliable your evidence is (have you got enough results? do they show a clear pattern? have you repeated measurements to check them?)

▶ suggest some improvements or extra data you could collect to be more confident in your conclusions

Creating a Case Study

Where do I start?

Sources of information could include:

▶ Internet
▶ school library
▶ your science textbook and notes
▶ local public library
▶ TV
▶ radio
▶ newspapers and magazines
▶ museums and exhibitions

Information can come from specific people or organisations.

You could:

▶ interview a scientist

▶ write a letter to an organisation

To get useful information from other people, make sure you have detailed questions beforehand.
Speak or write to them and explain who you are and what you are doing.
Make sure you ask for just the information you really need.

When will you do this work?

▶ Your Case Study may be done in class time.
▶ You may also do some research out of class.
▶ Your Data Analysis must be based on a practical you do in class.
▶ Your school or college will decide when you do your internal assessment. If you do more than one Case Study or Data Analysis, they will choose the best one for your marks.

Tip

The best advice is 'plan ahead'. Give your work the time it needs and work steadily and evenly over the time you are given. Your deadlines will come all too quickly, especially as you will have coursework to do in other subjects.

B1

Why study genes?

What makes me the way that I am?
Your ancestors probably asked the same
question. How are features passed on from
parents to children? You may look like your
relatives, but you are unique. Only in the last
few generations has science been able to
answer questions like these.

The science

Your environment has a huge effect on you, for
example, on your appearance, your body, and
your health. But these features are also
affected by your genes. In this Module you'll
find out how. You'll discover the story of
inheritance.

Ideas about science

In the future, science could help you to change
your baby's genes before it is born. Cloned
embryos could donate cells to cure diseases.
But, as new technologies are developed we
must decide how they should be used. These
can be questions of ethics – decisions about
what is right and wrong.

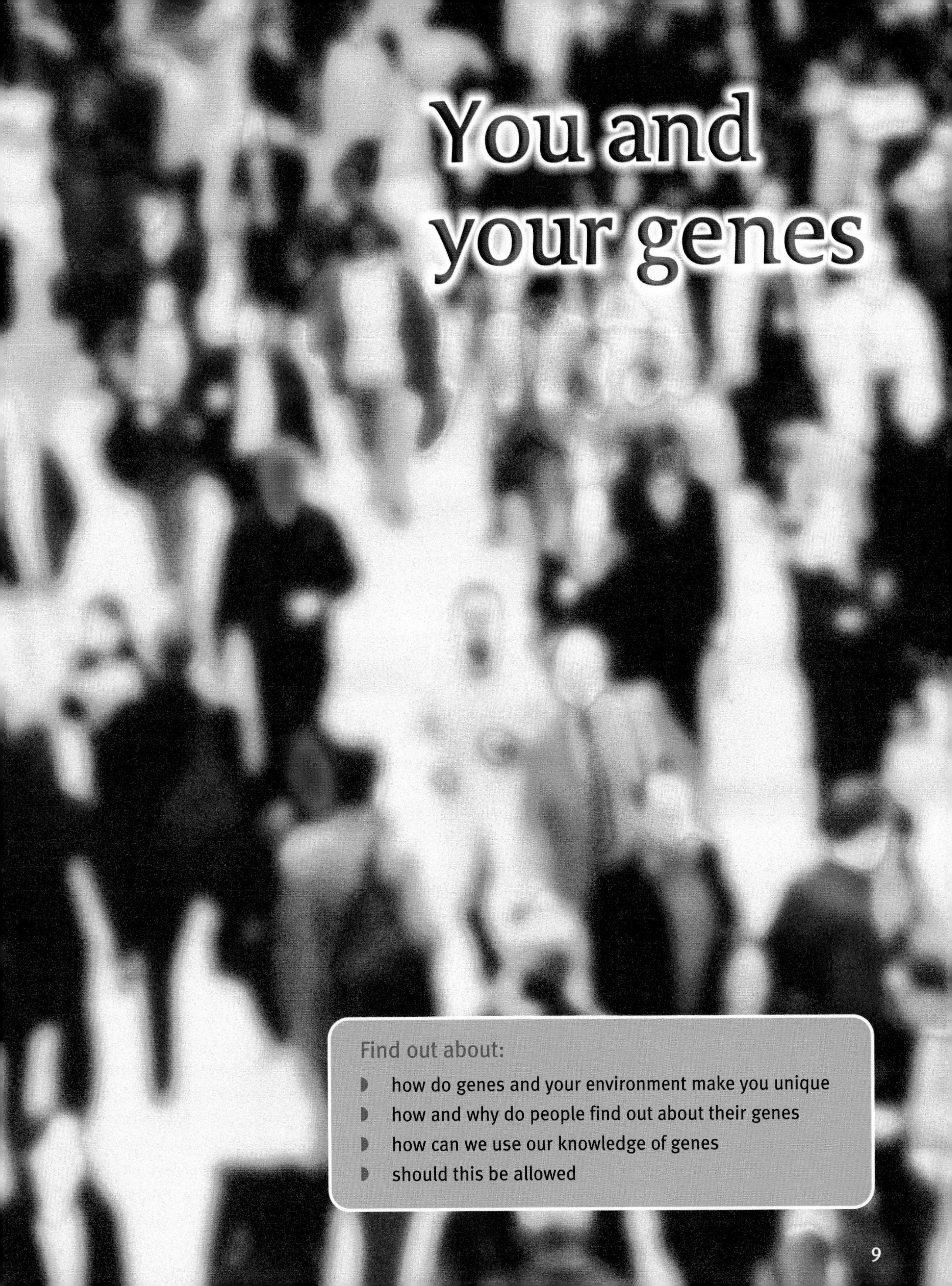

You and your genes

Find out about:

▶ how do genes and your environment make you unique
▶ how and why do people find out about their genes
▶ how can we use our knowledge of genes
▶ should this be allowed

Find out about:
▶ what makes us all different
▶ what genes are and what they do

Ⓐ The same and different

New plants and animals look a lot like their parents. They have **inherited** information from their parents. This information controls how they develop.

A lot of information goes into making a human being. So inheritance does a very big job pretty well. All people have most features in common. The differences between us are very, very small. But we're interested in them because they make us unique.

These sisters look like each other.

Environment makes a difference

Almost all of your features are affected by the information you got from your parents. For example, your eye colour depends on this information.

But most of your features are also affected by your **environment**. For example, your skin colour depends on inherited information. But if you spend more time in the sun, your skin will get darker.

Most features are affected by both the information you inherit and your environment.

Key words
inherited
environment

Questions

1 Choose two of the students in the photograph. Write down five ways they look different.

2 What two things affect how you develop?

3 Your eye colour depends on inherited information. Explain what is meant by inherited information.

Inheritance – where does it happen?

All living organisms are made up of cells. If you look at a cell under a microscope you can see the **nucleus**. The information to make you is in the nucleus of all your cells.

Inside the nucleus are long threads called **chromosomes**. Each chromosome is made up of thousands of **genes**. Genes control how you develop.

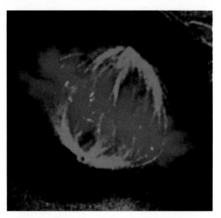

These cells have been stained to show up different parts. The long blue threads are the chromosomes. (Mag: × 6500 approx)

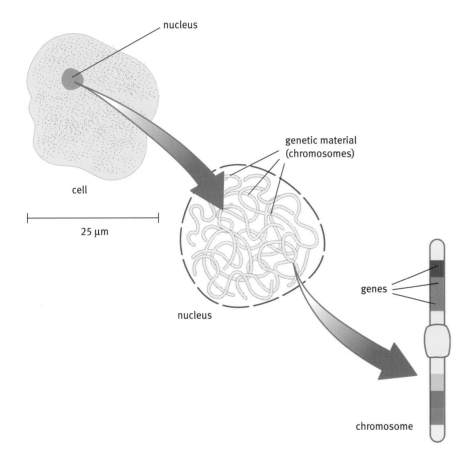

All the information needed to create a whole human being fits into the nucleus of a cell. The nucleus is just 0.006 mm across!

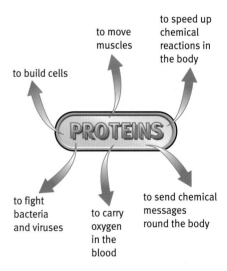

There are about 50 000 types of proteins in the human body.

How do genes control how you develop?

Genes are instructions for the cell. They tell the cell how to make **proteins**. Each gene is the instruction for making a different protein. Proteins are very important chemicals for cells.

Questions

4 Write these cell parts in order starting with the smallest:

chromosome, gene, cell, nucleus

Key words

nucleus   genes
chromosomes proteins

Find out about:
- how you inherit genes
- Huntington's disorder (an inherited illness)

B Family values

Have you inherited a feature you don't like? Maybe your dad's big ears or your mum's freckles. For some people, family likenesses are very serious.

Craig's story

My grandfather's only 56. He's always been well but now he's a bit off colour. He's been forgetting things – driving my Nan mad. No one's said anything to me, but they're all worried about him.

Robert's story

I'm so frustrated with myself. I can't sit still in a chair. I'm getting more and more forgetful. Now I've started falling over for no reason at all. The doctor has said it might be **Huntington's disorder**. It's an inherited condition. She said I can have a blood test to find out, but I'm very worried.

Craig and his grandfather, Robert

Huntington's disorder

Huntington's disorder is an inherited condition. You can't catch it. It is passed on from parents to their children. The symptoms of Huntington's disorder don't happen until middle age. The person has problems controlling their muscles. They get forgetful. They find it harder to understand things. After a few years, people with Huntington's disorder can't control their movements. Sadly, the condition is fatal.

Key words

Huntington's disorder

Questions

1 Look at the photos of Craig's family. Write down any features Craig looks like he's inherited.

2 Write down the symptoms of Huntington's disorder.

3 Explain why Huntington's disorder is called an inherited condition.

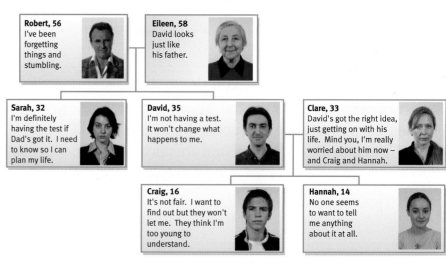

Robert, 56
I've been forgetting things and stumbling.

Eileen, 58
David looks just like his father.

Sarah, 32
I'm definitely having the test if Dad's got it. I need to know so I can plan my life.

David, 35
I'm not having a test. It won't change what happens to me.

Clare, 33
David's got the right idea, just getting on with his life. Mind you, I'm really worried about him now – and Craig and Hannah.

Craig, 16
It's not fair. I want to find out but they won't let me. They think I'm too young to understand.

Hannah, 14
No one seems to want to tell me anything about it at all.

Craig's family tree

Why don't brothers and sisters look the same?

Brothers and sisters are different because they each get a different mixture of genes from their parents. Except for identical twins, each one of us has a unique set of genes.

How many chromosomes does each cell have?

- Chromosomes in body cells come in pairs.
- Every human body cell has **23 pairs** of chromosomes.
- The chromosomes in each pair are the same size and shape.
- They carry the same genes in the same place.
- This means that your genes also come in pairs.
- Human beings have about 30 000 pairs of genes.

How did you inherit your genes?

Parents pass on genes in their **sex cells**. In animals these are sperm and egg cells. Sex cells have copies of half the parent's chromosomes. They only have one chromosome from every pair.

This means that a fertilized egg cell will have the right number of chromosomes – 23 pairs. One chromosome from each pair comes from the egg cell. The other comes from the sperm cell. So half of the new baby's genes are from the mother. Half are from the father.

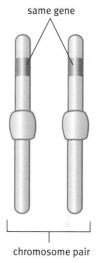

same gene

chromosome pair

These chromosomes are a pair.

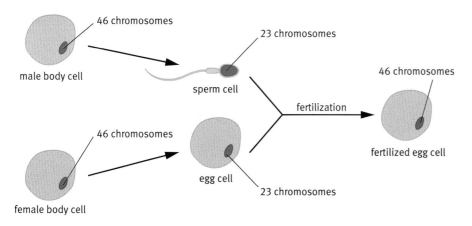

male body cell — 46 chromosomes

sperm cell — 23 chromosomes

female body cell — 46 chromosomes

egg cell — 23 chromosomes

fertilization

fertilized egg cell — 46 chromosomes

The cells in this diagram are not drawn to scale. A human egg cell is 0.1 mm across. This is 20 times larger than a human sperm cell.

> **Key words**
> 23 pairs
> sex cells

> **Questions**
>
> **4 a** Draw a diagram to show a sperm cell, an egg cell, and the fertilized egg cell they make.
>
>   **b** In each cell write down the number of chromosomes it has in the nucleus.
>
>   **c** Explain why the fertilized egg cell has pairs of chromosomes.
>
> **5** Explain why children may look a bit like each of their parents.

13

C The human lottery

Most of your features may be affected by your environment. Most are also affected by more than one gene. A few – like dimples – are controlled by just one gene. These are the easiest features to learn about.

Genes come in different versions

The diagrams on the left show pairs of chromosomes. They carry the genes that control dimples.

Genes in a pair may not be exactly the same. They may be slightly different versions. You can think about it like football strips – a team's home and away strips are both based on the same pattern, but they are slightly different. Different versions of the same genes are called **alleles**.

dimples

This person inherited a D allele from both parents. They have dimples.

Dominant alleles – they're in charge

The gene that controls dimples has two alleles. The D allele gives you dimples. The d allele won't cause dimples.

The D allele is **dominant**. You only need one copy of a dominant allele to have its feature. The d allele is **recessive**. You must have two copies of a recessive allele to have its feature.

no dimples

This person inherited a d allele from both parents. They don't have dimples.

Which alleles can a person inherit?

Sex cells get one chromosome from each pair the parent has.

dimples

This person inherited one D and one d allele. They have dimples.

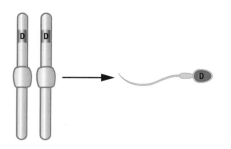

This man has two D alleles. This is all he can pass on to his children.

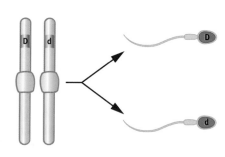

This man has one D and one d allele. Half of his sex cells get the D allele and half get the d allele.

We cannot predict which egg and sperm cells will meet at fertilization. The diagram shows the four possibilities for one couple.

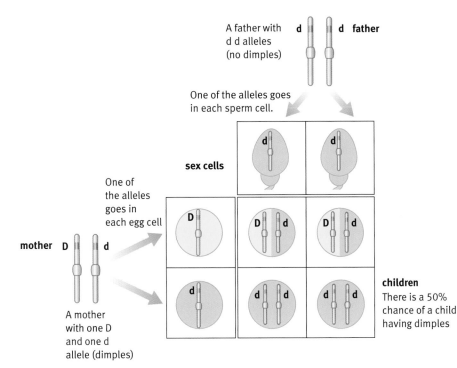

A father with d d alleles (no dimples)

d   d father

One of the alleles goes in each sperm cell.

sex cells

One of the alleles goes in each egg cell

mother D   d

A mother with one D and one d allele (dimples)

children
There is a 50% chance of a child having dimples

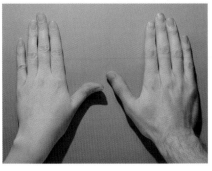

The allele that gives you straight thumbs is dominant (**S**). The allele for curved thumbs (**s**) is recessive.

The allele that gives you hair on the middle of your fingers is dominant (R). The allele for no hair is recessive (r).

What about Craig's family?

Huntington's disorder is caused by a dominant allele. You only need to inherit the allele from one parent to have the condition. Craig and Hannah's grandfather, Robert, have Huntington's disorder. So their dad, David, may have inherited this faulty allele. At the moment he has decided not to have the test to find out.

Key words

alleles   recessive
dominant

Questions

1 You inherit two of every gene. Explain why.

2 A gene may have different versions. What are diferent versions of a gene called?

3 Sam has alleles Dd for his dimples genes.

  a Does Sam have dimples?

  b Use the key words to explain your answer.

4 Would a person with these alleles have:

  a dd - dimples?

  b Ss - straight thumbs?

  c RR - hair on the middle of their finger?

5 Explain the difference between a dominant and a recessive allele.

Dear Clare,

Please help us. My husband and I have just been told that our baby has cystic fibrosis. Did I do something wrong during my pregnancy? I'm so worried.

Yours sincerely

Emma

Dear Emma,

What a difficult time for you all. First of all, nothing you did during your pregnancy could have affected this, so don't feel guilty. Cystic fibrosis is an inherited illness ...

Dear Doctor

We've had a huge postbag in response to last month's letter from Emma. So this month we're looking in depth at **cystic fibrosis**, *a disease which one in twenty-five of us carries in the UK …*

What is cystic fibrosis?

You can't catch cystic fibrosis. It's a genetic illness. So it's passed on from parents to their children.

Cells that make mucus in the body don't work properly. The mucus is too thick. It blocks the lungs and stops enzymes getting to the gut.

People with cystic fibrosis get breathless and have lots of chest infections. Their food isn't digested properly and they can be short of nutrients.

How do you get cystic fibrosis?

Babies with cystic fibrosis (CF) are usually born to healthy parents. But how can a healthy parent pass a disease on to their children?

There are two versions (or alleles) of the CF gene. One is dominant. It makes cells produce normal mucus. The other is a faulty recessive allele. It leads to CF.

So a person who has one normal allele and one faulty allele will not have CF. But they are a **carrier** of the faulty allele. They can pass it on to their child. If both parents do this, the child will have CF. One in every 25 people in the UK carries the CF allele.

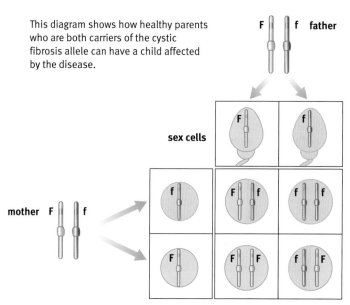

This diagram shows how healthy parents who are both carriers of the cystic fibrosis allele can have a child affected by the disease.

F   f   father

sex cells

mother F   f

children There is a 25% chance that a child from the carrier parents will have cystic fibrosis.

Can cystic fibrosis be cured?

Not yet. But treatments are getting better. Life expectancy is increasing all the time. Physiotherapy helps to clear mucus from the lungs. Sufferers take tablets with the missing gut enzymes in. Antibiotics are used to treat chest infections. Scientists hope to find a cure in the future.

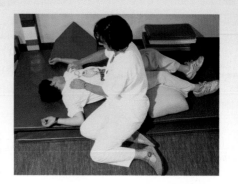

Tom has cystic fibrosis. He has physiotherapy every day to clear thick mucus from his lungs.

Can cystic fibrosis be prevented?

Yes, if a couple know they may have an ill child. But this involves a very hard decision for the parents. When the woman is pregnant, cells can be taken from the fetus. One way of getting the cells is by an amniocentesis test. Doctors look at the genes. If there are two alleles for cystic fibrosis, the child will have the disease.

The parents may choose to end the pregnancy. This is done with a medical operation called a **termination** (an abortion).

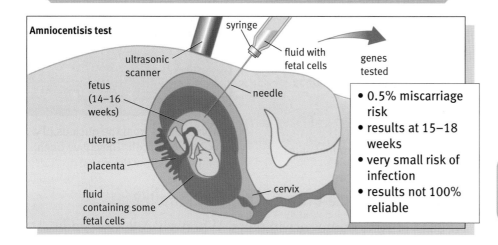

Amniocentisis test

- ultrasonic scanner
- syringe
- fluid with fetal cells
- genes tested
- fetus (14–16 weeks)
- needle
- uterus
- placenta
- cervix
- fluid containing some fetal cells

- 0.5% miscarriage risk
- results at 15–18 weeks
- very small risk of infection
- results not 100% reliable

Key words

cystic fibrosis   termination

carrier

Questions

6 The magazine doctor is sure that nothing Emma did caused her baby to have cystic fibrosis. How can she be so sure?

7 People with cystic fibrosis make thick, sticky mucus. Describe the health problems that this may cause.

8 Someone who is not a carrier or sufferer of CF has the alleles FF. What alleles does:

   a a sufferer have?

   b a carrier have?

9 Two carriers of cystic fibrosis want to have children. What is the chance that they will have:

   a a child with cystic fibrosis?

   b a child who is a carrier of cystic fibrosis?

   c a child who has no cystic fibrosis alleles?

Find out about:
▶ what makes a person male or female
▶ what hormones are

D Male or female?

Ever wondered what it would be like to be the opposite sex? Well, if you're male there was a time when you were – just for a short while. Male and female human embryos are very alike until they are six weeks old. Then their sex organs start to develop.

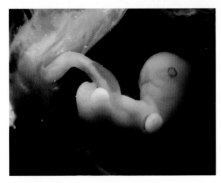

This embryo is six weeks old.

What decides an embryo's sex?

A fertilized human egg cell has 23 pairs of chromosomes. Pair 23 are the sex chromosomes. Males have an X chromosome and a Y chromosome – **XY**. Females have two X chromosomes – **XX**.

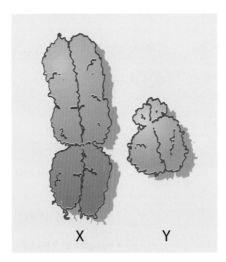

Women have two X chromosomes. Men have an X and a Y.

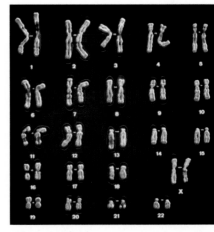

Chromosomes from the nucleus of a woman's body cell. They have been arranged to show the pairs.

What's the chance of being male or female?

Parents' chromosomes are in pairs. When sex cells are made they only get one chromosome from each pair. So half the sperm cells get an X chromosome and half get a Y chromosome. All egg cells get an X chromosome.

When a sperm cell fertilizes an egg cell the chances are 50% that it will be an X or a Y sperm. This means that there is a 50% chance that the baby will be a boy or a girl.

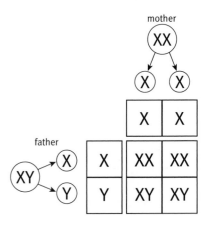

Questions

1 What sex chromosome(s) would be in the nucleus of:

   a a man's body cell

   b an egg cell

   c a woman's body cell

   d a sperm cell

2 Draw a diagram to show the chance of a baby being male or female.

How does the Y chromosome make a baby male?

The diagram shows a gene on the Y chromosome. This gene is the instruction to make a male sex **hormone**. This hormone causes the embryo to grow into a male. If this hormone is not made, the embryo is female.

Hormones are another group of proteins.

Different hormones control many things that happen in the body.

Jan's story

At eighteen Jan was studying at college in the US. She was very happy, and was going out with a college football player. She thought her periods hadn't started because she did a lot of sport.

Then in a science class Jan looked at the chromosomes in her cheek cells. She discovered that she had male sex chromosomes – XY.

Sometimes a person has X and Y chromosomes but looks female. This is because their body makes male sex hormone but the cells take no notice of it. About 1 in 20 000 people have this condition. They have small internal testes and a short vagina. They can't have children.

Jan had no idea she had this condition. She found it very difficult to come to terms with. But she has now told her boyfriend and they have stayed together.

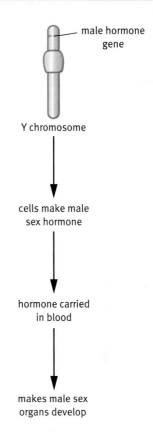

male hormone gene

Y chromosome

↓

cells make male sex hormone

↓

hormone carried in blood

↓

makes male sex organs develop

The male sex hormone causes an embryo to develop into a male.

Jan on holiday, aged eighteen.

Key words

XY   hormone
XX

Questions

3 Imagine you are Jan or her boyfriend. How would you have felt about her condition?

4 What are hormones?

5 How do hormones get around the body?

Find out about:
▶ how people make ethical decisions

E Ethics – making decisions

Elaine's nephew has cystic fibrosis. So Elaine and her husband Peter were worried about any children they might have. Tests showed that they were both carriers for cystic fibrosis.

Elaine and Peter decided to use genetic testing when Elaine was pregnant. Later on they had to make a very hard decision.

'We had genetic tests when I was pregnant,' says Elaine. 'Sadly we felt we had to terminate the first baby, because of CF. We are lucky now to have two healthy children. And we know we haven't got to watch them suffer.'

Not everyone would have made the same decision as Elaine and Peter.

Elaine and Peter had to decide what was the right or wrong way to behave. Deciding about right or wrong is called **ethics**.

Ethics – right or wrong

In some cases the right choice is very clear. For example, should you feed and care for your pet? Of course. But in some cases people don't agree on what is right.

When you believe that an action is wrong

For some people having a termination is completely wrong. They believe that an unborn child has the right to life. Other people believe that terminating a pregnancy is unnatural. They don't think that we should interfere. People may have these views because of their own personal beliefs, or because of their religious beliefs.

Key words

ethics   false positive

false negative

Elaine and Peter felt that they had weighed up the consequences of either choice. They thought about:

» how each choice – continuing with the pregnancy or having a termination – would affect all the people involved
» the difficulties their child would face with cystic fibrosis
» if they felt able to look after an ill child
» if having an ill child would affect their other children

Different choices

Not everyone thinking about these questions would make the same decision. Some people feel that any illness would have a very bad effect on a person's quality of life. But people lead very happy, full lives in spite of very serious disabilities.

How reliable are genetic tests?

Genetic tests look for alleles that cause genetic disorders. The information may be used to make very serious decisions. People must be told that the tests are not completely reliable. Current tests for CF detect about 90% of cases. A genetic test on an embryo is even more accurate. In a very, very few cases only it will not detect CF. This is called a **false negative**. **False positive** tests are not as common, but they can happen.

Jo has a serious genetic disorder. Her parents believe that termination is wrong. They decided not to have more children, rather than use information from an amniocentesis test.

This couple are both carriers of cystic fibrosis. They had an amniocentesis test during their pregnancy. The results were unclear. When their daughter was born she was completely healthy.

Questions

1 Write down what is meant by 'ethics'.

2 Describe three different points of view that a couple in Elaine and Peter's position might take.

3 What are 'false negative' and 'false positive' results?

4 Why is it important for people to know about the chance of false results?

5 What is your viewpoint on genetic testing of a fetus for a serious illness? Explain why you think this.

Find out about:

▶ how new technologies can allow people to select embryos
▶ how people think this technology should be used

'Huntington's disorder is a very serious condition. We don't want our children to inherit it.'

(F) Can you choose your child?

Bob and Sally want children. Bob has the allele for Huntington's disorder. So their children could inherit this disease.

Sally has already been pregnant twice. A genetic test was done for each fetus. Both had inherited Huntington's disorder. Bob and Sally decided to terminate both pregnancies.

Like many people they are unhappy about having terminations. They have decided not to try for any more children.

A new treatment?

Then Sally's doctor offered them a new treatment. They can find out about their child before Sally is pregnant. It works like this:

Doctors take out some of Sally's eggs.
Bob's sperm cells are added to the eggs.

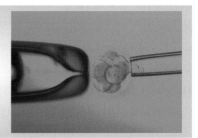

The fertilized egg cells start to grow.
They are called embryos.
One cell is taken from each embryo. Doctors test the embryo cells for the Huntington's allele.

Embryos clear of Huntington's disorder are put into Sally's womb.

So Sally and Bob could choose embryos that won't develop Huntington's disorder.

This method for choosing an embryo is called **embryo selection**.

Key words

embryo selection

Is it right to choose embryos?

Embryo selection is a new technology. This means there are new decisions to make. You have probably seen stories about it in the news. Not everyone agrees that it is right.

Feb 2002: Zain Hashmi has a serious inherited blood disorder. He needs a bone marrow transplant to give him normal blood-making cells. A matching donor cannot be found. Zain's only hope is for a new brother or sister who is a match. Blood from their umbilical cord could be used to make the cells that he needs. This month his parents were given permission to use embryo selection to find a matching donor embryo.

Dec 2002: An anti-abortion group takes the case to the High Court. They think that embryo selection is wrong. 'It is creating one human being to benefit another. This says that the new human life is not as valuable.' The judges decide that Zain's parents cannot use embryo selection unless the law is changed.

April 2003: People appeal against the High Court's decision. They win. Doctors can try to choose an embryo who is a match for Zain.

Zain and his parents.

It's wrong to create one person to help another.

It's just another step on the slippery slope to designer babies. People should let nature take its course.

It's not natural! They'll be producing babies as organ donors next.

It's wonderful! Think of all the misery this could prevent.

People had different opinions about Zain's case.

Questions

1 For Sally's first two pregnancies, write one sentence about:

   a where fertilization happened

   b what test was done

   c what happened after the test

2 Repeat question one for Sally's third pregnancy.

③ Why did Sally prefer embryo selection to a genetic test during pregnancy?

④ Write down one viewpoint that embryo selection:

   a should not be done because it is wrong

   b should be done because it is the best decision for all involved

⑤ Which viewpoint do you agree with? Give your reasons.

Find out about:
▶ treatments to replace faulty genes

G Gene therapy

Paul and Kamni look fine, but they have health problems.

Paul has cystic fibrosis.

Kamni has a bad cold.

Doctors cannot cure a cold or cystic fibrosis. But Kamni's body will fight off her cold. Paul's body cannot fight cystic fibrosis.

Finding a new treatment for cystic fibrosis

Cystic fibrosis is caused by a faulty allele. Scientists are trying to find a cure.

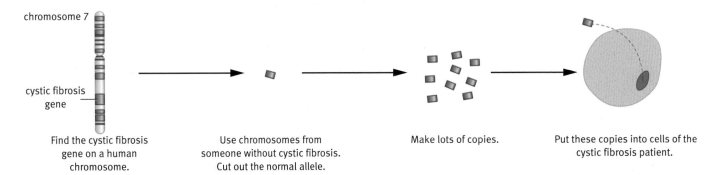

chromosome 7

cystic fibrosis gene

Find the cystic fibrosis gene on a human chromosome.

Use chromosomes from someone without cystic fibrosis. Cut out the normal allele.

Make lots of copies.

Put these copies into cells of the cystic fibrosis patient.

This is a new type of treatment. It is called **gene therapy**. Unfortunately it isn't working yet for cystic fibrosis. Doctors cannot find a good way of getting the new alleles into the cells that need it most. These cells are in the lungs and digestive system.

Key words

gene therapy

Questions

1 Draw a flow chart to explain the steps in gene therapy.

2 In the 1990s some people thought that gene therapy would soon be able to treat cystic fibrosis. Describe one problem scientists have had trying to do this.

Gene therapy success story?

Rhys Evans is a happy, healthy four year old. But when he was just four months old Rhys got a chest infection. He didn't seem to be getting better. Doctors soon realized that Rhys was very seriously ill.

Rhys's mother, Marie, remembers this frightening time: 'It was a bit of a mystery really, he lived on a knife edge. The doctors told us "We don't know if your child is going to live today".'

Rhys was sent to Great Ormond Street Hospital. Doctors at the hospital found that Rhys's immune system was missing an important protein. So, Rhys wasn't able to fight off diseases by himself. The gene for this protein was faulty.

Rhys's disease was caused by a faulty gene. The disease is called Severe Combined Immunodeficiency Disease (SCID).

People with SCID have to live in a sterile 'bubble'. This protects them from microorganisms which could kill them.

Rhys was given gene therapy treatment to replace the faulty gene. His treatment was a success. Another boy with SCID in the UK has also been cured this way.

Future possibilities

In the future it may be possible to use gene therapy to prevent some genetic diseases. New genes could be put into a person's sex cells or fertilized egg cells. At the moment gene therapy of sex cells is illegal. Many people are worried that replacing genes in sex cells would be a dangerous step. The same method could be used to control features like eye colour. People think this could be a step on the road to 'designer babies'.

Questions

3 Why did Rhys's faulty gene make him so ill?

4 The media often use the term 'designer babies'.

   a What do they mean by this term?

   b Why are some people worried that gene therapy could be misused in this way?

Ⓗ Cloning – science fiction or science fact?

Many living things only need one parent to reproduce. This is called **asexual reproduction**. Single-celled organisms like the bacterium in the picture use asexual reproduction.

The new bacteria only inherit genes from one parent. So their genes are identical to their parent's genes. They are **clones**. Any differences between clones are caused by their environment.

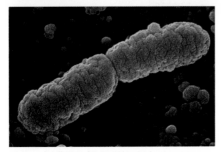

The bacterium cell grows and then splits into two new cells.
(Mag: × 7500 approx)

Asexual reproduction

Larger plants and animals have different types of cells for different jobs. As an embryo grows, cells become **specialized**. For example, blood cells, muscle cells, or nerve cells.

Plants keep some unspecialized cells all their lives. These cells can become anything that the plant may need. For example, they can make new stems and leaves if the plant is cut down. These cells can also grow whole new plants. So they can be used for asexual reproduction.

This strawberry plant has made many many new plants by asexual reproduction.

Hydra

Some simple animals, like the *Hydra* in the picture above, also use asexual reproduction. Larger animals do not have unspecialized cells after they have grown. So cloning is very uncommon in animals.

Sexual reproduction

Most animals use sexual reproduction. The new offspring have two parents so they are not clones. But clones are sometimes made naturally. We call them identical twins.

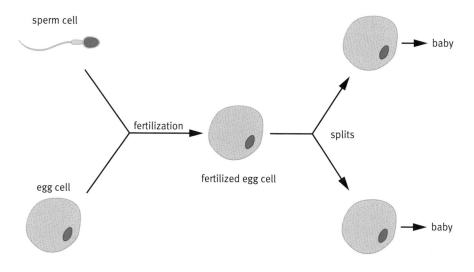

Identical twins have the same genes. But their genes came from both parents. So they are clones of each other, but not of either parent.

Questions

1 How many clones are shown in the *Hydra* picture?

2 Why is natural cloning more common in plants than animals?

3 Why are a pair of identical twins genetically identical to each other, but not to their parents?

④ Describe how Dolly the sheep was cloned.

5 Where did Dolly inherit her genes from?

Cloning Dolly

Scientists can also clone animals. But this is much more difficult. Dolly the sheep was the first cloned sheep to be born.

Is it safe to clone mammals?

Dolly died in 2003, aged 6. The average lifespan for a sheep is 12–14 years. Perhaps Dolly's illness had nothing to do with her being cloned. She might have died early anyway. One case is not enough evidence to decide either way.

But it took 277 attempts before Professor Wilmut's team managed to clone Dolly. Many other cloned animals have suffered unusual illnesses. So scientists think that more research needs to be done before cloned mammals will grow into healthy adults.

Professor Ian Wilmut and Dolly.

Who would you clone?

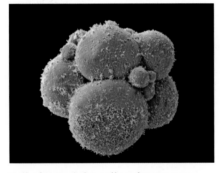
Cells from eight-cell embryos can develop into any type of body cell. (Mag: × 500 approx)

Cloning humans

Cloning humans – what does that make you think of? A double of you, or someone else? Scientists are trying to improve methods for cloning animals. So in the future it may be possible to clone humans. But most scientists don't want to clone adult human beings.

Some scientists do want to clone human embryos. They think that some cells from cloned embryos could be used to treat diseases. The useful cells are called **stem cells**.

What are stem cells?

Stem cells are unspecialized cells. They can grow into any type of cell in the human body.

Stem cells can be taken from embryos that are a few days old. Researchers use human embryos that are left after a fertility treatment.

Scientists want to grow stem cells to make new cells to treat patients with some diseases. For example, new brain cells could be made for patients with Parkinson's disease.

But these new cells would need to have the same genes as the person getting them as a treatment. When someone else's cells are used in a transplant they are rejected.

What's cloning got to do with this?

Cloning could be used to produce an embryo with the same genes as the patient. Stem cells from this embryo would have the same genes as the patient. So cells produced from the embryo would not be rejected by the patient's body.

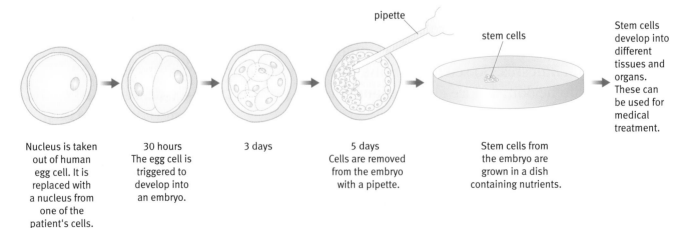
Nucleus is taken out of human egg cell. It is replaced with a nucleus from one of the patient's cells.

30 hours The egg cell is triggered to develop into an embryo.

3 days

5 days Cells are removed from the embryo with a pipette.

Stem cells from the embryo are grown in a dish containing nutrients.

Stem cells develop into different tissues and organs. These can be used for medical treatment.

Doctors have only started to explore this technology. Success is still years away, but millions of people could benefit if it is made to work.

Should human cloning be allowed?

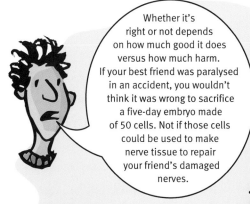

Whether it's right or not depends on how much good it does versus how much harm. If your best friend was paralysed in an accident, you wouldn't think it was wrong to sacrifice a five-day embryo made of 50 cells. Not if those cells could be used to make nerve tissue to repair your friend's damaged nerves.

Research on embryos is legal up to 14 days. If something is 'legal' it can't be wrong.

An embryo is human so it has human rights. Its age doesn't make any difference. You can't experiment on a child or an adult.

With some things there's no argument. Murder is just wrong – in the same way that lying and stealing are wrong. Killing an embryo at any age is as wrong as killing a child or an adult.

Creating embryos for medical treatments is wrong. It's creating a life which is then destroyed. This lowers the value of life.

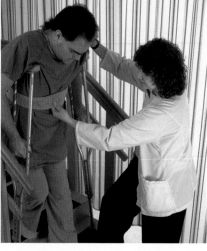

James has Parkinson's disease. His brain cells do not communicate with each other properly. He cannot control his movements. Scientists think stem cells could be used to treat this disease.

> **Key words**
> stem cells

Questions

6 How are stem cells different from other cells?

7 Explain why scientists think stem cells would be useful in treating Parkinson's disease.

8 Explain how this is different from cloning an adult.

9 For each of these cells, say whether or not your body would reject it:

  a bone marrow from your twin

  b your own skin cells

  c a cloned embryo stem cell

10 For embryo cloning to make stem cells:

  a describe one viewpoint in favour

  b describe two different viewpoints against

11 People often make speculations when they are arguing for or against something. This is something they think will happen, but may not have evidence for. Write down a viewpoint that is a speculation.

B1 You and your genes

Science explanations

How living things develop is one of the most complex scientific explanations. In this Module you've begun to explore the science behind what makes you the way you are.

You should know:

▶ most of your features are affected by your environment and your genes

▶ genes are found in the nuclei of cells and are instructions for making proteins

▶ your chromosomes, and genes, are in pairs

▶ genes have different versions, called alleles

▶ the difference between dominant and recessive alleles

▶ men and women have different sex chromosomes

▶ why you may look like your parents

▶ why you may look like your brothers and sisters, but not be identical

▶ how to interpret family trees

▶ how to complete genetic cross diagrams

▶ the symptoms of cystic fibrosis and Huntington's disorder

▶ why people can be carriers of cystic fibrosis, but not of Huntington's disorder

▶ doctors can test embryos, fetuses, and adults for certain alleles by genetic tests

▶ what happens during embryo selection

▶ how gene therapy could be used to treat some genetic disorders

▶ that some organisms use asexual reproduction and have offspring that are clones

▶ how animal clones are produced naturally

▶ that cells in multicellular organisms become specialized very early on in the organism's development

▶ what stem cells are, and how they could be used to treat certain diseases

Ideas about science

It is difficult to make decisions about some uses of science. Many of the issues in this module have ethical questions. Ethics is about deciding whether something is a right or a wrong way to behave. Just because science can help us to do something doesn't mean it is right or that it should be allowed.

People may disagree about some ethical questions. Often they agree about the facts of an issue, but disagree about what should be done. For example, it is possible to test for some alleles that cause disease. People disagree about whether these tests should be done. They disagree about whether people should be allowed to terminate a pregnancy if a fetus has a genetic disorder.

There are different viewpoints presented for each of the issues discussed in this Module:

▶ some people think that certain actions are wrong whatever the circumstances

▶ some people think that you should weigh up the benefit and harm for everyone involved and then make a decision

People may make different decisions because of their beliefs, and/or their personal circumstances. When you consider an ethical issue you should be able to:

▶ say clearly what the issue is

▶ describe some different viewpoints people may have

▶ say what you think and why

You've looked at different issues in this Module:

▶ should we test fetuses for particular genetic disorders?

▶ should other people, like insurance companies and employers, be allowed to have information about a person's genes?

▶ should we use genetic tests to choose embryos without certain genetic disorders?

▶ should doctors be allowed to use gene therapy to treat people with some genetic disorders?

▶ should doctors be allowed to clone stem cells from embryos to treat certain illnesses (therapeutic cloning)?

Why study air quality?

We breath air every second of our lives. If it contains any pollutants they go into our lungs. If the quality of the air is poor then it can affect people's health.

Chemicals that harm the air quality are called atmospheric pollutants. To improve air quality we need to understand how atmospheric pollutants are made.

The science

Most air pollutants are made by burning fossil fuels. When a fuel burns, the chemicals in the fuel combine with oxygen from the air. They form new chemicals. Some of the new chemicals are air pollutants which escape into the atmosphere. Burning is a chemical reaction. Knowing about chemical reactions helps people understand better what needs to be done to improve air quality.

Ideas about science

Scientists who are trying to improve air quality measure the amounts of pollutants in the air. They use special methods to make sure their data are as accurate as possible. Some scientists use their data to see if they can find a link between air quality and illnesses such as hay fever.

Air quality

Find out about:
▶ the gases that make up the Earth's atmosphere
▶ some of the main air pollutants

(A) The Earth's atmosphere

The Earth's atmosphere provides a protective blanket that supports life. It is a fragile environment that can be easily damaged by pollution.

The table below shows the gases in 'clean' air.

Gas	Percentage by volume
nitrogen (N_2)	78
oxygen (O_2)	21
argon (Ar)	1
carbon dioxide (CO_2)	0.04
water (H_2O)	Variable 0–4

The main gases in 'clean' air.

The Earth from space. White clouds of water vapour can be seen in the atmosphere.

The Earth's atmosphere is just 15 km thick. That sounds a lot but the diameter of the Earth is over 12 000 km. The atmosphere is like a very thin skin around the Earth. The mixture of chemicals it contains is just right to support life. Human activities have altered the balance of these chemicals and this can affect the air quality.

Air pollutants

Human activities can add **pollutants** to the atmosphere. These include:

- sulfur dioxide (SO_2)
- carbon monoxide (CO)
- nitrogen dioxide (NO_2)
- particulates (microscopic particles of carbon)

A lot of the air pollution comes from burning fossil fuels. The main ones are gas, coal, and oil.

This air pollution reduces the quality of the air that you breathe.

Carbon dioxide and the Earth's temperature

Even though there is only a tiny amount of carbon dioxide in the atmosphere, it helps to keep the Earth warm enough for life.

But the concentration of carbon dioxide in the atmosphere has doubled in the century since humans started burning fossil fuels in huge amounts. Climate scientists are very concerned about possible effects of this increase.

You will learn more about this in Module P2: *Radiation and Life*.

Questions

1 Oxygen, carbon dioxide, and water vapour are three of the gases in the atmosphere.
   a Why do you think oxygen is important?
   b Why do you think carbon dioxide is important?
   c Why do you think water vapour is important?

2 Draw a bar graph showing the different gases in the Earth's atmosphere. Use data from the table on page 34

3 List three gases that cause air pollution.

4 Look at the picture of Earth from space on page 34. It shows that the atmosphere is a very thin layer of gases surrounding the Earth. Write a note to a friend explaining how seeing this picture has helped you understand the importance of air quality.

Key words
pollutants

Find out about:
▶ the most important air pollutants
▶ the problems pollutants cause

B What are the main air pollutants?

Smoke is a pollutant that can easily be seen. This is because it contains billions of tiny bits of solid. These float in the air. They are called 'particulates'. Smoke makes things dirty and it can give you health problems if you breathe it in.

Most of the harmful pollutants are usually invisible.

The table lists air pollutants that scientists are most concerned about.

The clouds coming from the cooling towers are just harmless water vapour. 'Invisible' pollutants are coming out of the tall chimney.

smoke magnified many times

Smoke contains microscopic particles of carbon. They are called 'particulates'. Some of these are just 10 micrometres (10 millionths of a meter) in size. These are called PM10 particles. Although they are very small, they are very much bigger than atoms or molecules. Each particle contains billions of carbon atoms.

Name	What problem does it cause?
sulfur dioxide SO_2	Acid rain.
carbon monoxide CO	A poisonous gas. It reacts with blood and can kill you.
nitrogen dioxide NO_2	Acid rain. Causes breathing problems. Can make asthma worse.
particulates (tiny bits of solid suspended in the air)	Make things dirty. Can be breathed into your lungs. Can make asthma worse. Can make lung infections worse.

How can you find out about air quality?

Some people suffer from asthma or hay fever. They may be able to feel when the air quality is poor. But most people would need to look at a newspaper or a government web site to find out about air quality.

Does it matter where you live?

Nitrogen dioxide (NO_2) is an air pollutant. The bar chart below compares the concentration of NO_2 on the same day at three different places. It shows that they have different levels of NO_2 in their air.

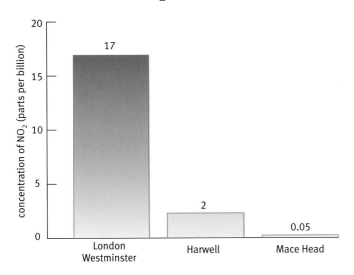

The concentration of NO_2 in three places: London (large city), Harwell (rural part of Britain), and Mace Head (west coast of Ireland).

The concentration of NO_2 depends a lot on the amount of road traffic in the area. London has lots of traffic and so has a high level of NO_2.

Mace Head, in Ireland, has very pure air. It gets air that has travelled over the Atlantic Ocean.

Most of us live in environments where the air quality is much poorer than at Mace Head.

Measuring the concentration of a pollutant

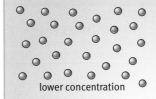

lower concentration

A low concentration of pollutants. There are very few pollutant molecules in a certain volume of air. This is an indication of good air quality

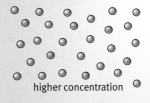

higher concentration

A high concentration of pollutants. There is a large number of pollutant molecules in a certain volume of air. This shows that the air quality is poor.

- molecules of pollutant
- other molecules in air

Concentration is the amount of pollutant in a certain volume of air.

Note: the air molecules are normally much more spread out than shown in the diagrams.

Key word

concentration

Questions

1 Write down one problem that can be caused by each of these air pollutants:
   a SO_2 b NO_2 c particulates

2 A newspaper article included a photograph of white clouds that come out of power station cooling towers. Write a note to the newspaper explaining why the clouds are not polluting the atmosphere.

3 Explain why there is less air pollution at Mace Head in Ireland than in the centre of London.

Find out about:
▶ how air quality is measured
▶ how data are checked for reliability

(c) Measuring an air pollutant

If you measure the concentration of NO_2 in a sample of air several times, you will probably get different results. This is because:

▶ you used the equipment differently
▶ there were differences in the equipment itself

If you take just one reading, you cannot be sure it is very accurate. So it is better to take several measurements. Then you can use them to estimate the true value.

The true value is what the measurement should really be. The **accuracy** of a result is how close it is to the true value.

How can you make sure your data are accurate?

Read the table on page 39. It shows what you should do to get a measurement of the NO_2 level that is as accurate as possible.

The mean value is 19.1 ppb. This is the best estimate of the concentration of NO_2 in the sample of air. You cannot be absolutely sure that it is the true value. But you can be sure that:

▶ the true value is within the range, 18.8 – 19.4 ppb
▶ the best estimate of the true value is 19.1 ppb

If you had taken only one measurement, you wouldn't have been sure it was accurate. If the range had been more narrow, say 19.0 – 19.3 ppb, you would have been even more confident about your best estimate of the true value.

This map shows the concentration of NO_2 over parts of England. It is based on measurements from government monitoring sites. Red shows the highest levels of NO_2. Why do you think the high levels follow motorway routes?

What you do	Data	Describing what you do
Take several measurements from the same air sample. Not all the measurements will be the same.	Concentration of NO_2 in parts per billion (ppb) 18.8, 19.1, 18.9, 19.4, 19.0, 19.2, 19.1, 19.0, 18.3, 19.3	The measurements (10 in this case) are called the data set.
Plot the results on a graph. This shows that the 18.3 ppb measurement is very different from the others.	this result is an outlier – so leave it out of the mean	A result that is very different from the others is called an **outlier**.
The outlier must have been a mistake so you ignore it. Add the other nine results together. Divide the total by 9. The answer is 19.1 ppb of NO_2.	Total of nine readings = 171.8 $\frac{171.8}{9}$ = 19.1 ppb	19.1 is called the **mean value** of the nine measurements.
You can use the mean value rather than any of the nine measurements.	The best estimate for the concentration of NO_2 is 19.1 ppb	The mean value is used as the **best estimate** of the true value.
When you write down the mean value you also record: • the lowest, 18.8 ppb, • and the highest, 19.4 ppb, measurements.	The range is 18.8 ppb – 19.4 ppb	18.8 ppb – 19.4 ppb is called the **range** of the measurements.

Questions

1 Jess measured the NO_2 concentration in the middle of a town. She took six readings:
22 ppb, 20 ppb, 16 ppb, 24 ppb, 21 ppb, 23 ppb.
   a Explain which one of these readings she should decide is an outlier?
   b Calculate the mean of the remaining five measurements.
   c Write down the best estimate and the range for the NO_2 concentration in this sample of air.

2 Repeat measurements on an air sample produced these results for the NO_2 concentration:

   Reading 1 – 39.4 ppb
   Reading 2 – 45.8 ppb
   Reading 3 – 42.3 ppb
   Reading 4 – 38.7 ppb
   Reading 5 – 39.7 ppb
   Reading 6 – 32.7 ppb

   a Draw a graph to show the range for these results?
   b Work out the mean NO_2 concentration and range for this sample.

3 A scientist took one measurement of NO_2 in an air sample. Explain why this would not give you much confidence in the accuracy of their result.

Key words
accuracy
outlier
mean value
best estimate
range

Find out about:
▶ the chemical changes that make atmospheric pollutants
▶ how these changes involve atoms separating and joining

D How are atmospheric pollutants formed?

Many air pollutants are caused by the burning of fossil fuels. This happens in the engines of vehicles and in power stations.

What happens when fuel burns in a car engine?

Vehicle engines burn petrol or diesel. Fuel and air go into the engine and exhaust fumes come out. Use the diagram to compare the chemicals that go into an engine with those that come out.

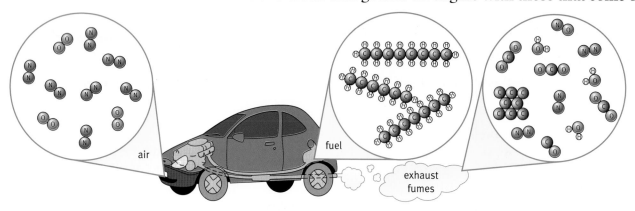

The chemicals going into and coming out of a car engine.

The overall change can be summarized as:

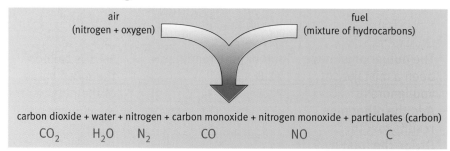

air
(nitrogen + oxygen)

fuel
(mixture of hydrocarbons)

carbon dioxide + water + nitrogen + carbon monoxide + nitrogen monoxide + particulates (carbon)
CO_2 H_2O N_2 CO   NO   C

CO_2, H_2O, and N_2 are the main chemicals in the exhaust fumes. The others are there in very small quantities. You can use these pictures to work out the chemical changes happening in the engine.

Chemical changes

New chemicals are formed when a fuel burns in an engine. Any change that forms a new chemical is called a **chemical change** or a **chemical reaction**.

For example, nitrogen monoxide (NO) is one of the new chemicals in the exhaust emissions. It must have been formed from nitrogen (N_2) and oxygen (O_2) in the air. These must have first split apart into **atoms** and then reformed to make nitrogen monoxide (NO).

Check that you know which of the pictures in the three circles represents each of the chemicals mentioned in the summary.

What happens when fuel burns in a power station furnace?

Most fossil-fuelled power stations burn:

▶ either coal which is mainly carbon (C)
▶ or natural gas which is mainly methane (CH_4)

You can compare what goes into a power station with what comes out. Then you can work out some of the chemical changes that take place inside the furnace.

The main product that comes out of the chimney at a coal power station is CO_2. It must have been formed by:

▶ oxygen atoms in O_2 separating
▶ the oxygen atoms then combining with carbon atoms to form CO_2

The main products from the burning of natural gas are CO_2 and H_2O.

These must have been formed by:

▶ carbon atoms and hydrogen atoms in CH_4 separating
▶ then carbon atoms combining with oxygen atoms to form CO_2
▶ and hydrogen atoms combining with oxygen atoms to form H_2O

Burning coal and gas can also produce smaller amounts of these air pollutants:

▶ particulates
▶ carbon monoxide (CO)
▶ nitrogen monoxide (NO)
▶ sulfur dioxide (SO_2)

Key words
chemical change/reaction
atoms

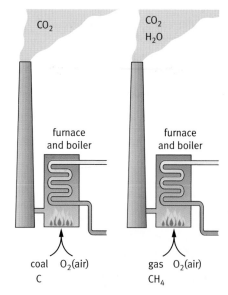

The chemicals going into and coming out of power station furnaces.

Questions

1 List the air pollutants released from a car engine when it burns fuel.

2 List the air pollutants that can be released from a power station which burns coal.

3 Use ideas about atoms separating and then joining together in different ways to explain how: carbon dioxide (CO_2) forms when coal (carbon, C) burns in oxygen (O_2) in a power station.

Find out about:
▶ the chemical changes involved in combustion
▶ different ways of representing chemical changes

E What happens during combustion reactions?

Some chemicals can react rapidly with oxygen to release energy and possibly light. This type of reaction is called **combustion** or burning.

A controlled combustion reaction between natural gas (methane) and oxygen occurs when you use a gas cooker.

Fuel has escaped during this racing car crash. An uncontrolled combustion reaction is happening. Either a spark or the hot engine has heated the mixture of fuel and air. This has made it hot enough to burn.

Burning charcoal

Burning charcoal on a barbeque is one of the simplest combustion reactions.

Charcoal is almost pure carbon. You can picture the surface of a piece of charcoal as a layer of carbon atoms tightly packed together.

Oxygen is a gas. All the atoms of this gas are joined together in pairs (O_2): O_2 is called a **molecule** of oxygen.

It will help you to understand this reaction if you can picture what happens to the atoms and molecules involved.

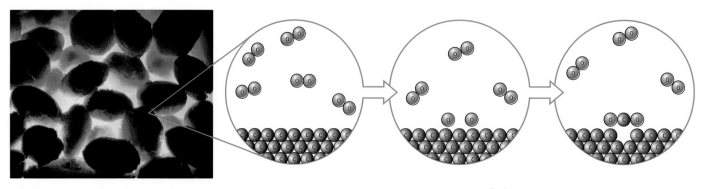

Air contains oxygen gas. One molecule of oxygen is two oxygen atoms joined together. Oxygen molecules split and react with carbon atoms in the charcoal. This forms carbon dioxide gas.

Describing combustion reactions

You can use pictures to describe the chemical change that happens when carbon burns.

The chemicals before the arrow are the ones that react together. They are called **reactants**.

The chemicals after the arrow are the new chemicals that are made. They are called **products**.

It would take a lot of time if you always had to draw pictures to describe chemical reactions. So scientists use equations to summarize the pictures.

The combustion of charcoal can be summarized in this **word equation**:

carbon + oxygen $\rightarrow$ carbon dioxide

The fire triangle

Three things are needed for a fire, or combustion reaction:

- a fuel mixed with
- oxygen (air) and a
- source of heat to raise the temperature of the mixture

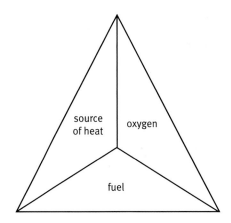

Questions

1 List the three things that are needed for a combustion reaction to happen.

2 a Draw a picture to describe the chemical change that happens when charcoal burns.
   b State if each of the following chemicals are reactants or products in the burning of charcoal.
   i oxygen
   ii carbon dioxide
   iii carbon

3 Use the fire triangle to help you explain why charcoal does not start to burn while it is stored in a cool place.

Key words

combustion
molecule
reactants
products
word equation

Find out about:

▶ what happens to atoms during chemical reactions

▶ how the properties of reactants and products are different

F Where do all the atoms go?

Look at the picture below. How many atoms of hydrogen (H) are there before and after the reaction? Count the atoms of oxygen (O) before and after. What does this show?

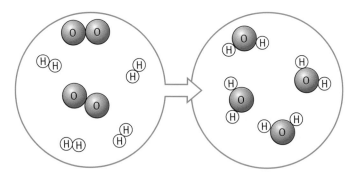

A picture showing the reaction of hydrogen and oxygen to form water.

When you have had a bonfire, some of the atoms that made up the rubbish are in the ashes left on the ground. The others are in the smoke and gases released into the air.

Conservation of atoms

All the atoms present at the beginning of a chemical reaction are still there at the end. No atoms are destroyed and no atoms are created. The atoms are conserved. They rearrange to form new chemicals but they are still there. This is called **conservation of atoms**.

Properties of reactants and products

The **properties** of a chemical are what make it different from other chemicals.

For example, some chemicals are solids, some are liquids, and some are gases at normal temperatures. Some are coloured, some burn easily, some smell, some react with metals, some dissolve in water, and so on. Each chemical has its own collection of properties.

If you compare the properties of the reactants and products of the reaction between sulfur and oxygen, you find:

▪ reactant 1: sulfur
  – is a yellow solid

▪ reactant 2: oxygen
  – is a colourless gas
  – has no smell
  – supports life

▪ product: sulfur dioxide
  – is a colourless gas
  – has a sharp, choking smell
  – is very harmful if you breathe it
  – dissolves in water to make an acid

In any chemical reaction all the atoms you start with are still there at the end. But they are combined in a different way. So the properties of the products are different from the properties of the reactants.

This is very important for air quality. For example:

▪ A piece of coal is a harmless black stone.
▪ The coal may contain a small amount of sulfur. When it burns the sulfur will change to the gas sulfur dioxide.
▪ The sulfur dioxide will escape into the atmosphere. It will harm the quality of our air.

The harmless piece of coal has produced a harmful gas.

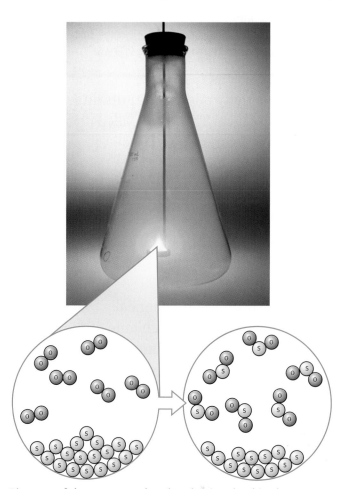

Pictures of the atoms and molecules involved in the burning of sulfur.

Questions

1 Burning rubbish gets rid of it forever. Is this a true statement? Think about the atoms in the rubbish. Fully explain your answer.

2 Look at the picture of sulfur atoms reacting with oxygen and add up the oxygen atoms and sulfur atoms in the left-hand circle. Then do the same for the right-hand circle.

3 Water (H_2O) is made by reacting molecules of hydrogen and oxygen together. Make a list of some properties of water that are different from the properties of the reactants it is made from.

Key words
conservation of atoms
properties

Find out about:
▶ what happens to pollutants when they are released into the air

G What happens to atmospheric pollutants?

CO_2 is absorbed by plants. It is also slightly soluble in water so it dissolves in the oceans and can react with other chemicals in the water.

Human activity adds pollutants directly to the atmosphere. These are called **primary pollutants**. Examples are:

▶ particulate carbon (C)
▶ carbon monoxide (CO)
▶ nitrogen monoxide (NO)
▶ sulfur dioxide (SO_2)
▶ hydrocarbons such as methane (CH_4) and hexane (C_6H_{14})

Some pollutants can chemically react in the air. They produce other chemicals which are called **secondary pollutants**. Nitrogen dioxide (NO_2) is an example of a secondary pollutant.

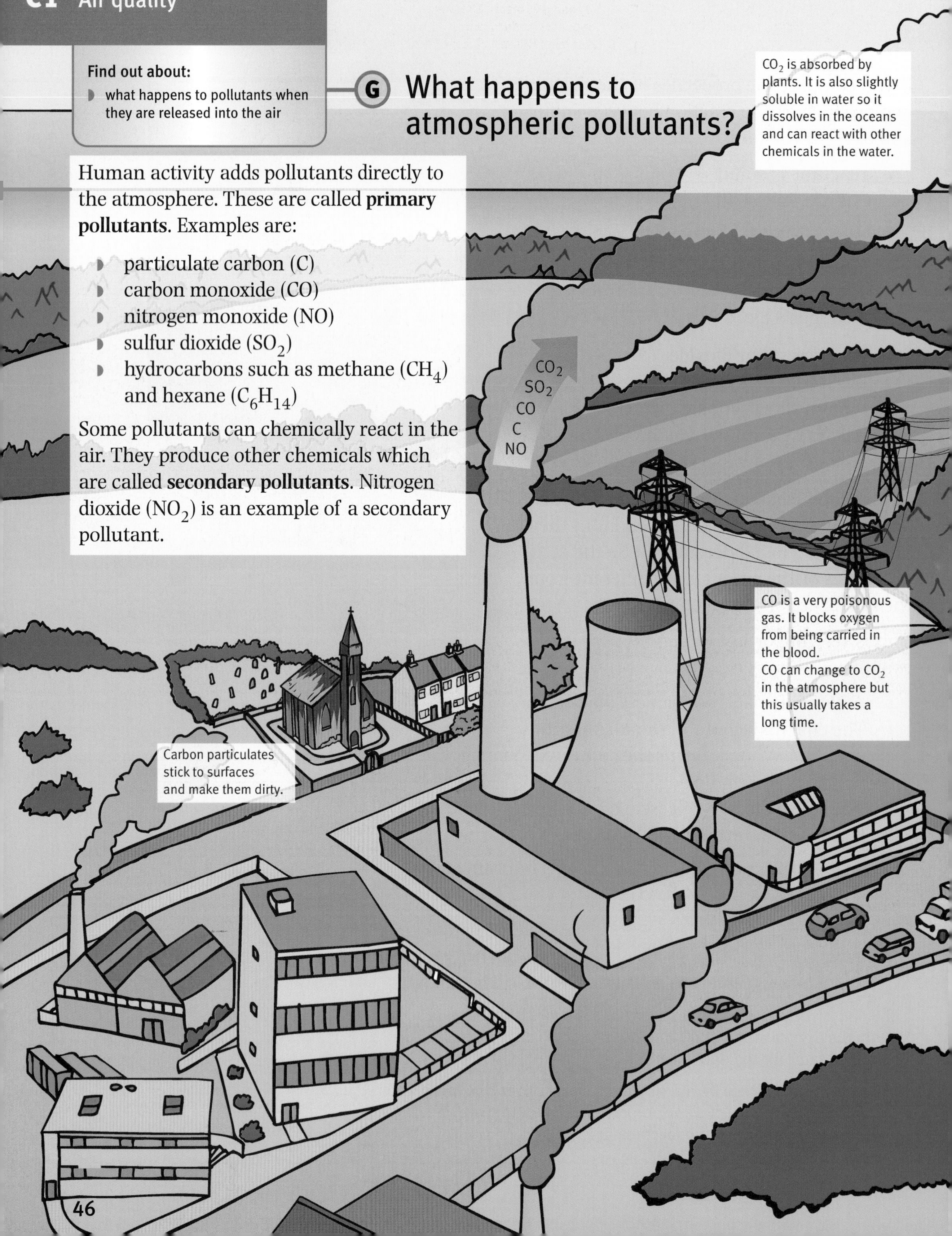

CO_2
SO_2
CO
C
NO

CO is a very poisonous gas. It blocks oxygen from being carried in the blood.
CO can change to CO_2 in the atmosphere but this usually takes a long time.

Carbon particulates stick to surfaces and make them dirty.

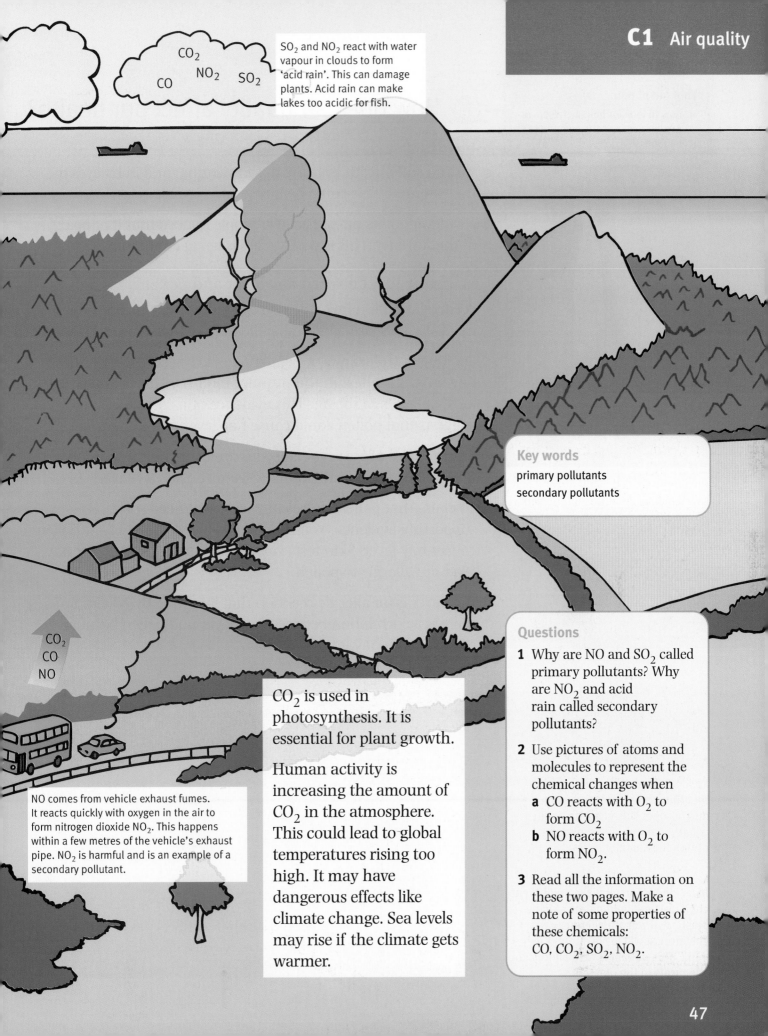

SO_2 and NO_2 react with water vapour in clouds to form 'acid rain'. This can damage plants. Acid rain can make lakes too acidic for fish.

CO_2

CO NO_2 SO_2

CO_2
CO
NO

NO comes from vehicle exhaust fumes. It reacts quickly with oxygen in the air to form nitrogen dioxide NO_2. This happens within a few metres of the vehicle's exhaust pipe. NO_2 is harmful and is an example of a secondary pollutant.

CO_2 is used in photosynthesis. It is essential for plant growth.

Human activity is increasing the amount of CO_2 in the atmosphere. This could lead to global temperatures rising too high. It may have dangerous effects like climate change. Sea levels may rise if the climate gets warmer.

Key words

primary pollutants
secondary pollutants

Questions

1 Why are NO and SO_2 called primary pollutants? Why are NO_2 and acid rain called secondary pollutants?

2 Use pictures of atoms and molecules to represent the chemical changes when
   a CO reacts with O_2 to form CO_2
   b NO reacts with O_2 to form NO_2.

3 Read all the information on these two pages. Make a note of some properties of these chemicals: CO, CO_2, SO_2, NO_2.

Find out about:
▶ how to look for links between air quality data and the symptoms of an illness

H How does air quality affect our health?

Hay fever

Do you suffer from a runny nose, sneezing, and itchy eyes in the summer? This could be hay fever.

Hay fever got its name because people noticed that it happens in the summer. This is when grass is being cut to make hay.

Is there a link between hay fever and pollen?

A **correlation** is a link between two things. In this case, does hay fever increase when the pollen count increases?

Looking at thousands of people's medical records shows that hay fever is highest in the summer months. This is also when most pollen is in the air. This evidence of a correlation suggests that pollen could **cause** hay fever.

But the sales of ice cream also increase during the summer. But nobody would say that ice cream causes hay fever.

To claim that pollen causes hay fever you need some supporting evidence. You need to be able to explain how pollen causes hay fever. Skin tests can show that people who get hay fever are allergic to pollen.

Hay fever is an allergic reaction that is caused by pollen. So there is a correlation between hay fever and pollen because pollen causes hay fever.

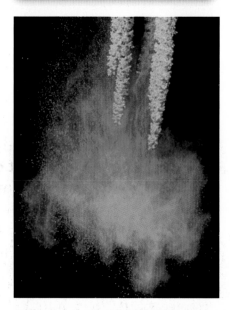

Pollen is released by plants and may travel many kilometres on the wind. Pollen grains are in the air that we breathe.

Pollen traps collect pollen grains so that they can be counted using a microscope. This gives the 'pollen count', that newspapers report during the summer.

In a skin test small disks of different chemicals are held on the skin by plasters. If you are allergic to a chemical, it will leave a round red mark. This patient is also allergic to chemicals in the plasters.

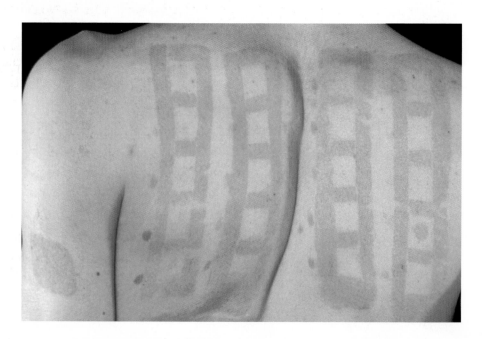

Asthma and air quality

Asthma is a common condition. During an asthma attack, the person's chest feels very tight. They find it difficult to breathe. This can be very frightening. A severe asthma attack can be very dangerous, especially for older people.

Asthma attacks are treated with inhalers. These contain medicines which help the lungs to 'open up' and breathe more freely.

Sometimes NO_2 levels stay high for several days. When this happens there is an increased number of asthma attacks. This may cause more people to die.

But asthma attacks may be triggered by many different factors. So, although there is a correlation between NO_2 levels and asthma attacks, there is no clear evidence that NO_2 causes asthma.

Things that can trigger asthma:

tree or grass pollen

animal skin flakes

dust-mite droppings

air pollution

nuts, shellfish

food additives

dusty materials

strong perfumes

getting emotional

stress

exercise
(especially in cold weather)

colds and flu

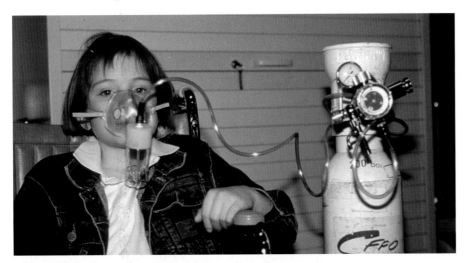
Inhalers are used to treat asthma attacks. Oxygen may be needed in severe cases.

Questions

1 Why is it useful to hay fever sufferers to report the levels of pollen in the air during the summer months?

2 Write a note to a friend explaining:
   a what is meant by 'there is a correlation between pollen count and hay fever symptoms'
   b why you are sure that pollen causes hay fever

3 One person who has asthma attacks lives in a busy city. Another lives in the countryside. Which person is more likely to have an attack? Explain your answers.

Key words
correlation
cause

Find out about:

▶ how new technology can reduce the harmful emissions from cars and power stations

① How can new technology improve air quality?

Scientists and technologists can find new ways of reducing the amounts of pollutants that escape into the air.

Cars and catalytic converters

Catalytic converters are added to the exhaust systems of modern cars. They remove carbon monoxide and nitrogen monoxide from the exhaust gases.

Inside the catalytic converter is a metal honeycomb. It is coated with a thin layer of platinum. This metal acts as a **catalyst**. It makes chemical reactions happen more quickly in the exhaust gases. These reactions convert the air pollutants CO and NO to less harmful gases.

Polluted water can be purified and delivered to people. Air is all around us. You do not get it out of a tap. So everyone should try to reduce pollutants getting into the air.

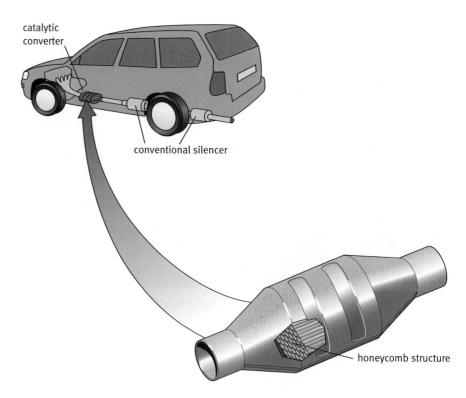

catalytic converter

conventional silencer

honeycomb structure

A catalytic converter

Questions

1 Catalytic converters remove harmful CO and NO by converting them to less harmful chemicals. What are the chemicals they are converted to?

The chemical reactions that occur in a catalytic converter are

carbon monoxide + oxygen → carbon dioxide

nitrogen monoxide + carbon monoxide → nitrogen + carbon dioxide

Reducing pollutants from power stations

Burning fossil fuels in power stations can produce the air pollutant SO_2. This can be removed from the waste gases before they leave the chimney.

Waste gases pass through a spray of powdered lime (calcium oxide), water, and air. The SO_2 in the gases combines with the mixture to form a new chemical called calcium sulfate. This is a solid so the SO_2 is captured before it can escape from the chimney.

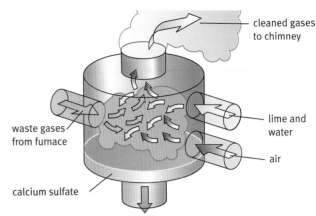

Removing sulfur dioxide to prevent it escaping from power station chimneys

Cleaner fuels make less pollutants

Sulfur compounds can be removed from natural gas. This reduces the SO_2 produced when it is burned. Also low-sulfur petrol is now available.

Cars are being developed that use hydrogen as the fuel. The hydrogen is converted to water so they do not produce any air pollution.

Electric trams and trains help to remove air pollution from congested cities. But some of the electricity they use will be produced by power stations that burn fossil fuels.

Questions

2 Sulfur dioxide can be removed from the waste gases before they escape from a power station chimney. What chemical is the SO_2 converted to?

3 Write a note to a friend explaining why it can be more difficult to supply people with clean air than clean water.

Key words
catalyst

51

Find out about:
▶ how laws and regulations can help to improve air quality

J How can governments and individuals improve air quality?

Governments pass laws and **regulations** that aim to improve air quality. Some of the older laws seem a little funny today. But they have all helped to tackle the problems of air pollution.

- ▶ **1845** A limit was placed on the amount of smoke released by steam train engines.
- ▶ **1847** The amount of smoke that factories could give out was reduced.
- ▶ **1863** The 'Alkali Act' controlled emissions from early chemical factories.
- ▶ **1956** The 'Clean Air Act' introduced smokeless zones in cities.
- ▶ **1991** Limits were set to control the emissions of carbon monoxide and particulates from vehicle exhausts.
- ▶ **1997** The National Air Quality Strategy set targets for a reduction in UK emissions.

Local emissions but global problems

The London smog of 1952 killed 4000 people. It led to the Clean Air Act which reduced pollution from coal fires.

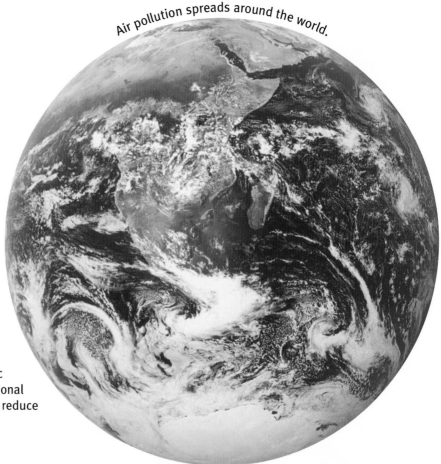

Air pollution spreads around the world.

There are international agreements that aim to reduce the emission of atmospheric pollutants. In 1997, there was an international meeting in Kyoto, Japan. People agreed to reduce CO_2 emissions.

What would you do if you were in control?

Sustainable development means giving people what they need without damaging the environment for future generations.

Financial incentives (or taxes) can be used to encourage people to produce less air pollution?

- Car tax

  In general, bigger cars, and cars with bigger engines, produce more air pollutants. Owners of these cars could pay a higher vehicle excise duty (car tax).

- Fuel duty

  Higher fuel prices could discourage people from using their cars. It would also encourage people to buy more fuel-efficient vehicles. Both of these results would help to reduce emissions.

- Energy efficiency grants

  These grants might include payments for fitting wall or roof insulation. They might also include the fitting of a high efficiency boiler, such as a condensing boiler.

Ordinary people, through the choices they make, can influence air quality.

Bad air pollution would affect your everyday life.

Questions

1 Feroz and Jay each have a car. Their cars are the same model and the same age. Each year Jay drives twice as many kilometres as Feroz. Explain why each year Feroz causes less air pollution than Jay.

2 The UK government has tried to encourage people to produce less air pollution. Write down the things it has done. For each one, say whether you think it will result in:
   a an increase in costs for people
   b a decrease in the convenience and quality of life
   c no change in costs or quality of life.

3 You want your friends and family to use less energy. Then they would produce less air pollution. Write down three things you would encourage them to do.

Key words

regulations
sustainable development
financial incentives

Science explanations

The atmosphere supports life and controls the temperature on the surface of the Earth. Human activity affects air quality. Understanding what happens in chemical reactions will help you to explain this

You should know:

▷ the gases that make up the Earth's atmosphere

▷ human activities add small amounts of chemicals to the atmosphere

▷ some of these chemicals are harmful and are called air pollutants

▷ power stations and vehicles that burn fossil fuels add:

   – small amounts of the gases carbon monoxide, nitrogen oxides, and sulfur dioxide to the atmosphere

   – small amounts of very small particles, such as carbon, called particulates, to the atmosphere

   – extra carbon dioxide that contributes to global warming

▷ primary pollutants are released directly into the atmosphere

▷ secondary pollutants, such as nitrogen dioxide and acid rain are produced by chemical reactions in the atmosphere

▷ that the fossil fuel coal, is mainly carbon

▷ fuels such as petrol, diesel, and natural gas are hydrocarbons - these are chemicals made up from carbon and hydrogen

▷ when a fuel burns the oxygen atoms from air combine with:

   – carbon atoms to form carbon dioxide

   – hydrogen atoms to form water

▷ in a chemical change/reaction atoms separate and recombine to form different chemicals

▷ chemical changes can be shown by pictures of the atoms and molecules involved

▷ during a chemical reaction, the number of atoms of each kind is the same in the products as in the reactants - the atoms are conserved

▷ the conservation of atoms means that combustion reactions affect air quality

▷ the properties of the reactants and products of chemical changes are different

▷ technological developments such as catalytic converters and flue gas desulfurization can reduce amounts of pollutants released into the atmosphere

Ideas about science

Scientists need to collect large amounts of data when they investigate the causes and effects of air pollutants. They can never be sure that a measurement tells them the true value of the quantity being measured. Data are more reliable if they can be repeated.

If you make several measurements of the same quantity, the results are likely to vary. This may be because:

▶ you have to measure several individual examples, for example, exhaust gases from different cars of the same make

▶ the quantity you are measuring is varying, for example, pollen levels

▶ the limitations of the measuring equipment or because of the way you use the equipment

Usually the best estimate of the true value of a quantity is the mean (or average) of several repeat measurements. The spread of values in a set of repeated measurements, the lowest to the highest, gives a rough estimate of the range within which the true value probably lies. You should:

▶ know that if a measurement lies well outside the range within which the others in a set of repeats lie, then it is an outlier and should not be used when calculating the mean

▶ be able to calculate the mean from a set of repeated measurements

Investigating the link between air pollution and illnesses:

▶ a correlation shows a link between a factor and an outcome, for example, as the pollen count goes up the number of people suffering from hay fever goes up

▶ a correlation does not always mean the factor causes the outcome

▶ a high pollen count does cause hay fever

▶ but although poor air quality can make people's asthma worse, there is no clear evidence that it causes people to suffer from asthma

Making decisions about improving air quality:

▶ official regulations such as the MOT test for motor vehicles can be used to improve air quality

▶ using less electricity and burning less fuel will improve air quality

Why study the Earth and the Universe?

Many people want to understand more about the Earth and its place in the Universe. Natural disasters, such as volcanoes and earthquakes, can be life-threatening. Can anything be done to predict them? The Earth is very fragile. It is a very, very small place in a huge and almost empty Universe. Some scientists think that an asteroid collision made the dinosaurs extinct. Could another big asteroid hit the Earth?

The science

Science can explain changes to the Earth. Some changes happen very quickly, and some happen very slowly. For example, over millions of years, whole mountain ranges grow, and then disappear. Astronomers study changes in stars and galaxies. These changes can take thousands of millions of years. Stars made the atoms found in everything: including everything on Earth and everything in your body.

Ideas about science

How can scientists be sure? Partly they depend on data and careful observations of the Earth and Universe. But scientists need to interpret the evidence they collect. So, imagination is also important.

How are scientific ideas tested? There are often many arguments put forward before scientists accept new data or agree with new explanations.

The Earth in the Universe

Find out about:

▶ evidence of the Earth's history found in rocks
▶ the movement of the Earth's continents
▶ how scientists develop explanations of the Earth and space
▶ the history of the Universe

Find out about:
▸ what is known about the Earth and the Universe

Ⓐ Time and space

Our rocky planet was made from the scattered dust of ancient stars. It may or may not be the only place in the whole Universe with life.

As the graphics on this page show, scientists know a lot about:

▸ the history of the Earth
▸ where and how the Earth moves through space

But there are many things that we still do not know. And there are some we may never know.

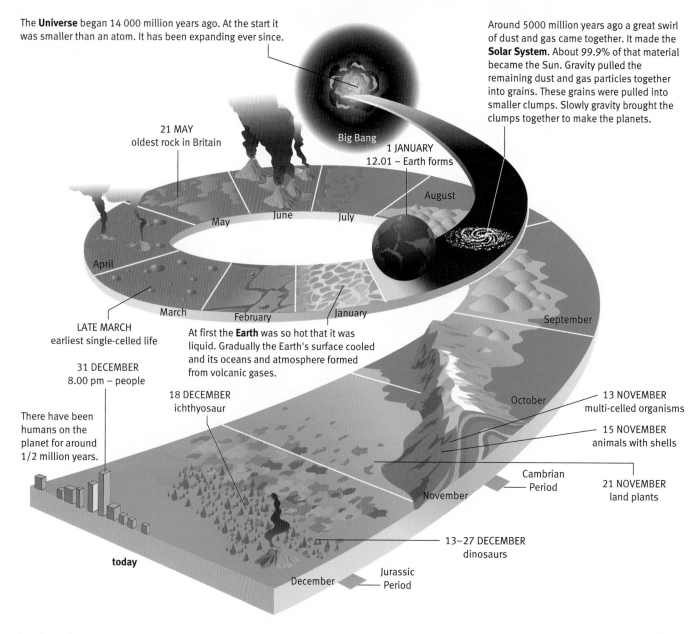

The **Universe** began 14 000 million years ago. At the start it was smaller than an atom. It has been expanding ever since.

Around 5000 million years ago a great swirl of dust and gas came together. It made the **Solar System**. About 99.9% of that material became the Sun. Gravity pulled the remaining dust and gas particles together into grains. These grains were pulled into smaller clumps. Slowly gravity brought the clumps together to make the planets.

Big Bang

1 JANUARY
12.01 – Earth forms

21 MAY
oldest rock in Britain

August

May   June   July

April

March   February   January

September

LATE MARCH
earliest single-celled life

At first the **Earth** was so hot that it was liquid. Gradually the Earth's surface cooled and its oceans and atmosphere formed from volcanic gases.

31 DECEMBER
8.00 pm – people

18 DECEMBER
ichthyosaur

13 NOVEMBER
multi-celled organisms

October

There have been humans on the planet for around 1/2 million years.

15 NOVEMBER
animals with shells

Cambrian
Period

21 NOVEMBER
land plants

November

today

13–27 DECEMBER
dinosaurs

December   Jurassic
Period

Timeline: from the big bang to the present day

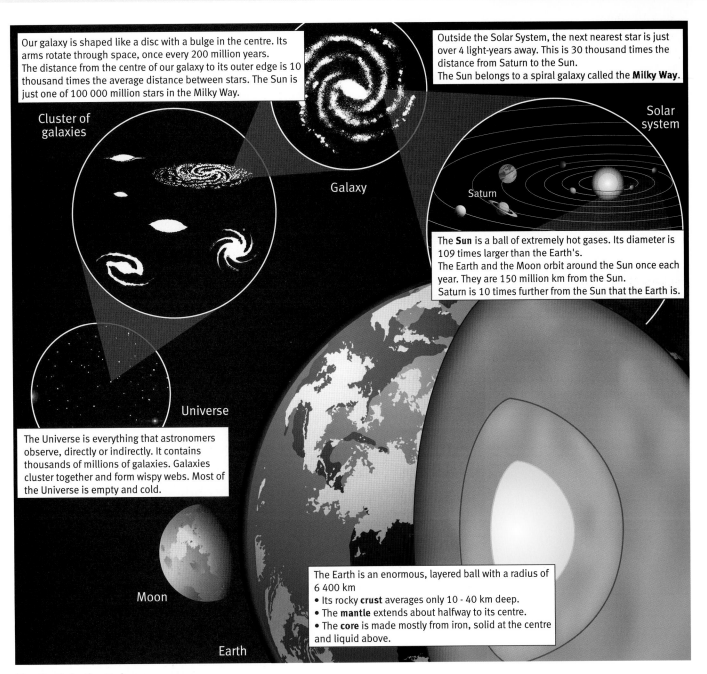

Our galaxy is shaped like a disc with a bulge in the centre. Its arms rotate through space, once every 200 million years.
The distance from the centre of our galaxy to its outer edge is 10 thousand times the average distance between stars. The Sun is just one of 100 000 million stars in the Milky Way.

Outside the Solar System, the next nearest star is just over 4 light-years away. This is 30 thousand times the distance from Saturn to the Sun.
The Sun belongs to a spiral galaxy called the **Milky Way**.

Cluster of galaxies

Galaxy

Solar system

Saturn

The **Sun** is a ball of extremely hot gases. Its diameter is 109 times larger than the Earth's.
The Earth and the Moon orbit around the Sun once each year. They are 150 million km from the Sun.
Saturn is 10 times further from the Sun that the Earth is.

Universe

The Universe is everything that astronomers observe, directly or indirectly. It contains thousands of millions of galaxies. Galaxies cluster together and form wispy webs. Most of the Universe is empty and cold.

Moon

Earth

The Earth is an enormous, layered ball with a radius of 6 400 km
• Its rocky **crust** averages only 10 - 40 km deep.
• The **mantle** extends about halfway to its centre.
• The **core** is made mostly from iron, solid at the centre and liquid above.

The Earth in the Universe

Questions

1 The timeline on page 58 shows the age of the Earth.

   a Redraw it as if it happened over a period of 14 years (roughly your lifetime).

   b On this scale, how long ago did the dinosaurs die out?

2 Make a list of the ways that scientists explore earlier times, or places that they cannot visit and observe directly. Think of as many ways as possible.

Key words

Universe	crust
Solar System	mantle
Milky Way	core
Sun	

Find out about:
▶ James Hutton's explanation for the variety of rocks he found
▶ how old rocks are and how scientists date them

B Deep time

James Hutton and the stories that rocks tell

Without some way of building new mountains, erosion would wear the continents flat.

Rivers carry sediment to the oceans, where it settles at the bottom as sand and silt.

Sediments form sedimentary rocks. In some places, layers of sedimentary rocks are tilted or folded.

Around 200 years ago, people were finding fossils of clamshells and other marine organisms in rocks at the tops of mountains. 'Why here?' they wondered.

James Hutton owned a big farm in Scotland. On journeys around England and Scotland, he studied rock formations and collected rock specimens (samples). Gradually, he learned to interpret rocks. An idea formed in his mind.

Use the present to interpret the past

In 1785 Hutton presented his startling new theory of the Earth. He explained it at a meeting of his local scientific club, the Royal Society of Edinburgh. Hutton described the rock cycle, like this:

'Over enormous periods of time, very slow processes such as **erosion** and deposition of sediment take place. They add up to huge changes in the Earth's surface. Heating inside the Earth too plays a part. The Earth has a history – it was not created all at once.'

The millions of years over which the Earth has changed are now called 'deep time'.

Dating rocks

Gradually, geologists learned to work out the history recorded in rocks. They used clues like these:

- deeper is older – in layers of rock, the youngest rocks are usually on top of older ones
- fossils are time markers – many species lived at particular times and later became extinct

But these clues only tell you which rocks are older than others. They don't tell you how old the rocks are.

Some rocks are radioactive. Scientists today estimate their age by measuring the radiation that these rocks emit (give off). This is called **radioactive dating**. The Earth's oldest rocks were made 3900 million years ago.

The development of scientific ideas

This first case study, about James Hutton, contains examples of:

- data
- expanations
- the role of imagination

Data

Fossils, rocks of different types, the way that rock types are layered, folded, or joined.

Explanations

Hutton's big idea, different ways of dating rocks.

Imagination

Most people in James Hutton's time believed in a young Earth. But Hutton could imagine the millions of years needed for familiar processes to slowly change the landscape.

Which layer has the fallen rock come from?

Key words

erosion

radioactive dating

Questions

1 In what time order did the creatures shown in the cliff above live?

Find out about:
▶ a scientific debate started by Alfred Wegener
▶ evidence that the continents are very slowly moving

C Continental drift

How are mountains formed?

In the 1800s, most geologists believed that the Earth began hot. They thought the Earth was like a drying apple. An apple shrinks as it dries. The skin of a drying apple becomes wrinkled. The Earth would have contracted (shrunk) as it cooled. Its surface would have wrinkled too. These geologists claimed that a mountain chain is one of those wrinkles.

Moving continents?

Many people can spot the match between the shapes of South America and Africa. The two continents look like pieces of a jigsaw. Alfred Wegener thought this meant that the continents were moving. They had once been joined together. He looked for evidence, recorded in their rocks.

In 1915 Wegener wrote his famous book, *The Origin of Continents and Oceans*. This presented his idea of **continental drift**. In the book he explained the evidence that backed up his idea.

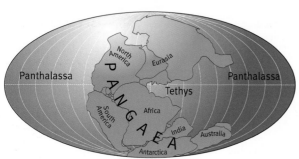

250 million years ago

Wegener showed how all the continents could once have formed a single continent, called Pangaea.

Key words

continental drift

Questions

1 In this case study, identify examples of

   a data

   b explanations

2 How did Wegener explain mountain building?

The Daily News   **2 November 1930**

POLAR EXPLORER DIES

The German meteorologist and polar explorer Alfred Wegener died yesterday. Aged 50, he was leading an expedition in Greenland. Unfortunately Wegener is likely to be remembered for being too bold in his science.

Wegener claimed that continents move, by ploughing across the ocean floor. That, he said, explains why there are mountain chains at the edges of continents.

As evidence of continental drift, he found some interesting matches between mountain chains, rocks, and fossils on different continents. But most geologists reject such an unlikely explanation for these observations.

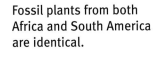

Mapping the seafloor

During the 1950s the US Navy paid for a lot of ocean science research. The Navy wanted to know how to:

- detect enemy submarines using magnetism, and
- move its own submarines near the ocean floor, where they could avoid detection

Ocean research completely changed our understanding of Earth processes.

From zebra stripes to seafloor spreading

Scientists started to make maps of the ocean floor. To their great surprise, they found a chain of mountains under most oceans. This is now called an **oceanic ridge**.

In 1960 a scientist called Harry Hess suggested that the seafloor moves away from either side of an oceanic ridge. This process, called **seafloor spreading**, could move continents.

Beneath a ridge, solid material pushes upwards on the ocean centre like warm toffee. Some of it melts to form magma. Hot magma erupts and cools to make new rock.

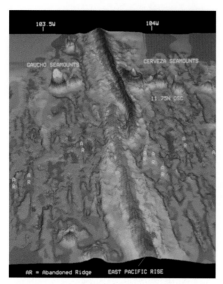

This computer-generated model shows part of the Pacific Ocean floor. (Water is not shown.)

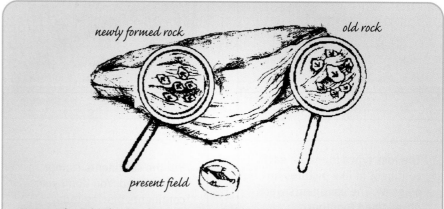

Now and again the Earth's magnetic field reverses. The magnetic North pole becomes the South pole, and vice versa. Iron-rich rocks record the Earth's field at the time that they solidified.

There is an identical zebra stripe pattern in rock magnetism either side of an oceanic ridge. The scientist Fred Vine worked out why this happens. Hot magma rises at a ridge and cools to make new rock. Fred Vine said that the new rock should be magnetized in the direction of the Earth's field at the time. That was in 1963.

By 1966 an independent group of scientists had found a clearer pattern of stripes in magnetic data either side of a different ridge. This forced other scientists to accept the idea of seafloor spreading.

Tanya Atwater was at university studying geology at that time. She describes a meeting of scientists. Fred Vine had shown them an especially clear pattern of magnetic stripes.

'[The pattern] made the case for seafloor spreading. It was as if a bolt of lightning had struck me. My hair stood on end. ... Most of the scientists [went into that meeting] believing that continents were fixed, but all came out believing that they move.'

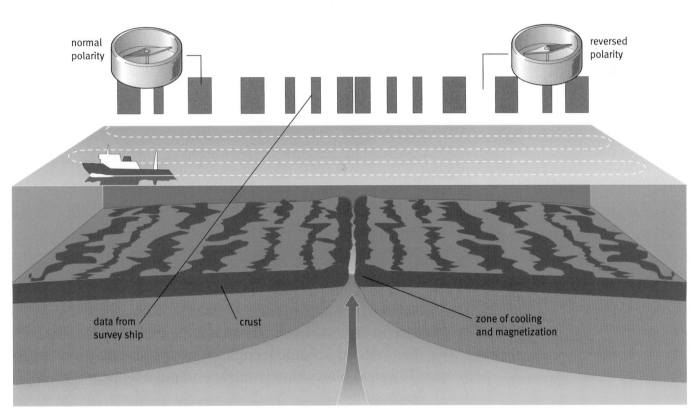

normal polarity

reversed polarity

data from survey ship

crust

zone of cooling and magnetization

New ocean floor is being made all the time at oceanic ridges. Rock magnetism either side of an oceanic ridge shows the same zebra stripe pattern.

Questions

3 In this case study, identify examples of:

a data

b explanations

c prediction

Key words

oceanic ridge

seafloor spreading

Find out about:

▶ a big explanation for many Earth processes

▶ ways to limit the damage caused by volcanoes and earthquakes

Ⓓ The theory of plate tectonics

By 1967, scientists had combined seafloor spreading with other things they knew about the Earth. They linked them together in one big explanation. It was called plate tectonics.

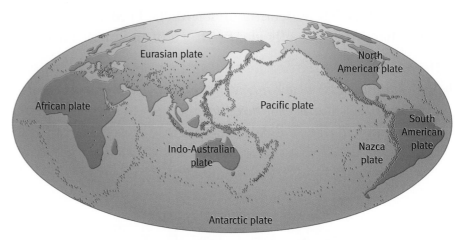

Each red dot on this a map represents an earthquake. Earthquakes happen at the boundaries between tectonic plates.

This is the plate tectonics explanation of the Earth's outer layer.

▶ The Earth's outer layer is made up of about a dozen giant slabs of rock. These are called **tectonic plates**.

▶ Convection currents in the Earth's solid mantle carry the plates along.

▶ The ocean floor continually grows wider at an oceanic ridge by seafloor spreading.

▶ Ocean floor is destroyed where the plate dips down beneath an oceanic trench.

▶ The rigid plates slowly move and push against each other.

Global Positioning Satellites (GPS) measure the movement of continents. The Atlantic is growing wider by 2.3 cm every year. This is roughly how fast your fingernails grow. In some places, seafloors spread as fast as 20 cm each year.

Earthquakes and volcanoes

Earthquakes are common at all moving plate boundaries. Because bits of plate get locked together like teeth, none of these movements are smooth or graceful. Each movement happens in a jolt, causing an **earthquake**.

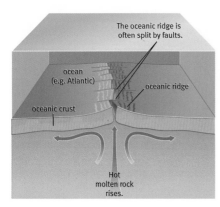

Constructive margin

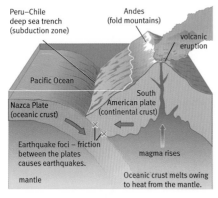

Destructive margin

Earth scientists record more than 30 000 earthquakes a year. On average, one of these is hugely destructive.

A **volcano** is simply a vent in the Earth's surface that erupts magma (molten rock). Volcanoes are common at plate boundaries. These are where the Earth's crust is being stretched or compressed.

Some volcanoes erupt regularly. Others store up pressure for thousands of years. Then they go off with a huge bang. Scientists monitor volcanoes and watch for warning signs. Each year there are about 50 eruptions from the world's 500 active volcanoes.

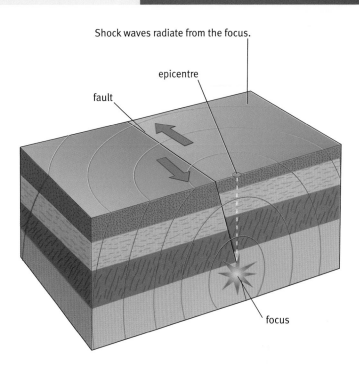

Shock waves radiate from the focus.

epicentre

fault

focus

Reducing the damage

Governments can try to reduce the number of people injured or killed in the event of a volcano erupting or a serious earthquake.

Sometimes a volcanic eruption can be predicted. These people need to be evacuated from the affected area.

Governments can prepare for an earthquake or a tsunami. They can:

- educate people, so they will know what to do.
- enforce building regulations. These can reduce the chance of buildings collapsing.
- prepare emergency plans. Then trained staff can respond quickly.

Questions

1 a How far does the Atlantic spread in 100 years (a lifetime)?

b How far has it spread in 10 000 years (all of human history)?

c How far has it moved in 100 million years?

2 a Where do most earthquakes and volcanoes occur?

b Why do they occur there?

Key words
tectonic plates
earthquake
volcano

Find out about:
▶ reasons for studying craters
▶ possible explanations for the extinction of dinosaurs

(E) The Solar System – danger!

Attack from space

Look up into a starry sky. You might see a streak of light dash across the sky. That's a meteor. Most meteors are tiny grains of dust. They shower down from space all the time. There will be quite a few micrometeorites on your school roof. They have diameters of less than 1 mm.

Only a few ever reach the Earth's surface. The bigger ones that hit the ground are called meteorites. A few times during the Earth's history a massive **asteroid** or **comet** has struck.

Barringer crater

The Barringer crater, Arizona, USA. The crater floor is 200 m below the rim. It is the size of 20 football pitches.

There is a huge crater in Arizona, USA. The first scientists to see it thought it was made by a volcano. But in 1902, a mining engineer, Daniel Barringer, suggested another explanation. The crater contains many fragments of iron. He knew meteorites also contain iron. He thought that a violent impact had made the crater.

Other scientists weren't all so sure at first. They found:

▶ quartz dust particles that are only created by huge pressures
▶ layers of rock in reverse order

Observations like this supported the impact explanation.

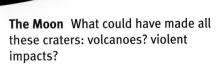

The Moon What could have made all these craters: volcanoes? violent impacts?

The age of the Solar System

Scientists have tested rocks from the Earth, from meteorites, from Mars, and from the Moon. None are older than 5000 million years. So, the Solar System is probably about 5000 million years old.

Crater work

Michelle Boast is a research scientist doing research at the Sudbury crater in Canada. A long time ago a major impact made this crater. The Earth has changed a lot since then. Michelle and her team are studying the layers of rock to work out the crater's history. Their aim is to find copper and nickel resources in the rocks.

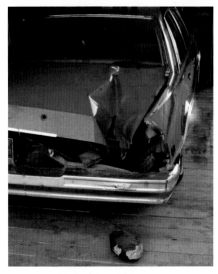

An iron-rich meteorite hit this car in Peekskill, New York. Fortunately no one was injured. Meteorites hit the Earth's surface with speeds of 12 to 70 km/s.

Michelle, on the right, and her assistant Tamara after a day's work at the Sudbury crater.

Michelle's team is writing scientific papers about their research. She'll present these to science journals for publication. Then, geologists all over the world will read them.

Michelle has no ordinary job. At the crater site she often has to camp. And she has an assistant with her for safety as one of the main hazards there is wild bears!

Questions

1 Look carefully at the photograph of the Moon. Describe any evidence there is that the craters were not made all at once.

2 **a** What metals are found at the Barringer and Sudbury crater sites?

   b Why are metals found there?

3 Why do Michelle Boast and her team write scientific papers?

Key words
asteroid
comet

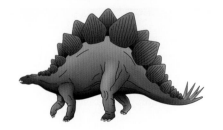

What killed off the dinosaurs?

A **mass extinction** is dramatic. A lot of the world's plants and animals die out. The most famous mass extinction was 65 million years ago. That was when the dinosaurs disappeared.

What caused these extinctions is something that scientists cannot yet agree about. It is still an area of scientific uncertainty.

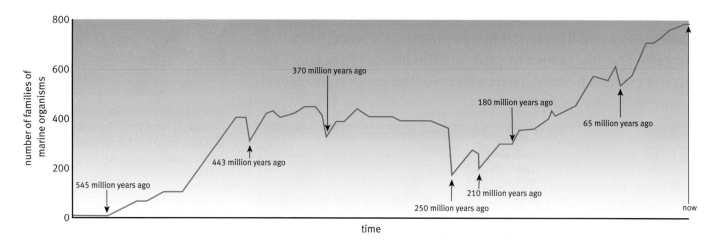

Asteroid collision – evidence and explanation

Luis and Walter Alvarez found an unusual, thin layer of clay in rocks in Italy. The clay contained a metal called iridium. The iridium was in amounts that are common in meteorites or asteroids.

They worked out that the clay arrived there 65 million years ago.

In 1980 they published a scientific paper. They suggested that the clay layer was the dust from an asteroid collision. They also said that this could explain the extinction of the dinosaurs.

They knew that they could be wrong. But in 1991, some other scientists dated a huge impact crater at Chicxulub, Mexico. It was 65 million years old. Others found iridium-rich deposits at different places, all around the world.

So there *was* a violent impact 65 million years ago. The impact must have partly vaporized the ground and the asteroid. Wind would have carried the material all around the planet. Eventually it would have settled into a layer of dust on the ground.

The big BUT

But we still can't be totally sure that an asteroid impact wiped out the dinosaurs. There are reasons to be uncertain. For example, many plants, dinosaurs, and other animals were becoming extinct before the asteroid hit.

Another explanation – enormous eruptions

In India there are huge layers of rock called basalt. It must have arrived there in floods of molten rock. There were hundreds of lava flows from a super-volcano. Eruptions release poisonous gases.

The eruptions that made India's basalt were strongest 65 million years ago. But they started before then. These eruptions could explain why extinctions began earlier than 65 million years ago.

There are flood basalts in Siberia, too. Those are much older – 250 million years. In the worst mass extinction ever, 95% of all the world's species died out at that time.

Basalt in India now. It took many eruptions to produce this rock, all between 63 and 68 million years ago.

Another big BUT

But there were also flood basalt events that did not cause any mass extinction. Some of the rocks of Scotland and Northern Ireland are flood basalts. They became solid 58 million years ago. There was no mass extinction then.

> **Key words**
> mass extinction

> **Questions**
>
> **3** Copy and complete this table, using the information above:
>
> | Explanation for dinosaur mass extinction | Evidence that supports the explanation | Problems with the explanation |
> | --- | --- | --- |
> | Asteroid collision | | |
> | Flood basalt events | | |
>
> **4** Do these problems prove that either explanation is **a** wrong **b** right?
>
> **5** What points do the two explanations agree about?

Find out about:
▶ how scientists know what stars are made from
▶ the process that releases energy in stars and produces new elements

(F) What are we made of?

Everything on Earth is made from just 92 kinds of atom, or elements. Salt, soil, ants, trees, and humans are all made from the same stuff.

Stars and Earth stuff

Scientists can spread light into spectra and study the colours present. This tells them two things about a light source:

1 its temperature. For example, a white-hot spark is hotter than a red-hot bar of iron

2 what it is made of

The Sun is a light source. Sunlight reveals how hot the Sun is. It can also show what the Sun is made of.

When astronomers first looked at the spectrum of sunlight, they were amazed. They looked at other stars. Exactly the same 92 elements, everywhere.

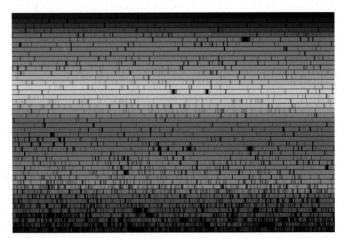 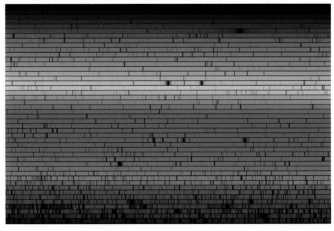

The spectra of the bright star Arcturus (left) and the Sun (right) – similar but not identical. The colours in its light show that the Sun is hotter.

Nuclear fusion

Scientists once struggled to understand the Sun. It could not be a great ball of fire. Fire needs fuel and oxygen. Any oxygen would have run out long ago.

Then scientists found that joining hydrogen atoms together forms helium. This releases energy in a process called **nuclear fusion**. It happens in stars. Fusion is what produces the light and warmth of the Sun.

Star birth

This is an explanation of how nuclear fusion begins in stars:

> There is an enormous cloud of hydrogen gas spread out in space.
> Gravity pulls the atoms together.
> The hydrogen cloud collapses, faster and faster.
> Some of the atoms hit each other hard enough to join together. Nuclear fusion starts.
> Fusion releases energy. The energy keeps the temperature high. It also keeps the atoms moving fast.

This photograph, taken by the Hubble Space Telescope, shows new solar systems forming in a dense gas region called the Eagle nebula. Dusty discs surround baby stars.

Star death

Sooner or later a star begins to run out of hydrogen. No star lasts forever. Stars, like people, frogs, and trees, have **life cycles**.

Heavy elements are made in stars

The most common element in the Universe is hydrogen. In stars, fusion makes heavier and heavier elements. When fusion stops, big stars explode as supernovae. Their debris is scattered through space. It contains all 92 elements.

When our Solar System formed, it gathered debris from dead stars. The chemical elements that make up everything on Earth come from stars. We are made of stardust.

This star exploded in 1987. This second image shows its gassy remains. The supernova behaved as scientists had predicted.

Questions

1 Copy and complete this table to summarize some key information.

What scientists know	How scientists know it
how hot stars are	
what stars are made of	
the Sun is not a ball of gas on fire	
stars run out of hydrogen	

2 The text above says, 'We are made of stardust'. Give the explanation for this statement, in a short sentence or two.

Key words
nuclear fusion
life cycles (star)

Find out about:
▶ ways of measuring the distance to stars
▶ planets around stars other than the Sun

G Are we alone?

In good conditions, you can see more than 2000 stars at a time with your unaided eyes. People have talked for centuries about other possible worlds. Now a scientific search for aliens has begun.

The Sun, Moon, and planets appear to move against a fixed background of stars. This means that stars are not part of the Solar System.

Star distances

The stars are a long way away. Here are two ways scientists use to work out their distances.

1 Parallax

The Earth moves from one side of the Sun to the other, every six months. Nearby stars shift their position against the background of more distant stars. The nearer a star is, the more it seems to shift. This effect is called **parallax**.

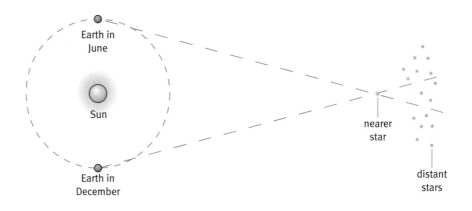

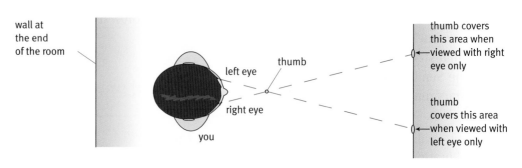

To see the parallax effect, hold up your thumb and look at it with each eye in turn.

2 Brightness

Imagine a large number of lights of different brightness. Some are much further away than others. It could be hard to tell the difference between a nearby torch and a distant searchlight. But if you know whether a light is a torch or a searchlight, then you can judge its distance.

That's how it is with stars. You need to know what kind of star you are looking at. Then you can use its apparent brightness to estimate its distance. The nearer a star, the brighter it seems.

These streetlights all shine with the same brightness. But the further away a streetlight is, the less bright it appears.

Light-years away

Proxima Centauri is the closest star outside the Solar System. Parallax measurement shows that it is 4.22 light-years away.

Light moves fast. It could travel the length of Britain in a few millionths of a second. A **light-year** is the enormous distance that light travels in a year.

Are we alone?

Astronomers have so far (in 2005) found 130 stars that have planets. The number keeps rising. Planets around distant stars are called **exoplanets**. Perhaps a few of these planets are suitable for life.

In 1992, NASA began a Search for Extra-Terrestrial Intelligence. It looks for radio signals from aliens, checking one star at a time. About 50 000 people around the world use their home computers to help process the data that SETI collects.

So far there is no evidence of life elsewhere.

In 2004, astronomers made the first ever image of an exoplanet. They called it 2M1207.

Questions

1 Some light from Alpha Centauri is reaching Earth as you read this. How old were you when that light left Alpha Centauri?

2 There may be intelligent life forms on exoplanets. What risks and benefits could there be in communicating with them?

Key words
parallax
light-year
exoplanets

Find out about:
▶ clusters of stars called galaxies
▶ an explanation called 'big bang'

Ⓗ How did the Universe begin?

The stars that you can see are part of the Milky Way. On a cloudless night you might also see one or two faint patches of light. These are nebulae.

New telescopes

Around 1920, astronomers in America built big new telescopes. These were on mountaintops, far away from cities. There is less **light pollution** from streetlights at these locations.

Astronomers looked closely at some of the nebulae. They could see that some of them are dense clusters of stars. The distance to these clusters seemed to be more than 100 000 light-years.

This is the view towards the centre of our own Milky Way galaxy. Each speck is a star. The distance across our galaxy is over 100 000 light-years.

More than one galaxy

Some nebulae have a spiral shape. Andromeda, for example.

Edwin Hubble used a new telescope to try to find out how far away Andromeda is. The result was stunning. It seemed Andromeda was a *million* light-years away. It is another collection of stars, far away from our own but not so different.

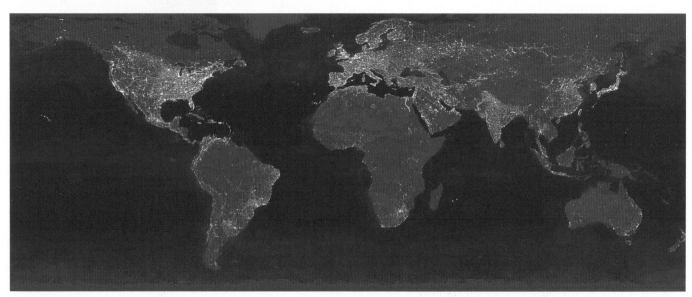

Satellites produced this night image of the Earth. Many parts of the Earth are affected by light pollution.

A huge collection of stars held together by gravity is called a **galaxy**. The Milky Way and Andromeda are both galaxies.

Generations of stars

The galaxies in the picture (on the right) are very far away. The light that made the image left them long before the Sun and the rest of the Solar System existed.

Their stars died thousands of millions of years ago. Debris from these stars included atoms of oxygen, carbon, and iron. Those atoms may now be inside later generations of stars and planets.

The Universe

The Universe is everything. It's stars and galaxies. It's clouds and oceans. It's bacteria and birds. You are part of the Universe.

The big bang

The light from distant galaxies shows that clusters of galaxies are all moving away from each other. The Universe is big and getting bigger. Space itself is expanding.

Imagine filming this expanding Universe. If you ran the film backwards, you could see how it all began.

The Universe once had no size at all. It burst into existence from nothing. It was incredibly hot. This is called the **big bang** theory. Most scientists agree with this explanation. There are several lines of evidence for it. The most convincing evidence comes from microwaves.

The Universe is about 14 000 million years old. Its future is very difficult to predict

This is a Hubble Space Telescope image of very distant galaxies.

Subrahmanyan Chandrasekhar's studies of the structure and evolution of stars won him the Nobel Prize in 1983. NASA's Chandra X-ray telescope was named in his honour. It was launched in 1999.

Questions

You will also need to look back at page 59 of this chapter.

1 a What is the 'Milky Way'?

  b Roughly how many stars make up the Milky Way?

2 a Imagine there is a clear night sky across all of Britain. Where would you see more stars from: a city full of street lights, or the dark countryside?

  b Look at the night image of Earth from space. Which parts of the world are affected by light pollution?

3 How and when did the Universe begin?

Key words
light pollution
galaxy
big bang

Science explanations

In this Module you have seen how scientists gather evidence (data and observations) and try to persuade others of their explanations of it.

You should know:

▶ how rocks provide evidence for changes in the Earth

▶ Alfred Wegener's explanation of mountain-building

▶ the Earth must be older than its oldest rocks

▶ some evidence for continental drift and tectonic plates

▶ where earthquakes, volcanoes, and mountain building generally occur

▶ several things that public authorities can do to reduce the damage caused by geohazards

▶ what is in our Solar System

▶ fusion of hydrogen is the source of the Sun's energy

▶ possible consequences of an asteroid collision with the Earth

▶ light travels at very high speed

▶ distant objects in the night sky are observed as younger than they are now

▶ the Sun is a star in the Milky Way galaxy.

▶ all chemical elements with a larger mass than helium were made in earlier stars.

▶ distant galaxies are moving away from us

▶ the Universe began with a 'big bang' about 14 000 million years ago.

▶ the relative ages of the Earth, the Sun, and the Universe; and the relative diameters of the Earth, the Sun, and the Milky Way.

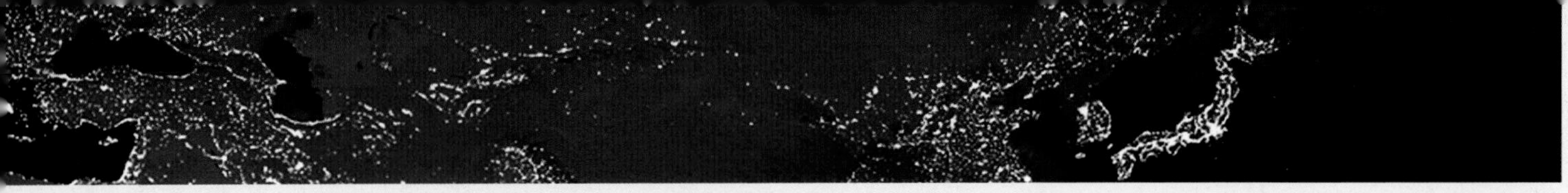

Ideas about science

New scientific data and explanations become more reliable after other scientists have critically evaluated them. This process is called peer review. Scientists communicate with other scientists through conferences, books, and journals.

Scientists test new data and explanations by trying to repeat experiments and observations that others have reported.

The chapter includes many Case Studies. From these you should be able to identify:

▶ statements that are data

▶ statements that are all or part of an explanation

▶ data or observations that an explanation can account for

▶ data or observations that don't agree with an explanation

Scientific explanations should lead to predictions that can be tested. You should know:

▶ how observations that agree or disagree with a prediction can make scientists more or less confident about an explanation

Scientists don't always come to the same conclusion about what some data means. The debate about Wegener's idea of continental drift provides an example of this. You should know:

▶ working out an explanation takes creativity and imagination

▶ why Wegner's explanation was rejected at the time

▶ some scientific questions have not been answered yet

▶ distances to many stars and galaxies are not known exactly, because they are so difficult to measure

▶ the ultimate fate of the Universe is difficult to predict

These ideas are illustrated through Case Studies, including: James Hutton; Alfred Wegener; Fred Vines; Daniel Barringer; Michelle Boast; Luis and Walter Alvarez; Edwin Hubble; and Subrahmanyan Chandrasekhar.

Why study keeping healthy?

Good health is something everyone wants. Stories about keeping healthy are all around you, for example, news reports about what to eat, new viruses and 'superbugs'. New evidence is reported everyday. So the message about how to stay healthy often changes. It's not always easy to know which advice is best.

The science

Some diseases are caused by harmful microorganisms. Your body has ways to stop them getting in. If you are infected it has amazing ways of fighting back. Vaccines and drugs can help you survive many diseases, and doctors are always trying to develop new ones. But, not all diseases are caused by microorganisms. Your lifestyle may also put you at risk. Media reports often warn about the dangers of smoking, eating badly, and not exercising.

Ideas about science

So, how do you decide which health reports are reliable? Knowing about correlation and cause and peer review will help. There are also ethical questions (arguments about right and wrong) to consider when deciding how we should use vaccines and drugs.

Keeping healthy

Find out about:

▶ how your body fights infections

▶ arguments people may have about vaccines

▶ where 'superbugs' come from

▶ how new vaccines and drugs are developed and tested

▶ how scientists can be sure what causes heart disease

Find out about:
▶ how some microorganisms (MOs) make you ill
▶ how your body keeps MOs out
▶ infections and lifestyle diseases

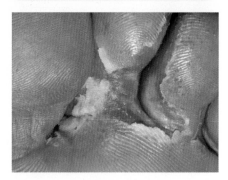

The fungus that causes athlete's foot grows on the skin.

A What's up, Doc?

Most days you don't think about your health. But everyone gets ill sometimes. Usually it is minor – like a cold. Other illnesses may be life-threatening, like heart disease or cancer.

There are lots of reasons for feeling ill. In the doctor's waiting room:

▶ the man with the painful knee has arthritis
▶ the young woman feeling sick and tired is pregnant – she doesn't know yet
▶ the man having his monthly check-up has had heart disease

No one else could 'catch' these conditions. They can't be passed on to other people.

But the other patients all have **infectious** diseases. Infections can be passed from one person to another.

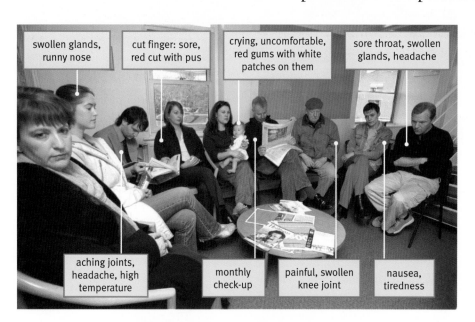

swollen glands, runny nose

cut finger: sore, red cut with pus

crying, uncomfortable, red gums with white patches on them

sore throat, swollen glands, headache

aching joints, headache, high temperature

monthly check-up

painful, swollen knee joint

nausea, tiredness

Passing it on

Infections are caused by some **microorganisms** that invade the body.

Microorganisms (MOs) are **viruses**, **bacteria**, and **fungi**.

Disease MOs can reproduce very quickly inside your body. This causes **symptoms** – the ill feelings you get when you are unwell. Symptoms may be caused by:

▶ damage done to your cells when the MOs reproduce
▶ poisons made by the MOs

	Virus	**Bacterium**	**Fungus**
Size	20–300 nm	1–5 μm	50+ μm
Appearance			
Examples of diseases caused	flu, polio, common cold, AIDS, measles	tonsillitis, tuberculosis, plague, cystitis	athlete's foot, thrush, ringworm

What are MOs like?

Microorganisms are very small. You need a microscope to see bacteria.

And viruses are even smaller. They are measured in nanometres. One nanometre is only one millionth of a millimetre.

Every breath of air you take has billions of MOs in it. And every surface you touch is covered with them. But most of the time you don't get ill. This is because:

) most MOs do not cause human diseases
) your body has barriers that keep most MOs out

Chemicals in tears destroy microorganisms .

If microorganisms get in through your mouth, acid in the stomach destroys most of them.

Your skin produces chemicals that make it hard for microorganisms to grow.

The skin is a physical barrier to microorganisms.

The human body has barriers to stop harmful MOs getting inside.

Are we safe from infections?

One hundred years ago most people died from infectious diseases. Today we have better hygiene and health care. So infections can usually be controlled. But some infections are becoming more common, for example, food poisoning.

Lifestyle diseases

Now **lifestyle diseases** are much more common than they were. These include heart disease and some cancers.

Lifestyle diseases aren't caused by infections. For example, most things that increase the risk of heart disease are to do with a person's lifestyle. These are factors like a high-fat diet, smoking, and lack of exercise.

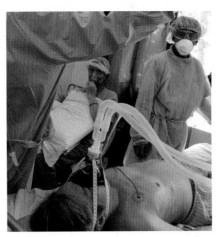

In 2003 a new infection called SARS appeared. Infections can still be very dangerous.

Questions

1 Choose one patient. Write down their symptoms. Say what you think is wrong with them.

2 Name three types of MOs that can cause disease.

3 Write down two different diseases caused by each type of MO you have named.

4 Explain two ways that MOs make you feel ill.

5 Describe three defences your body has to stop MOs from getting in.

Key words

infectious
microorganisms (MOs)
viruses
bacteria
fungi
symptoms
lifestyle diseases

Find out about:
▶ how white cells fight infections
▶ what antibodies do

B Microbe attack!

Jolene cut her finger when she was gardening. She didn't wash it quickly, so bacteria invaded her body. Inside they started to reproduce quickly.

How do bacteria reproduce?

Bacteria reproduce by a cell splitting into two new cells. These grow and then split again. The bacteria need warmth, nutrients, and moisture. If the conditions are right they can split every 20 minutes.

It was just a small cut, so I ignored it. By the time I went to bed it was a bit sore and red. Now it's all swollen and shiny. It really hurts.

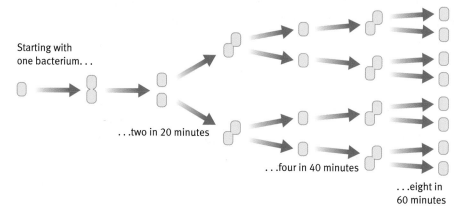

Starting with one bacterium. . .

. . .two in 20 minutes

. . .four in 40 minutes

. . .eight in 60 minutes

Bacteria can reproduce rapidly inside the body.

The battle for Jolene's finger

Conditions inside Jolene's body are ideal for the bacteria. But they don't have everything their own way.

Extra blood is sent to the cut finger. This makes it red and swollen. The blood is carrying the body's main defenders – the **white blood cells**. One type of white blood cell surrounds the bacteria and digests them.

The worn-out white blood cells and dead bacteria make pus. So redness and pus show that your body is fighting an infection. As the bacteria are killed the cut heals up.

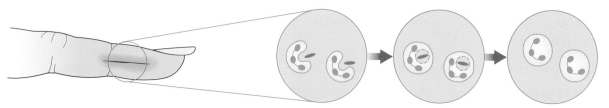

Jolene's body sends more blood to the area.

White blood cells surround the bacteria and digest them.

And the winner is?

Jolene's body should destroy the bacteria. She should keep the cut clean and use antiseptic cream. But there is a risk that the bacteria will get into her blood. This could make Jolene very ill.

Because her cut is quite deep, Jolene's doctor gives her a course of **antibiotics**. Antibiotics are chemicals that kill bacteria and fungi. Jolene's finger heals up in a few days.

Do antibiotics have side effects?

But Jolene is soon back at the doctor's. She has a common disease called thrush. Jolene's friend says that taking antibiotics gives you thrush. But she's not got the story quite right.

There is a link – a **correlation** – between some antibiotics and thrush. A person is more likely to get thrush if they have had a course of antibiotics than if they have not. But they won't definitely develop thrush. The diagram below explains the full story.

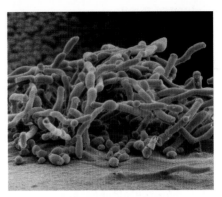

Candida albicans is the fungus that causes thrush. It lives on warm, moist body surfaces. Thrush usually infects the vagina or the mouth. (Mag: × 800 approx)

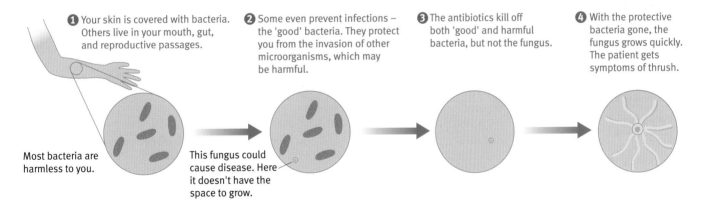

1 Your skin is covered with bacteria. Others live in your mouth, gut, and reproductive passages.

Most bacteria are harmless to you.

2 Some even prevent infections – the 'good' bacteria. They protect you from the invasion of other microorganisms, which may be harmful.

This fungus could cause disease. Here it doesn't have the space to grow.

3 The antibiotics kill off both 'good' and harmful bacteria, but not the fungus.

4 With the protective bacteria gone, the fungus grows quickly. The patient gets symptoms of thrush.

Questions

1 Write down the best conditions for bacteria to reproduce.

2 You have a small cut. How can you reduce your risk of an infection?

3 What two types of MOs are treated with antibiotics?

4 Describe why taking antibiotics may lead to thrush. You could do this in a flowchart.

Key words

white blood cells
antibiotics
correlation

Find out about:
▶ how white blood cells fight infections
▶ how you become immune to a disease

I've had a bad cold for four days. My neck is really swollen, and the stuff I'm blowing out of my nose is really horrible. Mum's worried about me missing school. She wants the doctor to give me antibiotics.

c Everybody needs antibodies – not antibiotics!

A bad cold can make you feel awful. All you feel like doing is staying in bed. And there's not usually much sympathy – 'What's all the fuss about? It's just a cold!'

Natalie goes to her doctor. He doesn't give her any antibiotics because colds are caused by viruses. Antibiotics have no effect on viruses. But the doctor knows that Natalie will get better. Her own body is fighting the infection by itself.

Your body's army – fighting a cold

The parts of your body that fight infections are called your **immune system**. White blood cells are a part of your immune system. Natalie's neck glands are swollen. This is because millions of new white blood cells are being made there. These white blood cells are fighting the virus in her body. The diagram explains how this is happening.

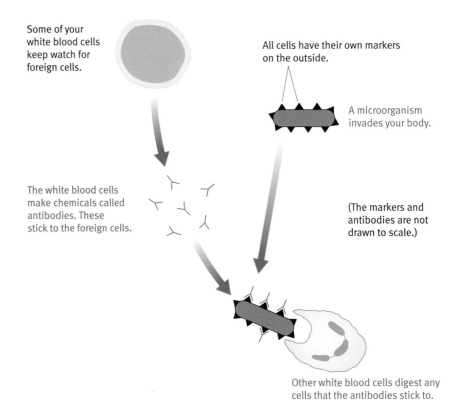

Some of your white blood cells keep watch for foreign cells.

All cells have their own markers on the outside.

A microorganism invades your body.

The white blood cells make chemicals called antibodies. These stick to the foreign cells.

(The markers and antibodies are not drawn to scale.)

Other white blood cells digest any cells that the antibodies stick to.

One type of white blood cell makes **antibodies** to label MOs. A different type digests the MOs.

If antibodies are so good, why do I get ill?

Every kind of MO is a different shape. For example, there are many different cold viruses. Your body must make a different antibody to fight each one. This takes a few days. So you get ill before your body kills the MOs.

This doesn't really matter if you've got a cold. But it does matter if the disease is serious. A person may die before the MOs are destroyed.

Once your body has made an antibody it is not forgotten. Some of the white blood cells make the antibody stay in your blood. If you are invaded again by the same MO, these white blood cells react straight away.

▶ They reproduce very quickly – so there are lots of them.
▶ They start making the right antibody straight away.

So your body reacts much faster the second time you meet this MO. Your body destroys them *before* they can make you feel ill. You are **immune** to this disease.

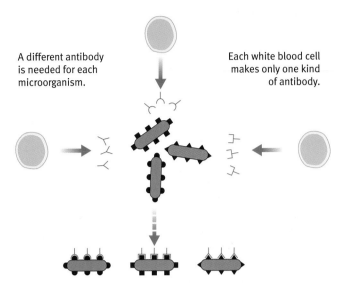

A different antibody is needed for each microorganism.

Each white blood cell makes only one kind of antibody.

Only the correctly shaped antibody can fight each MO.

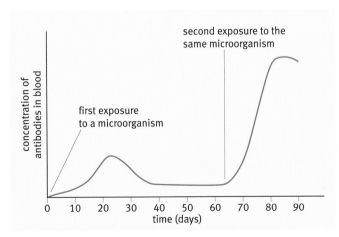

A person is infected twice by a disease MO. Their white blood cells make antibodies much faster the second time.

Key words

immune system   immune
antibodies

Questions

1 Why didn't Natalie's doctor give her antibiotics?

2 Write down one sentence to describe the job of the immune system.

3 Explain two ways that white blood cells protect the body from disease MOs.

4 Explain why different antibodies have to be made for every MO.

5 Draw a flowchart to explain how you can become immune to the chicken-pox virus.

6 Write a few sentences to explain to Natalie why she will never be immune to catching colds.

Find out about:
▶ how vaccines work
▶ deciding if vaccines are safe to use

D Vaccines

Small amounts of disease MOs are put into your body. Dead or inactive forms are used so you don't get the disease itself. Sometimes just parts of the MOs are used.

White blood cells recognise the foreign MOs. They make the right antibodies to stick to the MOs.

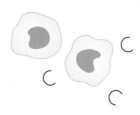

The antibodies make the MO's clump together. White blood cells digest the clump.

If you meet the real disease MO, the antibodies you need are made very quickly.

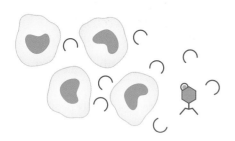

The MOs are destroyed before they can make you ill.
(Not to scale.)

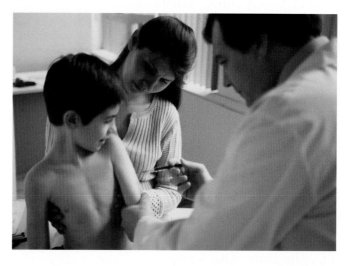

Vaccines are most important against infections that may be fatal.

This child is having a **vaccination**. It may not be much fun having the injection, but it's better than catching the disease. And the **vaccine** can protect him from this.

Age	Immunization
2, 3, and 4 months	polio, DTP-Hib (diphtheria, tetanus, pertussis, and hib – causes pneumonia and meningitis), meningitis C
13 months	MMR (measles, mumps, and rubella)
3–5 years	polio, DTaP (diphtheria, tetanus, and acellular pertussis), and MMR
10–14 years	BCG (against tuberculosis)
13–18 years	tetanus and polio

Many childhood diseases are very rare in the UK. This is because of vaccines.

How do vaccines work?

Vaccinations use your body's own defence system. They kick-start your white blood cells into making antibodies. So you become immune to a disease without catching it. The diagrams on the left shows how vaccines work.

Key words
vaccination
vaccines

Questions

1 Name two diseases you have been vaccinated against.

2 What is a vaccine made of?

3 Write a flowchart to explain how vaccines can stop you getting ill.

Are vaccines safe?

Any treatment you have if you are ill should:

- improve your health
- be safe to use

Vaccines protect you from disease. They are also tested to make sure that they are safe to use.

But remember that no action is ever completely safe. People react differently to all medical treatments. This includes vaccines. So a vaccine may cause some harmful effects in a few people.

Doctors decide that a treatment is safe to use when:

- the risk of serious harmful effects is very small
- the benefits outweigh any risks

You can read more about how new treatments are tested in Section F.

Should Tom have a flu vaccine?

Tom is weighing up the pros and cons of having a flu vaccine. Flu is a very serious disease. It kills thousands of people each year. Most of them are elderly or have other illnesses. Doctors ask these groups of people to have a new flu vaccine every year.

Why new flu vaccines each year?

If you catch flu you should get better, But you could catch this disease again. This is because small changes often happen to the virus. There are hundreds of different types. Your body must make different antibodies to fight each one. A different vaccine is needed for each one.

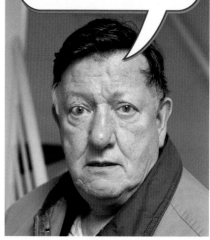

I've come for my flu vaccine. It seems like a waste of time to me – I had one last year. And my neighbour was ill straight after her vaccination. What's the point if it makes you ill?

Costs

small risk of a reaction to the vaccine – Tom might feel a bit ill for a few days

cost of providing Tom's flu vaccine is about £3.70

Benefits

much smaller risk of suffering from flu

saving to the NHS if Tom does not get flu could be £1000s

Questions

4 Explain why a vaccine can never be 'completely safe'.

5 Why must a new flu vaccine be made each year?

6 An elderly relative or friend has been offered a 'flu jab'. They are worried it may not be safe. What would you advise them to do? Explain your reasons.

In 2001 the media wanted to know if Prime Minister Tony Blair's baby son, Leo, had been given the MMR vaccine.

Amina had the MMR vaccine. Her mum says: 'I was worried. But my doctor explained how dangerous measles can be.'

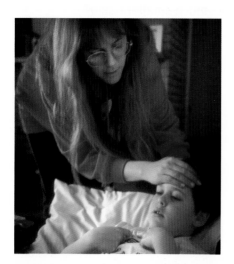

James has measles. He's very ill, but is getting better. His mum says: 'I didn't want James to have the vaccine. I was worried about whether it was safe. I didn't want to take the risk.'

Vaccines in the news

The MMR vaccine protects against three diseases – measles, mumps and rubella. But media stories about the MMR vaccine have worried many parents.

Whose choice is it?

The government knows that vaccines stop lots of people getting diseases. But to do this almost everyone in the population must be vaccinated.

The MMR vaccine means that only a very few people in the UK catch measles.

Which choice has the greatest risk?

Doctors ask parents to have their children vaccinated with MMR. Parents have to balance the risks of measles against the possible risk from the MMR vaccine:

- almost everyone who has the vaccine notices no harmful effects
- harmful effects from MMR can be mild (3 in every 100 000 children), or a serious allergic reaction (1 in every million children)
- some children who catch measles are left severely disabled (1 in every 4 000 cases)
- measles can be fatal (1 in every 100 000 cases)

What would you do?

It is better for our whole society if people have vaccinations. It makes the chance of anyone catching a disease much smaller.

But for a worried parent it is a hard choice. People need clear information to help them decide.

In the 1990s there were media reports about MMR and a link with autism. These reports have not been proven.

What is autism?

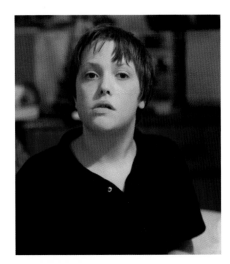

James has autism. He does not look disabled. This can make it harder for other people to understand his condition.

People with autism can find it hard to communicate. They may have problems with language or some thinking skills.

> Reality to an autistic person is a confusing, interacting mass of events, people, places, sounds, and sights. There seems to be no clear boundaries, order, or meaning to anything. A large part of my life is spent just trying to work out the pattern behind everything.

27 February 1998

MMR LINKED TO AUTISM?

A scientist claims that his work shows a connection between the MMR jab and autism. His comments have spread panic in parents. New figures show that fewer children in the UK are having the MMR vaccine.

Two children in Ireland have already died, and many were left disabled in a recent measles epidemic.

The World Health Organisation suggests that ideally 95% of children should receive the measles vaccination. In the UK in some areas, that figure has sunk as low as 61%, leaving the door open to an epidemic and all the problems this brings.

24 January 2004

'No link' between MMR and autism

Scientists have reported the strongest evidence yet that MMR does not cause autism.

Researchers looked at number of autism cases in a city in Japan, before and after the MMR vaccine was withdrawn in 1993.

Autism rates kept on rising, even after the vaccine was withdrawn. 'These results rubbish the claim that MMR has an effect on the rate of autism' said a leading scientist. He also suggested that cases of autism are going up because doctors are better at diagnosing it.

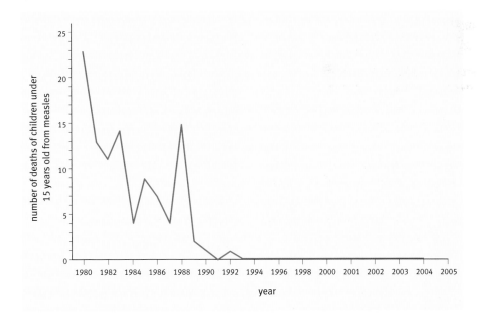

Questions

7 Write down three pieces of evidence about the safety of the MMR vaccine.

8 Describe two points of view parents may have about giving their child the MMR vaccine.

9 For each of these points of view list the main benefits and drawbacks for:

   a the child

   b other children

Find out about:
- where 'superbugs' come from
- how *you* can help fight them

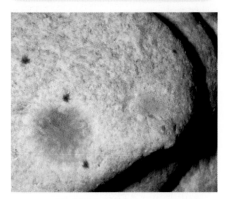

Antibiotics are made naturally by bacteria and fungi to destroy other MOs.

Tens of thousands of lives were saved during World War II by penicillin.

'SUPERBUGS' MRSA ON THE RAMPAGE

These killer bacteria are resistant to almost all known antibiotics. The bad news is that they have broken out of hospitals. People are dying of MRSA 'superbug' infections picked up at work, out shopping, and even at home. And the cause? The very antibiotics we've been using to kill them!

(E) The end for antibiotics?

The first antibiotics

This bread looks like it should be in the bin. But Ancient Egyptians used to put mouldy bread onto wounds. It could cure infections.

This mould is a fungus. It makes an antibiotic called **penicillin**. So the Egyptians may have been the first people to use antibiotics.

The wonder drug

In the 1940s scientists started growing moulds to make large amounts of penicillin.

At first penicillin was called a 'wonder drug'. Infections used to kill millions of people every year. Now many people could be cured by the antibiotic.

The bugs fight back

By 1950 doctors noticed that in a few cases penicillin didn't work. One type of bacteria was no longer killed by the antibiotic. It had become **resistant**.

Scientists found new antibiotics. But each time resistant bacteria soon developed.

Superbugs

The media often reports 'superbugs'. These bacteria are resistant to all known antibiotics, except one. How long that will last, we don't know.

Why are 'superbugs' developing so quickly?

Imagine your doctor gives you a five-day course of an antibiotic. After a few days you start to feel better. So you stop taking the medicine. This is one reason why superbugs are developing so quickly.

The bacteria MRSA is resistant to almost all antibiotics.

How can I make a difference?

If you take a full course of antibiotic, all the bacteria making you ill are killed.

But if you stop taking the antibiotic too soon some of the bacteria survive. These are most resistant to the antibiotic.

The resistant bacteria reproduce. So a population of antibiotic resistant bacteria soon grows.

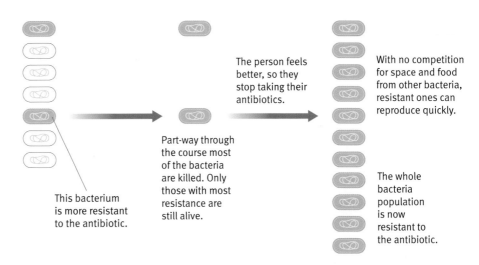

This bacterium is more resistant to the antibiotic.

Part-way through the course most of the bacteria are killed. Only those with most resistance are still alive.

The person feels better, so they stop taking their antibiotics.

With no competition for space and food from other bacteria, resistant ones can reproduce quickly.

The whole bacteria population is now resistant to the antibiotic.

How antibiotic resistant bacteria develop.

Can the superbugs be stopped?

Antibiotic resistant bacteria happen in nature. So scientists can't stop them developing. What they can do is try to stay one step ahead of the bacteria.

Using antibiotics as little as possible also helps. The fewer times bacteria meet antibiotics, the smaller the chance of a superbug developing.

You can help slow down the superbugs by:

 ▶ only using an antibiotic when you really need it
 ▶ always finishing a course of an antibiotic (unless side effects develop)

New drugs in strange places?

Crocodiles could give us new drugs to fight bacteria. A scientist wondered why they didn't die of infection when they bit each other's legs off. He has found a chemical in crocodile blood that kills bacteria.

Crocodiles have an anti-bacterial chemical in their blood.

Key words

penicillin   resistant
antibiotic

Questions

1 Remember the last time you had an antibiotic. Why did you have it?

2 What are antibiotic resistant bacteria?

3 Write bullet points to explain how antibiotic resistant bacteria can develop.

4 Write down two things everyone can do to help stop antibiotic resistant bacteria developing.

Find out about:
- how new drugs are developed
- how drugs are tested

F Where do new medicines come from?

Think of the last medicine you took. You will have checked how much to take. If you had a chance, you might want to ask some other questions.

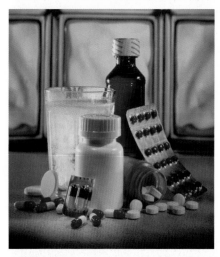

Medicines save thousands of lives in the UK every day.

Is it safe?

How much should I take?

Are there any side effects?

How did you discover the drug?

Has it been tested properly?

I'm not sure if I should have the new drug. Could I be risking my health?

Before the tests Anna would sign a patient consent form. She must have time to ask all her questions. She can leave the tests at any time.

Are drugs tested on people?

Five years ago Anna had breast cancer. She has been asked to take part in tests of a new drug to treat the disease.

Anna is worried about taking a new drug. Before she decides about the test she asks her doctors lots of questions.

Any new drug is checked in other ways before it is tested on people. So, Anna's doctors can give her quite a lot of information.

Stage 1: Human cells

The first tests of a new drug are done on human cells. The cells are are grown in a laboratory. Scientists use different types of cells with the disease. They try different concentrations of the drug on the cells.

These tests give the scientists data about:

- how well the drug works
- how safe it is for the cells

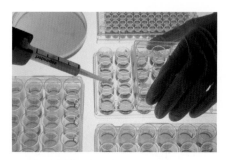

Drugs are first tested on cells grown in the laboratory.

Stage 2: Animal tests

If the drug passes tests on human cells it can be tested on animals. These tests give scientists data about:

- how well the drug works in whole animals
- how safe it is

Scientists must apply for a licence to test a drug on animals. Other scientists check the results of their work. Animal tests are only allowed if the early tests have shown that the drug could work.

Stage 3: Human trials

Tests on people are called **human trials** or **clinical trials**. It takes many years before scientists get to this stage. But if the drug passes animal tests, the scientists write a plan for human trials.

Again the scientists must apply for a licence to do the tests. Other scientists check that the plan is good enough.

- First the drug is tested on healthy people. This gives data about how safe it is to take.
- Then the drug is tested on people with the disease. This gives data about how well the drug works.

This last test is the one that Anna has been asked to take part in. Scientists have been working to develop this drug for over ten years.

Not everyone agrees that it is right to test drugs on animals.

The British Medical Association (BMA) believes that animal experimentation is necessary at present to develop a better understanding of diseases and how to treat them, but says that alternative methods should be used whenever possible.

Questions

1 Copy and complete the table:

Stage	Testing	To find out
one	Drug is tested on human cells grown in the lab.	• how safe the drug is for human cells • how well it works against the disease
two		
three		

2 What do you think Anna should do? Explain why you think this.

3 Developing a new drug is usually very expensive. Suggest why.

Key words
human trials
clinical trials

Find out about:
- what causes a heart attack
- how to look after your heart

G Circulation

Three weeks ago 45-year-old Oliver suffered a serious **heart attack**. He was very lucky to survive. Now he wants to try and make sure it doesn't happen again.

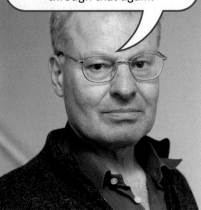

I'll never forget. I went cold and clammy, covered in sweat. And the pain – it wasn't just in my chest. It was down my arm, up my neck and into my jaw. I don't remember much else until I woke up in intensive care. I never want to go through that again.

Your body's supply route

Your heart is a bag of muscle. It pumps blood around your body. When you are sitting down your heart beats about 70 times each minute.

Tubes carry the blood around your body:

- **arteries** take blood from the heart to your body.
- **veins** bring blood back to the heart.

The diagram shows the flow of blood around your body.

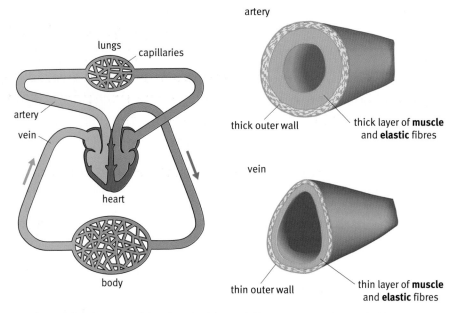

Arteries and veins carry blood to and from different parts of your body.

What is a heart attack?

Blood brings oxygen and food to cells. Cells use these raw materials for a supply of energy. Without energy the heart would stop. So heart muscle cells must have their own blood supply.

Sometimes fat can build up in the coronary arteries. A blood clot can form on the fatty lump. If this blocks an artery, some heart muscle is starved of oxygen. The cells start to die. This is a heart attack.

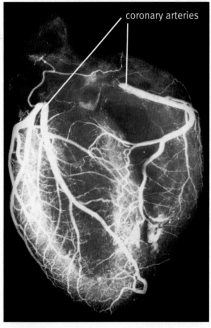

Coronary arteries carry blood to the heart muscle.

What causes heart disease?

Heart disease means any illness of the heart. So a blocked coronary artery and a heart attack are types of heart disease. Heart attacks are not normally caused by an infection. Your genes, your lifestyle, or most likely a mixture of both, decide if you suffer a heart attack.

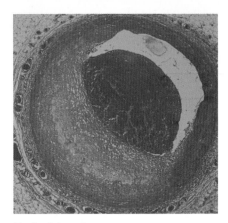

Fat build-up in a coronary artery.

How serious is the problem?

Each year in the UK 270 000 people have a heart attack. That is one every two minutes. Coronary heart disease is more common in the UK than in many poorer countries. This is because people on the UK do less exercise. Most people travel in cars and have machines to do many jobs. And a typical UK diet is high in fat.

Is Oliver at risk of another heart attack?

Oliver has a family history of coronary heart disease. He is also overweight and often eats high-fat, high-salt food. This diet has given Oliver high blood pressure and high cholesterol levels. He likes sport – but he'd rather watch it on TV than do exercise himself. The advice leaflet Oliver was given by his doctor is useful for everyone.

Key words

heart attack	veins
arteries	coronary arteries

Questions

1 Draw a diagram to show the inside of an artery and vein.

2 Label your diagrams to explain how these two blood vessels are suited to their jobs.

3 Explain why heart cells need a good blood supply.

4 Explain how too much fat in a person's diet can lead to a heart attack.

5 List four lifestyle factors that increase a person's risk of a heart attack.

6 Your next-door neighbour wants to do more exercise. But she gets bored easily, and doesn't want to spend money going to a gym. Suggest some ways that she could get more exercise into her daily life.

7 Why is coronary heart disease more common in the UK than in some other countries?

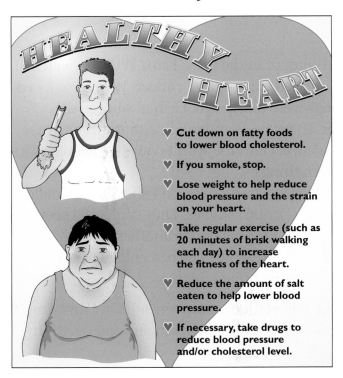

HEALTHY HEART

♥ **Cut down on fatty foods to lower blood cholesterol.**

♥ **If you smoke, stop.**

♥ **Lose weight to help reduce blood pressure and the strain on your heart.**

♥ **Take regular exercise (such as 20 minutes of brisk walking each day) to increase the fitness of the heart.**

♥ **Reduce the amount of salt eaten to help lower blood pressure.**

♥ **If necessary, take drugs to reduce blood pressure and/or cholesterol level.**

Find out about:
▶ how scientists learn about the causes of lifestyle diseases

Ⓗ Causes of disease – how do we know?

It's usually easy for doctors to find the cause of infectious diseases. It's harder to find the causes of lifestyle diseases, like heart disease or cancer.

Smoking and lung cancer

Government health warnings have been printed on cigarette packets since 1971.

But in 2003 the message was made much stronger.

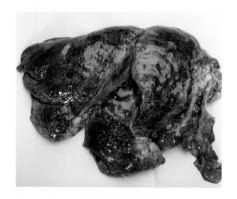

Lung tissue blackened by tar from cigarette smoke.

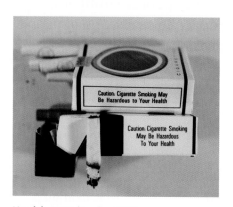

Health warning in 1971

Health warning in 2003

What evidence showed a link – a *correlation* – between smoking and lung cancer? And how did doctors prove that smoking *caused* lung cancer?

Early clues

In 1948 a medical student in the USA, Ernst Wynder, watched an autopsy. The man had died of lung cancer. Wynder noticed that the man's lungs were blackened. He had smoked 40 cigarettes a day for 30 years. Wynder knew that this one case wasn't enough evidence. One case won't convince people of a link between any two things.

In 1950, two British scientists, Richard Doll and Austin Bradford Hill, started a series of scientific studies. They compared people admitted to hospital with lung cancer, to another group of people in hospital for other reasons. The percentage of smokers in the lung cancer group was much higher.

So there is a link – a correlation – between smoking and lung cancer. But a correlation doesn't always mean that one thing *causes* the other.

Cigarettes smoked per day	Number of cases of cancer per 100 000 men
0 – 5	15
6 – 10	40
11 – 15	65
16 – 20	145
21 – 25	160
26 – 30	300
31 – 35	360
36 – 40	415

The table shows how the number of cases of lung cancer in men is affected by the number of cigarettes smoked.

How reliable was the claim?

Doll and Hill published their results in a medical journal. Other scientists looked at the results. This is called 'peer review'. The claim is more reliable if other scientists:

▸ can't find faults in the results, or how the study was done
▸ can get more data that shows the same thing

It wasn't long before lots more evidence was reported linking smoking to lung cancer.

A major study

In 1950 Doll and Hill started a much bigger study. They followed the health of 40 000 British doctors for over 50 years. They showed that:

▸ smokers die on average ten years younger than non-smokers
▸ stopping smoking at any age reduces this risk

Last piece of the puzzle – an explanation

Many doctors were now sure that smoking caused lung cancer. But cigarette companies did not agree. They said other factors could have caused the increases in lung cancer. For example, more air pollution from motor vehicles.

The missing piece of the puzzle was an explanation of *how* smoking caused cancer. In 1998 scientists discovered just this. They were able to explain *how* chemicals in cigarette smoke damage cells in the lung. This confirmed that smoking causes cancer.

Before 1920 lung cancer in the USA was very rare. As smoking became more popular with men, the numbers of lung cancer cases rose. This happened later for women, because very few women smoked until after World War II. The same pattern was seen in the UK.

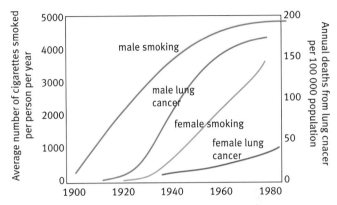

Questions

1 Write down one example of an everyday correlation.

2 Draw a graph to show how the number of cases of lung cancer in men is affected by the number of cigarettes smoked.

3 Explain briefly what happens during 'peer review'.

4 Explain why scientists think it is important that a scientific claim can be repeated by other scientists.

5 It's unlikely that many people would have agreed with Wynder if he'd reported the case he saw in 1948. Suggest two reasons why.

6 If a man smokes 20 cigarettes a day from age 16 to 60, will he definitely develop lung cancer? Explain your answer.

Looking at the health of lots of people can show scientists the risk factors for different diseases.

What makes a good study?

On the TV you see a news report. It says that using a mobile phone may damage your health. You want to know if the study has been done well. There are two things you can look for.

How many people were involved in the study?

A good study usually looks at lots of people. This means that the results are less likely to be affected by chance. In 1948, a study of heart disease began in Framingham, USA.

For the study, 5209 men and women aged 30–62 were recruited.

In 1971, their children were also recruited – another 5124 people.

Now the third generation – the grandchildren – are joining the study.

Every two years the researchers record each person's medical details. They also ask about the person's lifestyle. For example, if they smoke, and how much exercise they do.

In total the Framingham study is looking at over 13 000 people.

How well matched are the people in the study?

Health studies sometimes compare two groups of people. One group has the risk factor, the other group doesn't. For example, a study that compares people who use a mobile phone with people who do not. In these studies, it is important to **match** the people in the two groups as closely as possible. You can read more about this in Module P2 *Radiation and life*.

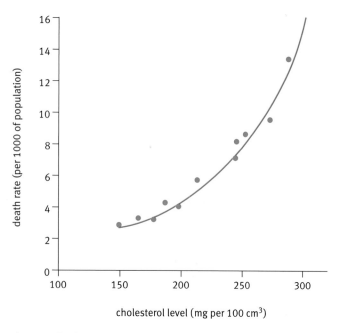

The graph shows some of the data from the Framingham study.

In many studies, like Framingham, people cannot be matched at the start of the study. The researchers are following the health of a particular group of people.

When the results of these studies are analysed, researchers check for differences between the people who have a disease and those who have not. If the two groups are very different, for example, they are not of the same ages, the researchers must make allowances for this in their conclusions.

The British Regional Heart Study

The British Regional Health Study began in 1975 in 24 towns across the UK. The researchers selected 8000 people at random. For 25 years the study measured factors that could affect their risk of heart disease.

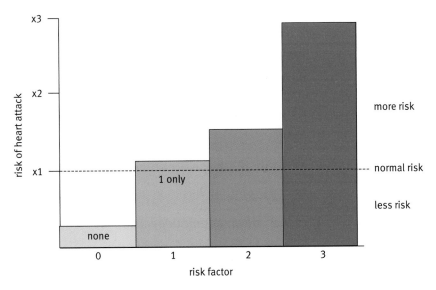

Data from the British Regional Heart Study shows that the more risk factors you are exposed to, the greater your risk of a heart attack.

The people in this study were all:

▸ men
▸ middle-aged at the start of the study

So the results of the study gave a true picture of heart disease risks. But *only* for men of this age group.

Key words
match

Improving the study

Age and gender both affect your risk of heart disease. The British Regional Heart Study results could not be used to decide about risk factors for women, or older men.

So, in 2001 the study was made bigger. It is now collecting data from men in other age groups, and women.

Questions

7 a Name one factor that increases a person's risk of heart disease.

 b Use information from the graphs on these pages to support your answer.

8 Suggest two factors you should look for when deciding whether a study was well planned.

Science explanations

In this chapter you have found out how your body fights disease. You have also seen how scientists learn about the causes of diseases.

You should know:

▶ diseases are caused by some microorganisms, and by a person's lifestyle, for example, smoking, poor diet

▶ natural barriers help to stop harmful microorganisms entering the body

▶ these microorganisms may reproduce very quickly in good conditions, damaging cells or producing poisons which cause symptoms of disease

▶ white blood cells are part of the immune system to fight infections

▶ white blood cells can destroy microorganisms by digesting them or producing antibodies

▶ different antibodies are needed to fight every different microorganism

▶ once you have made one type of antibody you can make it again very quickly, so you are immune to that disease

▶ vaccines trigger the body to make antibodies before it is infected with a particular microorganism

▶ vaccines contain a harmless form of the microorganism

▶ no action can be completely safe, including vaccinations and other medical treatments

▶ new vaccines must be made against flu every year because the virus changes quickly

▶ antibiotics are chemicals that kill bacteria and fungi

▶ an antibiotic may stop working because the bacteria or fungi have become resistant to it

▶ to slow down antibiotic resistant bacteria you should:
  - only use antibiotics when really needed
  - always finish the course

▶ new drugs are tested for safety and how well they work on:
  - human cells grown in the laboratory
  - animals
  - healthy human volunteers
  - people with the illness

▶ heart muscle needs its own blood supply to bring food and oxygen to the cells

▶ how the structures of arteries and veins are suited to the jobs they do

▶ fatty deposits in blood vessels supplying the heart can produce a heart attack

▶ heart disease is usually caused by lifestyle factors

Ideas about science

It is not always easy to make decisions about personal health. It can be difficult to decide whether information about health risks is reliable.

You should also be able to:

▸ correctly use the ideas of correlation and cause when discussing the issues in this module

▸ suggest factors that might increase the chance of an outcome

▸ explain that individual cases do not provide convincing evidence for or against a correlation

▸ evaluate a health study by commenting on sample size or sample matching

▸ describe what happens in 'peer review'

▸ know that scientific claims which have not been evaluated by other scientists are less reliable than ones which have

▸ know that if data cannot be repeated by other scientists it makes any scientific claim based on the data less reliable

People may have different viewpoints for personal and social decisions:

▸ some people think that certain actions are wrong whatever the circumstances

▸ some people think that you should weigh up the benefit and harm for everyone involved and then make your decision

People may make different decisions because of their beliefs, and their personal circumstances. When you consider an ethical issue such as vaccination policy you should be able to:

▸ say clearly what the issue is

▸ describe some different viewpoints people may have

▸ say what you think and why

Why study materials and their uses?

All the things we buy are made of 'stuff'. That stuff must come from somewhere. When you have finished with it, it has to go somewhere. The products people use every day are made of many different kinds of materials. Materials are chosen to do a job because of their properties. Everyone can make better choices about uses of materials if they understand more about these properties.

The science

Scientists use their knowledge of molecules to explain why different materials behave in different ways. This gives them the ability to design new materials with just the right properties to meet everyday needs.

Ideas about science

Scientists test products to check that they can do the job, are good value and safe. You can use data from these tests when you buy a product. So you need to be able to judge whether or not the results can be trusted.

Science can also help us to save money and cut down waste. Scientists make a careful analysis of the energy used, and materials needed, for each stage in the life of a product.

Material choices

Find out about:

▶ the testing and measurement that helps people to make good choices when buying products

▶ some of the explanations scientists use to design better materials

▶ ways to weigh up the costs and benefits of using different materials

▶ the choices people can make to reduce waste

Find out about:
- materials and their properties
- natural and synthetic materials
- long-chain polymers

A Choosing the right stuff

The newest fashion

The newest fashion

CHOCOLATE SHOES

Glossy shoes with a perfect fit. No rubbing, no corns, making your feet comfy, tasty, and attractive. Just dip your feet in luxurious molten chocolate to form a close-fitting slipper in one of three gorgeous colours: milk, dark, or white.

What the advertising agency didn't tell you

Of course this is a joke. Chocolate is not a good **material** for making shoes. Here are some reasons:

- it would crack
- it would melt in warm weather.
- dogs might follow you and lick your feet
- it would wear away
- it would leave a mess on the carpet

Maybe not chocolate

Although chocolate does not have the right **properties**, the idea of moulded shoes is not new. South American Indians used to dip their feet in liquid latex straight from the rubber tree. They would sit in the sun to let the latex harden, forming the first, snug-fitting, wellies. So latex is more suitable than chocolate for making shoes. It has some different properties that make it better.

Key words

material	natural
properties	synthetic
flexible	polymers

106

Fantastic elastic

The most obvious difference between latex and chocolate is that latex is **flexible**. The material of our shoes needs to be flexible. It also needs to be:

- hard wearing because you walk on it
- waterproof
- a solid at room temperature
- elastic so it keeps its shape
- flexible so you can bend your feet

Latex has all these properties. Chocolate does not.

Fit for purpose

Latex is not the only material for making shoes. Shoe designers decide on the properties they need. Then they choose from a number of different materials. As well as latex, they can use **natural** materials like cotton or leather. Or they can use a **synthetic** material like nylon, neoprene, or Gore-tex.

What's in a name?

These synthetic materials are all **polymers**. They have been made using chemicals and chemical reactions. We sometimes call them 'plastic' but this is a fairly loose, everyday word. The word 'polymer' is more useful because it tells us something about the material and its make up.

What are polymers?

All polymers have one thing in common: their molecules are long chains of repeating links. Each link in the chain is a smaller molecule which is joined up in the repeating pattern. This is true for natural polymers like cotton, silk, and wool and synthetic polymers like polythene, nylon. and neoprene.

You will find natural and synthetic polymers all around you.

Latex is a natural polymer that can be tapped from rubber trees. After treatment, it is used in a wide variety of products, including the soles of shoes.

Questions

1 Look at the picture of young people in a car. Identify items that can be made from:

   a natural polymers

   b synthetic polymers

2 The word 'synthetic' can mean different things at different times. Write down up to four words that come to mind when you hear the word synthetic.

Find out about:
▶ synthetic polymers made to meet our needs
▶ examples of plastics and their uses

Key words
plastic

B Polymers everywhere

What's in a name?

Polymers are all around us. Some are natural and some are man-made or synthetic. Many of these are what we would call **plastic**. They have often been created for a specific purpose or to meet a specific need.

Meeting our needs

Polymers can be made into products that meet our needs and improve our lives. These include:

▶ physical needs: providing shelter, warmth, and transport
▶ bodily needs: helping to supply food, water, hygiene, and health care
▶ social and emotional benefits: aiding human contact, leisure, and entertainment
▶ improving our minds: stimulating thinking, and creativity

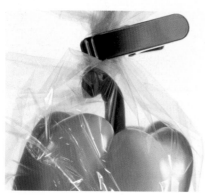
Polythene bags help people to protect, store, and carry food.

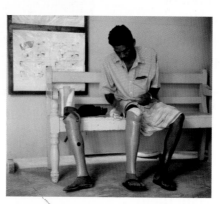
This patient in Sri Lanka is fitting a new leg made of polypropylene.

The world's first inflatable church made from PVC.

PET is a polyester used to make soft-drinks bottles and other food containers.

Polyester is used to make hulls and sails.

This acrylic painting was on show in a shop in Zanzibar.

Polycarbonate glass in the roof of the Manchester City stadium.

Kevlar helmets have saved the lives of many soldiers.

Austrians on a sleigh in traditional woollen dress with their old wooden skis. Wood and wool are both made from natural fibres. They are now often replaced with synthetic polymers.

A wet suit made from neoprene offers warmth and protection.

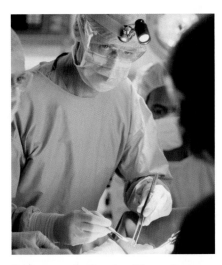

Doctors and other health workers wear gloves made of natural rubber (latex) for protection and to prevent infection.

Questions

1 Which products on these two pages meet our:
a physical needs **b** social needs?

2 Choose one of the products.

a Describe how it can help us improve our minds.

b It is made from a polymer. Write two sentences about where you think the polymer has come from.

3 a Write down two products made from synthetic polymers.

b i Write down two products made from natural polymers.

ii Choose one of these. Write down whether it could be improved by using a synthetic polymer.

iii Explain your answer.

Find out about:
- ▶ words scientists use to describe materials
- ▶ testing materials to ensure quality and safety

c Testing times

Getting the right material

Manufacturers and designers have to choose the right materials to make their products. Often, they choose a synthetic polymer. They decide which polymer to use based on its properties.

Here are two examples:

1 the soles of shoes have to be flexible, hard wearing, and **strong**. A synthetic rubber is a good choice.
2 A computer case needs different properties. It has to be **stiff** rather than flexible. Good ones are resistant to scratches – they are **hard**. Polypropylene and polycarbonate are both suitable.

Material words

When scientists describe the properties of materials, they use special words. Some of these, like strong, have everyday meanings that are similar to their technical meaning. Others are a little different.

- ▶ A stiff material is one that is difficult to stretch. It is the opposite of **flexible**
- ▶ hard and **soft** are also opposites. The softer a material, the easier it is to scratch it. A harder material always scratches a softer one
- ▶ a strong material does not break easily. A big force is needed to break it. Nylon and concrete are both strong materials

Climbers can pull on nylon ropes without them breaking. They are strong in **tension**.

Concrete is strong in **compression**. Whole buildings can rest on concrete foundations without breaking them.

Measuring the words

These words help us to describe materials. Sometimes it is also useful to measure their **values**. This lets engineers compare materials and test their quality.

Modern materials with special properties.

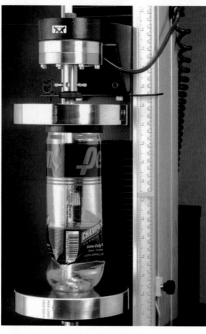

A testing machine for plastic packaging. Measuring the force needed to crush the container gives a value for the strength of the pack.

Key words

strong	soft
stiff	tension
hard	compression
flexible	values

For example, rope makers need to find strong, stiff fibres to make their climbing ropes. Their engineers test small samples to find the ones that are strong enough. The force that breaks each fibre tells them its strength.

They can also measure how much they stretch. A stretchy rope is not suitable for climbing mountains - but it would do for bungey jumping.

Nylon ropes are stiff, light and, most importantly, strong. It is reassuring to know that they have been tested.

	Stiffness	Hardness	Strength
chocolate	stiff	very soft	weak
polythene	flexible	soft	quite strong
cotton	flexible	soft	quite strong
leather	quite flexible	soft	strong
synthetic rubber	flexible	soft	strong
polycarbonate	quite stiff	quite hard	very strong

Quality control

The rope manufacturer also tests the strength of the final ropes. This is called 'quality control'.

The quality of a rope can be a matter of life and death. Sometimes it is less vital but still important.

John Fletcher is quality manager for Coates. This company makes sewing threads. He takes samples from every batch that leaves the factory and tests them. He makes sure that they have the correct strength and stiffness. His customers know they can rely on the quality of the threads.

John Fletcher tests his threads in this machine. It pulls on the threads with an increasing force. It measures the force when the thread snaps.

Questions

1 Look at the picture of skaters. Identify items which are: **a** flexible **b** stiff **c** strong **d** hard

2 Look at the entries in the table for chocolate and rubber. Find two properties for which they have opposite values. Use these to write two sentences explaining why rubber is better for making shoes than chocolate.

3 The skaters have chosen to practise on the asphalt path rather than on the grass.

   a What are the properties of asphalt that make it better for rollerblading?

If they were playing football, they would probably play on the grass.

   b What are the properties of turf that it make it better for playing football?

4 Engineers often test the properties of materials. Give two reasons why this is useful.

5 Draw up a table similar to the one here. Replace the words in the body of the table with numbers. Use a scale of 1 to 10 in each case. So, for example, the entry for the stiffness of chocolate could be 8 – stiff.

Find out about:
▶ materials under the microscope
▶ molecules and atoms in materials
▶ models of molecules

D Zooming in

A woollen jumper is very different from a silk shirt. The shirt is more formal and less stretchy than the jumper. They are both made from natural polymers but they are very different. Their properties depend on their make-up from the large scale to the invisibly small:

▶ what you can see – the weave of a fabric
▶ the microscopic shape and texture of the fibres
▶ the invisible molecules that make up the polymer

Silk

Magnification: x 20. Visible: to naked eye (just). Width of circle: 4 millimetres

Magnification: x 1000. Visible: down a microscope. Width of circle: 80 micrometres

Magnification: x 50 million. Visible: not even to a microscope. Width of circle: 1.5 nanometres

There are different levels of structure and detail.
(1000 micrometres = 1 millimetre and 1 000 000 nanometres = 1 millimetre)

What can you see?

Take a look at a woven shirt. You can probably see the weave – a criss-cross pattern of threads. It is difficult to stretch the fabric because the threads are held together so tightly.

A knitted jumper is different. It is stretchy and loose. Its stitches allow the threads to move around and reshape the garment.

You can see the weave and the stitches with your naked eye. They are visible in our macro-world so they are macroscopic.

The properties of a fabric also depend on smaller structures.

Get out the microscope

If you look at the fabrics under a microscope, you can see the individual fibres.

On the one hand, silk has smooth, straight fibres that slide across each other. On the other hand, wool fibres have a rough surface covered in scales. The wool fibres tend to cling to each other in the thread, and also make the threads cling together.

This is not the end of the story. In a test, a single wool fibre would be stronger than a single silk fibre. This is because their make-up is different in the world beyond the view of microscopes: the world of molecules.

The invisible world of molecules

Both wool and silk are polymers. Their molecules are long repeating chains. A molecule of silk has a repeating chain of carbon and nitrogen atoms. The arrangement of these atoms determines the strength, stiffness, and other properties of a silk fibre.

Models and molecules

No-one can ever see the atoms in the molecules – even with the most powerful instruments. So scientists build models and draw pictures to show how the molecules are arranged. Usually, the atoms are shown as little coloured spheres.

This does not mean that nitrogen atoms are actually like tiny blue billiard balls. But it helps if you think of them like that.

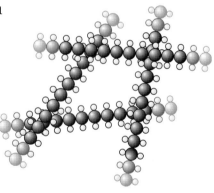

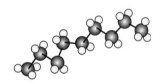

Gee. So that's what an atom looks like.

Atoms and molecules are too small to see. So no-one knows what they really look like. But it helps us to use models in the laboratory, in drawings, or in our mind's eye to help us understand what they do.

Questions

1 **a** Put these in order of size. Start with the largest: fibre, fabric, atom, thread, molecule.

   b Use the words in **a** to write four sentences that describe the decreasing structures. The first sentence might be: Fabrics are made by weaving together threads. Use linking words and adjectives to make the sentences interesting to read.

2 **a** How many chemical elements are there in silk?

   b Is silk a hydrocarbon?

3 A polymer molecule is about 1000 nanometres long. An atom is about 0.1 nanometres across.

   a How many atoms are there along the chain?

   b How many polymer molecules would fit into a millimetre?

Find out about:
- new technologies in war time
- polymer discoveries
- polymers as long-chain molecules

(E) The big new idea

The 1930s was the decade of the first polymers. The world was a tense place and war was on its way. Governments were looking for scientific solutions to give them an advantage. This speeded up many scientific developments. Some of these used the big new idea: polymers. The first synthetic polymer was discovered by accident.

Polythene appears by accident

In 1933, two chemists made polythene thanks to a leaky container. Eric Fawcett and Reginald Gibson were working for ICI. Their job was to investigate the reactions of gases at very high pressures. They had put some ethene gas into the container and squashed it to 2000 times its normal pressure. But some of the ethene escaped. When they added more ethene, they also let in some air.

In the Second World War, scientists were developing radar. But it was too heavy to take up in an aeroplane. They replaced its bulky insulators with polythene. The airmen called the system H2S. This sounds like it might be a chemical name but actually stood for Home Sweet Home.

What they found inside

Two days later, the chemists found a white waxy solid inside the apparatus. This was a surprise. The gas must have reacted with itself to form a solid. Somehow, the small molecules of ethene had joined with each other to make bigger molecules. The ethene molecules had **polymerized**.

The chemists worked out that the new molecules were like long chains. The chains were made from repeating links of ethene molecules.

The oxygen in the uninvited air had been the key. It helped to form the links between the ethene molecules.

A Polymer pioneer

Wallace Carothers was an American chemist who discovered neoprene and invented nylon. Neoprene was another accidental discovery. A worker in Carothers' laboratory left a mixture of chemicals in a jar for five weeks. Carothers discovered a rubbery solid in the bottom of the jar. He realized that this new stuff could be useful. During 1930, he developed it into neoprene – a synthetic rubber which is still used in wetsuits.

Neoprene tyres: America got its rubber from the Far East. The supplies were cut off during the Second World War (1939–1945). Neoprene replaced rubber during the Second World War.

Nylon

America and Japan were on bad terms in the years before the Second World War. Trade was difficult and the supply of silk was cut off. It became rare and expensive. Carothers started looking for a synthetic replacement. In 1934, his team came up with nylon. This is a polymer made from two chemicals. The different molecules join together as alternate links in the chain.

Sadly, Carothers died before he saw the effects of his discoveries. Nevertheless, they are both still in use today.

Silk stockings were rare in the Second World War. Some women used gravy browning to paint a seam on their legs to look like stockings.

What are polymers?

All polymers have one thing in common: their molecules are long chains of repeating links. Each link in the chain is a smaller molecule; it connects to the next one to form the chain. This is true for natural polymers such as cotton, silk, and wool and for synthetic polymers such as polythene, nylon, and neoprene.

Naming a polymer

Fawcett and Gibson called their material poly-ethene. We now call it polythene. The word poly means 'many'. A poly-ethene molecule is made from many ethene molecules joined together. The names of many polymers include poly followed by the name of the building block:

▸ Polystyrene is a chain made of styrene molecules
▸ Polypropylene is a chain made of propylene molecules
  and so on.

Key word
polymerized

Questions

1 a Write down the names of two polymers that were discovered by accident.

b Write down any other accidental discoveries that you know about.

2 Draw a timeline for the years from 1930 to 1950. Draw it running down the middle of a page. Put dates every five years.

a Put on the dates of the discovery of polythene, nylon, and neoprene. Mark these on the right of the timeline.

b Mark the dates for major world events in this period. You should include the Second World War. Do this on the left of the timeline.

c Mark on any other dates that you think are important to the stories of these polymers.

Find out about:
- long and short polymer chains
- explaining polymer properties

The molecules of candle wax are about 20 atoms long. Wax is weak and brittle.

The molecules of polythene are similar to those of candle wax. But they are about 5000 times longer. Polythene is much stronger than candle wax.

F Molecules big and small

The first synthetic polymers were discovered in the 1930s – sometimes by accident. Now chemists understand polymers much better. They can use their knowledge to explain their properties and develop new polymers. They can even choose what properties to give to new polymers. One of the key properties is strength.

The longer the stronger

The properties of a polymer depend on the length of its molecules. The molecules in candle wax are very similar to those in polythene. But wax is weaker and more brittle than polythene. This is because the wax molecules are much shorter. Wax molecules contain just a few atoms. A polythene molecule contains many hundreds of atoms. The molecule with the longer **chains** makes a stronger polymer. This is how.

A polymer tangle

A polymer is made up of long molecules. There are forces between the molecules. These forces hold the molecules together in a solid.

The molecules of wax are small. They are held together. But each one has only a few neighbours. This makes them easy to separate. This is why wax is so weak.

Breaking a lump of polythene is more difficult. Its long molecules are all jumbled up. Each molecule is held in by lots of other molecules. It is more difficult to pull the molecules apart.

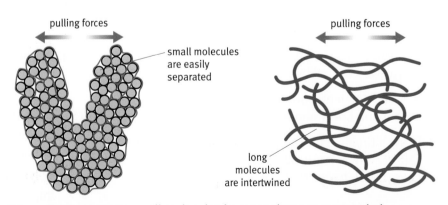

It is easier to separate small molecules because they are not tangled.

Using our imagination

No-one can ever see these molecules to find out what is going on. You have to use your imagination to think up a **model**. Sometimes a model is a kit that you put together. But sometimes it is a set of ideas. Often it helps to relate the model to something that you can see. This is called 'using an analogy'.

Imagine that wax and polythene are like bowls of pasta. You want to divide each bowl into two portions. Wax is like spaghetti hoops – small pieces of pasta. It is really easy to pull the pasta apart because all you have to do is separate a few hoops.

Polythene is more like a plate of proper spaghetti. This gets all tangled up. Each strand of spaghetti sticks to lots of other strands. It is difficult to prise them apart. The lump of spaghetti is stronger because of its long chains.

You can use your mind's eye to make models. You can imagine different models of the same situation. The model you choose is the one that is best at explaining what is happening.

> **Key words**
> chains
> model

Questions

1 Look at the section called *A polymer tangle*. Make a table to summarize the differences between wax and polythene. Include the size of their molecules, their properties, and how their molecules give them those properties.

2 Look at the section *Using our imagination*. It uses an analogy. The two polymers have been compared with bowls of pasta.

   a In the analogy, what represents a molecule?

   b What kind of pasta represents **i** wax **ii** polythene?

   c Explain why each kind of pasta is like **i** wax **ii** polythene.

   d What does the word 'analogy' mean?

3 Look at the section *Using our imagination*. Draw two diagrams: one of a plate of spaghetti hoops and one of a plate of proper spaghetti. Use these to explain why it is easier to divide a lump of spaghetti hoops. You can write on your diagrams and show movement and forces with arrows. Use the illustrations on page 116 to help you.

4 Jane has short hair and Tasha has long hair. Jane finds it easy to run a comb through her hair in the morning. Tasha finds it more difficult.

   a Who is more likely to break some of her hairs?

   b Explain why Jane finds it easier to comb her hair.

   c Use this as an analogy to help to explain why polythene is stronger than wax?

Find out about:
▶ using science to change polymer properties
▶ cross links to make polymers harder
▶ plasticizers to make polymers softer

G Designer stuff

Hardening rubber

Natural **rubber** is a very flexible polymer. But it wears away easily. This makes it good at rubbing away pencil marks. But not for much else.

In around 1840, Charles Goodyear was mixing sulfur and rubber in his American laboratory. He accidentally dropped some of the mixture on his hot stove. By the next morning it had hardened. He called the process vulcanization.

He started a business making tyres. He began with bicycles and prams. Now the business makes tyres for cars, motorcycles, and aeroplanes.

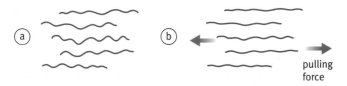

There are weak forces between the rubber molecules. They can slide over each other.

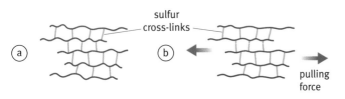

The sulfur atoms link across the chains. This stops the rubber molecules moving around.

Cross-links

Goodyear was the first person to alter the properties of a polymer. He did not know why vulcanization worked. He just knew that it did. Nowadays chemists know more about what is going on.

The sulfur makes **cross-links** between the long rubber molecules. This stops them from slipping over each other. The molecules are locked into a regular arrangement. This makes the rubber less flexible, stronger, and harder.

Hard polymers

Polymer science took off a hundred years later. Polymer chemists can now create new polymers with all sorts of properties. They know how different chains behave. They can also control the amount of cross-linking.

This means that they can control the properties of a material at the molecular level. Imagine you are the designer of a new mobile phone. You need a polymer with just the right balance of hardness, strength, and flexibility.

You use your old mobile to ring up a polymer scientist. She can produce exactly what you want.

Softening up

PVC is a good, safe polymer for making children's toys. But PVC is quite stiff. Toy manufacturers often need to make it a bit softer and more flexible. To do this, they add a **plasticizer**. This is usually an oily liquid with small molecules. The small molecules sit between the polymer chains.

The polymer chains are now further apart. This weakens the forces between them. Therefore, they can slide over each other more easily. This makes the polymer softer and more flexible.

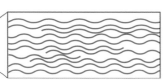

This PVC is unplasticized. It is called uPVC.

The chains of PVC lie close together. The closer they are, the stronger the forces.

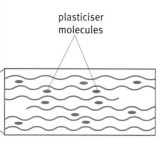

plasticiser molecules

This PVC has been plasticized to make it soft.

The molecules of plasticizer hold the PVC chains apart. This weakens their attraction.

Keeping it hard

You may have heard of uPVC. It is often used for making window frames. These need to be durable and hard. There is no need to add any plasticizer. You do not want soft window frames! So the PVC is left unplasticized. This is what the u stands for in uPVC.

Questions

1 There are five sections on these two pages. For each one, decide what the most important point is. Write a sentence that summarizes this point. For example, the first one might be: Charles Goodyear discovered that sulfur makes rubber harder.

2 Draw a design for a new mobile phone. You can draw it flat or in three dimensions. You can base it on a design that you have seen already – maybe in real life, in a magazine, or on the internet.

   a Label at least three parts of the phone that are made from polymers. Some should be hard and some should be soft.

You need to be able to brief the polymer chemists. So:

   b Under each part, list the properties the polymer needs to have.

   c Highlight the plasticized polymers in one colour and the unplasticized polymers in another colour.

   d Which of your polymers might have cross-links? Refer back to Section F?

Find out about:
▶ unsustainable development on Easter Island
▶ wood from sustainable forests

Ⓗ Is it sustainable?

Modern lifestyles depend on **natural resources**. Some of these resources provide us with warmth and light. Some of them make products. Either way, using them affects our future.

We have to think whether we can replace them and whether we can sustain this lifestyle. This lesson was learnt the hard way by the people of Easter Island.

These amazing carved heads are all around the coast of Easter Island. They stare sadly out to sea from their treeless landscape.

The Easter Island story

Easter Island is a remote place in the middle of the Pacific Ocean. It is famous for its gigantic carved rock faces. These were carved by the Polynesian people.

The Polynesians arrived by boat in about 600 AD. They found a lush, palm-covered island. It was an ideal place to live and they settled there. The population grew to several thousand.

Sadly, when Captain Cook landed there in March 1774, only a few islanders were left. They were barely surviving on a barren land. The statues were toppled and the trees were gone.

Wangari Maathi won the 2004 Nobel Peace Prize for her work promoting sustainable development. Her efforts have encouraged women in poor communities to plant over 300 million trees in Kenya.

What went wrong?

The islanders' main resource was wood. They used this to build houses, boats, and fires. It gave them a good, comfortable life. But they were felling too many trees. The stocks were being depleted. Eventually, the last tree was cut down. They could not even build a boat to escape.

If only they had not used up all the wood. If only they had noticed the dwindling stocks. If only they had replaced the trees they used. If only they had lived in a way that was **sustainable**.

It is easy to think they were foolish. But there are signs that we are doing the same with our own resources.

Are we sustainable?

Even now, there are forests that are dwindling. Their hardwood trees are being cut down to make furniture. These trees can take a hundred years to grow. This means that not many new trees reach maturity each year. Not as many as are being felled. This is not a sustainable use of timber.

The Easter Islanders used up their small forest in about a thousand years. The hardwood forests of South America may be big but they could still run out.

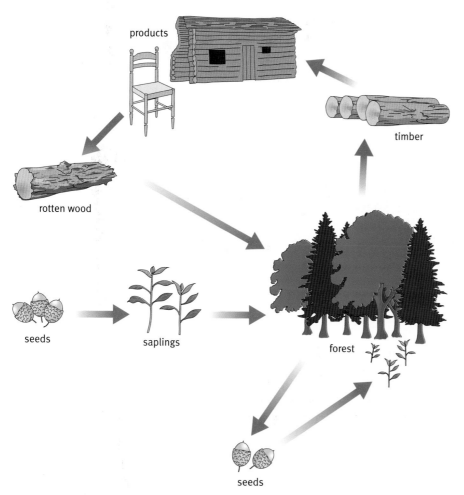

The life cycle of a forest works over hundreds of years.

Is it just trees?

Trees are not the only natural resource that is being depleted. We use materials made from metals, rocks, coal, and oil. These will not last for ever. We have to try to use them in a sustainable way. Otherwise, our isolated planet will run out of these as well.

Questions

1. Look at these things that people do: use hardwood trees for furniture; farm vegetables; use limestone for buildings; fish for cod in the North Sea; use wool for clothes; rely on crude oil.

   a In each case:

   i write down whether you think it is sustainable or not;

   ii explain your reasons.

   b Choose one example that you think is unsustainable. Describe how to make it sustainable.

2. Farming and forestry both involve growing and harvesting plants. They can both be sustainable.

   a Draw a diagram for the life cycle of a field of wheat. Include the timescale.

   b It is more difficult to make forestry sustainable. Explain why.

   c We use oil, coal, and stones.

   i Is it easier or more difficult to make this sustainable?

   ii Explain your answer.

Key words

natural resources
sustainable

Find out about:
▶ the life of products from cradle to grave
▶ assessing the impact of all the materials we use

① Life cycle assessment

Take a look around you. You are probably surrounded by manufactured goods such as books, clothes, carpets, and CDs.

Each of these products has a life with three distinct phases from cradle to grave:

1 a manufacturer makes it
2 people use it and then
3 they throw it away

Cradle to grave

Each phase uses resources:

▶ the raw materials for making the product
▶ the energy used to manufacture it
▶ the energy needed to use it (for example, petrol in a car)
▶ the energy needed to maintain it – cleaning, mending, etc
▶ the chemicals needed to maintain it
▶ the energy needed to dispose of it
▶ the space needed to dispose of it

Most items in a typical room are manufactured. There may be the odd pebble, seashell, or plant in its natural state.

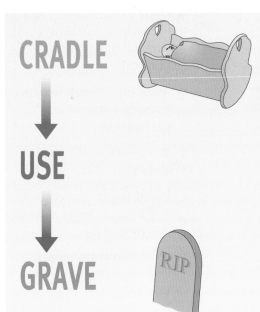

CRADLE
↓
USE
↓
GRAVE

• The raw materials for making the product

• The energy used to manufacture it

• The energy needed to use it (e.g. petrol in a car)

• The energy needed to maintain it – cleaning, mending etc

• The chemicals needed to maintain it

• The energy needed to dispose of it

• The space needed to dispose of it

Lives or life cycles?

Imagine a television that was bought in 1970 and thrown away in 1981. It contains glass, metals, plastics, and wood. It is now buried under 50 tonnes of rubble in a **landfill**. This is its grave.

The wood will eventually rot because it is biodegradable. But the rest of the materials are stuck there. This is not sustainable. The materials had a life but not a life-cycle.

Recycling materials once the life of a product is over is better. This is more sustainable.

Life cycle assessment

New laws are changing the way manufacturers work.

They have to assess the impact their products have on the environment. They do a **Life Cycle Assessment** (LCA) on each one. They add up all the resources it uses from its cradle to its grave. This encourages them to reduce its impact.

One part of the law deals with Waste Electrical and Electronic Equipment – known as WEEE.

A WEEE problem

Manufacturers have to pay the costs of dealing with WEEE. They can recycle, burn, or bury it. But they save money by recycling – especially if they make their products easy to recycle. The more they recycle, the more they save. And this keeps the price of the product down. It also reduces the impact on the environment.

A real waste: this rubbish is spread and buried. All the materials are lost for ever.

Weeeman is made from electronic waste. Its size shows the amount of waste that one person is likely to produce in a lifetime, from electronic toys to mobile phones. It weighs three tonnes.

Questions

1 A video player has a steel case, plastic knobs, and copper circuits.

   Imagine that the video player is put in landfill when it is thrown away.

   a Draw a diagram to show the life of the video player.

   b How can its grave be changed to give its materials a life cycle?

   c Add to the grave section of your diagram to show this life cycle.

2 Choose five items from the room you are in (you could do this randomly by spinning a pencil). Answer these questions for each item – put this in a table if it helps.

   a What is the product?

   b Has it been manufactured or is it still in its natural state?

   c Is it made from natural materials or synthetic ones?

   d About how long will the product last?

   e Can the product itself or its materials be reused or recycled?

Key words
landfill
recycling
life cycle assessment

J Life cycle of a synthetic polymer

All manufactured goods have a cost on the environment. Manufacturers are now being asked to assess this cost – from cradle to grave.

Here is a typical example. A polythene bottle.

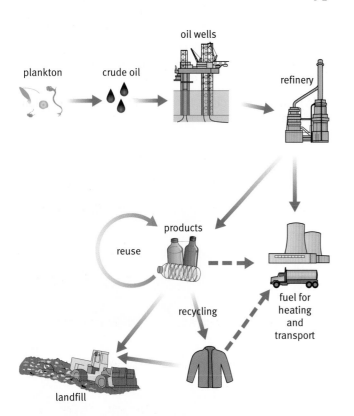

The life cycle of hydrocarbons from crude oil.

From the *cradle*

Polythene is a polymer made from ethene. This comes from **crude oil**. So the story starts millions of years ago under the sea bed where plankton died and were crushed. Eventually, their dead remains turned into crude oil.

Getting the oil

Oil companies extract the oil and transport it to their refineries.

Crude oil is a mixture of **hydrocarbons**. Most of them are used to provide energy for transport, homes, and manufacturing industry. Only about 4% is used for **chemical synthesis** to make polymers.

Making the polymer

The hydrocarbons are separated at an oil refinery. Some of the hydrocarbons are converted to ethene. This is piped to a chemical plant where it is turned into polythene. This uses the same process that Fawcett and Gibson invented in 1931.

Making the product.

The raw polythene is sent to a factory where it is heated and forced into a bottle-shaped mould. The bottle then emerges from its cradle.

You can see the pipes going into the oil wells. The world uses millions tonnes of oil every day.

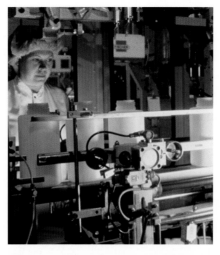

Blow moulding is a way of making plastic bottles. The plastic is heated and forced into a mould. This process uses energy and water for cooling.

Use

The polythene bottles are transported to a filling plant, filled, and sent to supermarkets and shops. People buy the drink and consume it. They might reuse the bottle a few times but eventually they throw it away.

To the *grave*

From here on, the story can follow different routes.

Landfill

Unfortunately, most synthetic polymers still end up being tipped into holes in the ground. We call this landfill.

Once it has been buried, the bottle's chemicals and energy are lost for ever.

Recovering the energy

Some polymers can be burnt. This reduces the need to use fresh fuel from crude oil. They are burnt in special **incinerators** at a very high temperature.

Recycling

Some regions recycle plastic. Others do not because it is too costly.

Waste contains a mixture of polymers – sometimes in a single product like trainers. These polymers have to be separated. Also, they have to be cleaned to get rid of food and mud. This all costs time, energy, and money.

Often the cost is more than the polymers are worth. So most plastic still goes into landfill.

This really is a waste. The crude oil that makes synthetic polymers is not being replenished. We cannot afford to lose the hydrocarbons that are locked up in synthetic polymers.

This man's Dutch company makes matting from recycled bottle caps.

Questions

1 Oil is used as a fuel and to make polymers.

  a Is its use sustainable: **i** as a fuel? **ii** for making polymers?

  b Explain your answers to part **a**.

  c In each case, describe how we might improve the situation.

2 People often wash and reuse products made from plastics.

  a What impact does this have on the environment?

  b Why might it be impossible or undesirable?

  c How many times would you reuse a drinks bottle?

3 Recycling makes our use of polymers more sustainable. Why do few councils recycle plastic products?

4 Burning waste polymers recovers their energy.

  a What impact does this have on the environment?

  b Why do you think people oppose having incinerators near their homes?

Key words

crude oil
hydrocarbons

chemical synthesis
incinerators

C2 Material choices

Science explanations

Knowledge of molecules can help chemists to develop new materials with useful properties. Some materials consist of very long chain molecules. One way of developing new plastics and fibres is to changing the length and arrangement of these big molecules.

You should know:

▶ one way of comparing materials is to measure their properties, including:

  – melting points;

  – strength (in tension or compression)

  – stiffness

  – hardness

  – density

▶ when choosing a material for use it helps to have an accurate knowledge of its properties

▶ polymers are materials which are made up of long-chain molecules

▶ there are natural polymers such as cotton, paper, silk, and wool

▶ there are synthetic materials which are alternatives to materials from living things

▶ there are many examples of modern materials made of synthetic polymers that have replaced older materials such as wood, iron, and glass

▶ crude oil is mainly made of hydrocarbons

▶ most of the products from oil are fuels and only a small percentage of crude oil is used to make new materials

▶ refining crude oil produces some small molecules which can join together to make very long-chain polymers; the process is called polymerization

▶ polymerization produces a wide range of plastics, rubbers, and fibres

▶ the properties of polymer materials depend on how the long molecules are arranged and held together

▶ it is possible to modify polymers to change their properties. This includes modifications such as:

  – increasing the length of the chains

  – cross-linking the molecules

  – adding plasticizers to lubricate the movement of molecules

Ideas about science

Scientists measure the properties of materials to decide what jobs they can be used for.

Scientists use data rather than opinion in justifying the choice of a material for a purpose.

You should be able to:

▶ suggest why a measurement may not be accurate

Scientists can never be sure that a measurement tells them the true value of the quantity being measured. Data is more reliable if it can be repeated. When making several measurements of the same quantity, the results are likely to vary. This may be because:

▶ you have to measure several individual examples, for example, several samples of the same material

▶ the quantity you are measuring is varying, for example, different batches of a polymer made at different time

▶ the limitations of the measuring equipment or because of the way you are using the equipment

Usually the best estimate of the value of a quantity is the average (or mean) of several repeat measurements. The spread of values in a set of repeated measurements give a rough estimate of the range within which the true value probably lies. You should:

▶ know that if a measurement lies well outside the range within which the others in a set of repeats lie, then it is an outlier and should not be used when calculating the mean.

▶ be able to calculate the mean from a set of repeated measurements

Making choices about the uses of materials:

▶ a life cycle assessment (LCA) tests:

 – a material's fitness for purpose

 – the effects of using the materials from its production from raw materials to its disposal

▶ the key features of a life cycle assessment include:

 – the main energy inputs

 – the environmental impact and sustainability of making the material from natural resources

 – the environmental impact of making the product from the material

 – the environmental impact of using the product

 – the environmental impact of disposing of the product by incineration, landfill, or recycling

▶ when making decisions about the uses of materials it is important to be able to:

 – know that some questions can be addressed using a scientific approach, and some cannot

 – identify the groups of people affected, and the main benefits and costs of a course of action for each group

 – explain whether the use of a material is sustainable

 – show you know regulations and laws control scientific research and applications

Why study radiation?

Human eyes see one type of radiation - visible light. But there are many other types of 'invisible' radiation. Some radiations are harmful. You hear a lot about the health risks of different radiations: for example, from natural sources such as sunlight, and from devices like mobile phones. Radiation is involved in climate change, and this is the biggest risk of all.

The science

Science shows that microwaves, X-rays, visible light, and other kinds of radiation all belong to one family. This is called the electromagnetic spectrum.

The Earth's atmosphere may seem transparent to sunlight. But its ozone layer absorbs the UV radiation in sunlight, protecting life on Earth. Science can explain how radiation warms the atmosphere, and uses computer modeling to predict global warming.

Ideas about science

To make sense of media stories about radiation you need to understand a few things about correlation and cause. It will also help if you know how to evaluate reports from health studies, and how to interpret statements about risks.

Radiation and life

gamma ray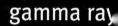

x-rays

ultraviolet

visible

infrared

microwave

radio

Find out about:

- how radiation affects living cells
- microwave radiation from mobile phones
- weighing up risks against benefits
- the evidence of global warming, and its possible effects

Find out about:
▶ benefits and risks of exposure to sunlight
▶ how the ozone layer protects life on Earth

(A) Sunlight, the atmosphere, and life

Skin colour

The **ultraviolet radiation (UV)** in sunlight can cause skin cancer. Skin cancer can kill.

Melanin is a brown pigment in skin. It provides some protection from UV radiation. People whose ancestors lived in sunnier parts of the world are more likely to have protective brown skin (See Module B3 *Life on Earth*).

Vitamins from sunlight

Human skin absorbs sunlight to make vitamin D. This nutrient strengthens bones and muscles. It also boosts the immune system, which protects you from infections. Darker skin makes it harder for the body to make vitamin D. So in regions of the world that are not so sunny there is an advantage in having fair skin.

Nowadays the links between UV, skin cancer, and vitamin D are clear. People with fair skin can keep healthy in sunny countries if they are careful not to expose their skin to too much UV. People with dark skin can keep healthy in less sunny countries if they get enough vitamin D from their food.

Feeling good

People like sunshine. It can alter your mood chemically and reduce the risk of depression.

Fair skin is good at making vitamin D. But fair skin gives less protection against skin cancer. One bad sunburn in childhood doubles the risk of serious skin cancer in later life.

A suntan is the body's attempt to protect itself against UV and skin cancer. A tanned skin has more melanin. But the protection is only weak.

Sri Lanka is the one of the world's sunniest places. A high level of protection from UV radiation is important.

Balancing risks and benefits

Is sunlight good for you? There is no simple answer. There are risks from exposure to UV in sunlight. There are also risks from staying indoors all the time. Protecting your health involves reducing risks, whenever possible. And balancing risks against benefits.

Correlation or cause?

A study of 2600 people found that people who were exposed to high levels of sunlight were up to four times more likely to develop a cataract (clouding of the eye lens). Exposure to sunlight is a **factor**. Eye cataracts are an **outcome**. There is a **correlation** between exposure to sunlight and eye cataracts. But doctors do not say that exposure to sunlight will **cause** cataracts. There are other risk factors involved, such as age and diet.

Questions

1 Exposure to sunlight increases your risk of developing skin cancer. List some benefits of staying indoors and avoiding direct sunlight. List some risks as well.

2 Describe at least three ways that a person could reduce the risk of skin cancer while enjoying a beach holiday.

Key words

ultraviolet radiation (UV)
factor
outcome
correlation
cause

131

Sunlight and life

When a material **absorbs** light, or any kind of electromagnetic radiation, it takes its energy from it. The radiation then ceases to exist.

Absorbing energy from sunlight

When leaves absorb light from the Sun, they gain energy. They use the energy to make starch. Leaves take in carbon dioxide from the air and release oxygen. This chemical process is called **photosynthesis**.

Respiration

Plants store the starch they make. They can use it later to produce energy, through a process called **respiration**. Leaves take in oxygen from the air and release carbon dioxide. The process of respiration is the reverse of photosynthesis.

Leaves absorb red and blue light. It gives them the energy they need for photosynthesis. They don't absorb green light. They **reflect** it. So leaves look green.

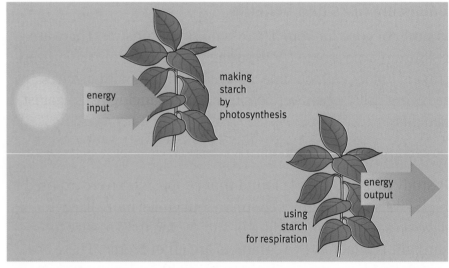

Photosynthesis needs an energy input. That comes from the light which leaves absorb. Respiration provides an energy output.

An absorbing atmosphere

The atmosphere is a thin layer of air around the Earth. It protects us from harmful radiations from Space.

The atmosphere is a mixture of gases, including oxygen. In the upper atmosphere some of the oxygen is in the form of ozone. It makes an **ozone layer**. Ozone is good at absorbing UV radiation.

UV is harmful to living things. Life on Earth depends on the ozone layer absorbing UV.

Ozone absorbs UV but not visible light. This is called selective absorption.

Humans have created a problem. Some synthetic (manufactured) chemicals, such as CFCs, have been escaping into the atmosphere. They turn ozone back into ordinary oxygen. So more UV radiation reaches the Earth's surface. This happens strongly over the North and South Poles. The thin ozone in those places is 'the hole in the ozone layer'.

Aerosol cans once contained CFCs. This use has been stopped worldwide. Old fridges are more of a problem. Waste fridges now go to special recycling centres so that CFCs can be removed from them.

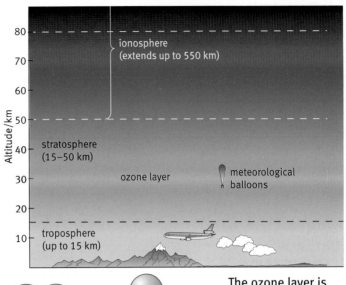

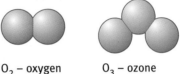

O_2 – oxygen O_3 – ozone

The ozone layer is good at absorbing harmful UV radiation.

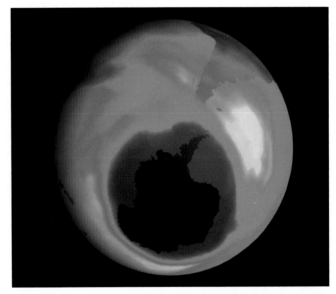

This image has been made by sensing ozone. Dark colours represent less dense ozone. There seems to be a 'hole' in the protective layer.

Old fridges waiting to have CFCs removed.

Key words

absorb	reflect	ozone layer
photosynthesis	respiration	

Questions

3 What are the names of the three main layers of the atmosphere? In which of these is the ozone layer?

4 What effect do CFCs have on ozone?

5 What action is being taken to reduce damage to the ozone layer?

Find out about:
▶ a family of radiations called the electromagnetic spectrum
▶ sources and detectors of radiation
▶ why some kinds of radiation are more dangerous than others

Ⓑ Radiation models

A beautiful world

All radiation has a source that **emits** it. Then it has a journey. It spreads out, or 'radiates'. Radiation never stands still.

Many materials can reflect light as it travels on its journey from its source to your eyes. The objects around you would be invisible if they did not reflect light.

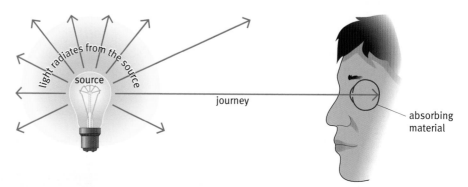

A journey of visible light from **source** to eye.

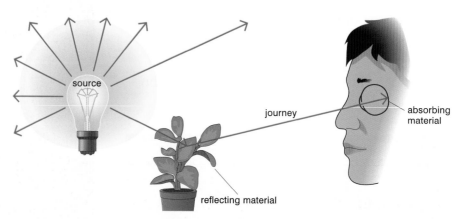

A journey of visible light, from source to reflector to eye.

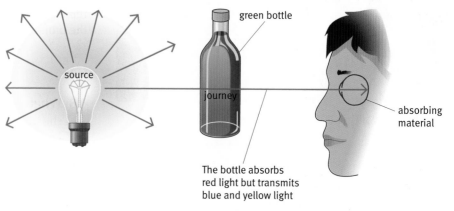

A journey of visible light, with partial absorption on the journey.

Glass is a good transmitter of light and a weak absorber. Coloured materials added to glass can absorb some colours of light and **transmit** others.

A single source of light, the Sun, made this picture possible.

▶ Air mostly transmits the light.

▶ Water surfaces are good reflectors, though some light also travels down into its depths.

▶ Tree leaves transmit some colours of light, and absorb others. But they also reflect light into the camera that took this picture.

Hidden messages

Look back at page 128. Detectors can make invisible radiation visible. There are also ways of detecting radiation without producing pictures at all. For example:

- gamma radiation can make clicks that you hear
- a bowl of soup in a microwave oven responds to radiation by getting hot
- the aerial of a radio detects radiation by making electrical signals in the radio's circuits

For all of these examples of electromagnetic radiation, there is a source, a journey, and a detector. The detector must absorb radiation for it to work.

Questions

1. Glass is a weak absorber of visible light. How would you show that it does absorb some light?

2. Can glass reflect light?

3. Materials can transmit, reflect, or absorb light. Which one of these is glass best at?

Communication

Radiation can carry information from a source to a detector by having coded patterns. The simplest way to do that is to turn the source on and off. You can do that with a torch. Digital radio communication uses the same idea, switching at incredibly high speeds. A TV 'remote' also uses flickering patterns in infrared radiation to send information to a TV set.

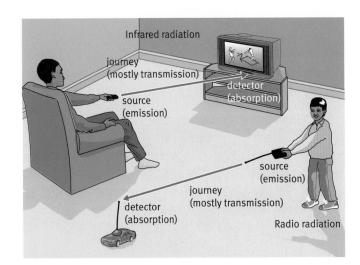

Radiation from source to detector.

Key words

emit	source	transmit

Absorbing electromagnetic radiation

When materials absorb electromagnetic radiation they gain energy. Exactly what happens depends on the energy absorbed.

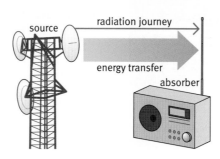

Metal aerials can absorb radio and microwave radiation.

Radiation can make patterns of electric current in metals

Patterns of microwave and radio radiation can make patterns of electric current in radio aerials.

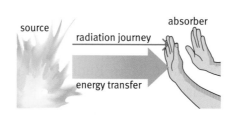

A fire transfers energy to the world around it. It warms its surroundings.

Radiation can have a heating effect

Radiation absorbed by a material may increase the vibration of its particles (atoms and molecules). The material gets warmer.

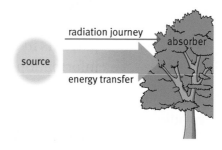

A leaf takes energy from the Sun's radiation so that photosynthesis can happen.

Radiation can cause chemical changes

If the radiation carries enough energy, the molecules that absorb it become more likely to react chemically. This is what happens in photosynthesis.

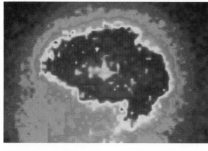
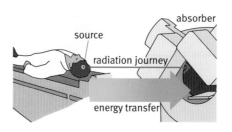

This medical image was made by a gamma camera. Each dot on the image was made by a single ionization event.

Ionization can damage living cells

If the radiation carries a large amount of energy, it can break up the molecules that absorb it into smaller 'bits', called **ions**. This process is called **ionization**. Ionization can damage living cells.

Radiation arrives in energy packets

It is useful to think about radiation in terms of **photons**. A photon is an energy packet of radiation:

▶ sources emit energy photon by photon
▶ absorbers gain the energy photon by photon

The energy deposited by a beam of electromagnetic radiation depends on both:

▶ the number of photons arriving
▶ and the energy that each photon delivers

Sitting in sunlight, infrared and visible radiations have a warming effect on you. UV ionizes and can (though not very often) be the start of skin cancer.

Ionizing radiation

Sources of gamma radiation, X-rays, and UV pack a lot of energy into each photon. So absorbers get a lot of energy from each photon. These photons have a strong local effect – so they can ionize.

Non-ionizing radiation

Sources of visible, infrared, microwave, and radio radiation pack less energy into each photon. These photons do not carry enough energy to ionize molecules. Their main effect is to warm things up. And radio photons produce hardly any heating effect.

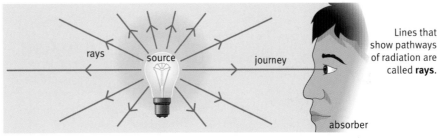

Lines that show pathways of radiation are called **rays**.

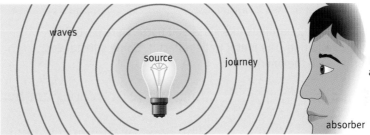

You can think about light spreading out like ripples on a pond. This is a **wave** picture.

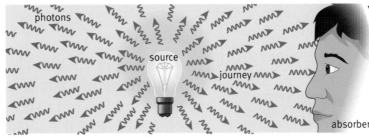

You can imagine the individual photons that transfer energy from the source to the observer.

Radiation transfers energy. There are different ways of thinking about how it travels between source and absorber.

Questions

There is radio radiation passing through your body right now.

④ Where does the radio radiation come from?

5 Why does it not have any ionizing effect?

6 Does it have a heating effect? Explain your answer.

Key words

ions	rays
ionization	wave
photon	
ionizing radiation	
non-ionizing radiation	

Find out about:
▶ how microwaves cause heating
▶ design features that make microwave ovens safe to use

ⓒ Using radiation

Microwave ovens

In a microwave oven, microwave radiation transfers energy to absorbing materials. Once the radiation is absorbed it loses all of its energy, and it ceases to exist.

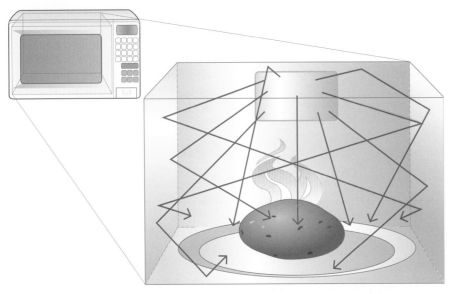

Inside a microwave oven, materials like glass and pottery are partially transparent to the radiation. The metal walls reflect it. Some substances, including water, absorb the energy.

Molecules of water, fat, and sugar are good absorbers of microwave radiation. Microwaves make these molecules vibrate. Food containing them gets hot. A potato, for example, is made mostly of water, with carbohydrate and just a little fat.

Other particles, like the particles in glass or crockery, take very little energy from the radiation. It does not increase their vibrations at all. So the radiation in a microwave oven does not heat a bowl or a mug directly.

The bowl or the mug is heated by the food or drink inside it.

How deep?

Absorption does not take place until the radiation enters the material. Water in a potato is good at absorbing microwave radiation. But it is not so good that the energy is all absorbed near the surface of the potato. Some energy is transferred quite deeply into the potato.

Absorption of energy by a potato. The plate does not absorb energy from the microwave radiation.

Questions

1 What radiations are on either side of microwave radiation in the electromagnetic spectrum? (Look at pages 128-9 for help.)

2 Why doesn't microwave radiation cause ionization?

③ In a conventional oven, how does energy reach the centre of a potato to cook it?

How cooked?

Using microwaves is an energy-efficient way of cooking. Most of the energy goes into heating the food. Microwave ovens are typically rated at 600–800 watts.

You can control the amount of cooking in a microwave oven by adjusting the power setting.

The heating effect of non-ionizing radiation on an absorbing material always depends on its **intensity**. This is the amount of microwave energy arriving every second.

Safety features

People contain water and fat. So a human body is a good absorber of microwave radiation.

Exposure to sufficient microwave radiation from an oven could cook you. The oven door has a metal grid to reflect the radiation back inside the oven. And a microwave oven cannot operate with its door open.

> **Key words**
> intensity

> **Questions**
>
> **4** Why is it important that the walls and door of a microwave oven reflect the microwave radiation?
>
> **5** How much larger is the power of a microwave oven than a 60-W lamp?

D Is there a health risk?

Mobile phones – gt th msg?

Mobile warning?

Local campaigns against new mobile phone masts are springing up everywhere. Why?

Scientific evidence suggests that radiation from mobile phones is 'unlikely' to be harmful. But this is not yet certain. Meanwhile, the experts say:

● Some people, particularly children, may be at greater risk of harm.

● People can choose to take care. They can make fewer and shorter calls.

● When buying a mobile, choose one with a lower SAR value (radiation exposure).

● Children under eight should not use mobile phones.

The UK government is paying for health studies to find out more.

UK report on mobile phone safety, January 2005

Cooked brain?

Mobile phones use microwave radiation. They receive microwave radiation from a nearby phone mast (or 'base station') and send microwave radiation back. Patterns in the radiation carry information. Phone masts radiate at powers up to 100 watt and mobile phones up to $\frac{1}{4}$ watt.

When you make a call some of this radiation warms your brain. But ever so slightly. Your brain can be warmed more when you take physical exercise.

Distance from a radiation source is important. The intensity of microwaves decreases with distance. Some people use a hands-free kit to keep the mobile phone away from their head.

Perfectly safe?

Nothing is completely safe. Even drinking a glass of water can be hazardous. You could choke on the water. Or drop the glass and get a cut from the broken glass.

There are usually ways of reducing risks to an acceptable level.

Health studies

Over 50 million people in the UK use mobile phones. But there may be harmful effects that people don't know about yet.

Are the results reliable?

The news often has reports of studies that compare people from two groups. These studies try to find out if something (called a factor) makes a difference to people's health.

When you think about studies like these, there are two things worth checking:

Scientists look for correlations between people's habits and their health.

What to check ...	... and why
Are the groups selected so that the comparison is fair?	Suppose there was a study to see whether mobile phone use increases the risk of brain cancer. It would need to compare health outcomes of two groups – a sample of mobile phone users and a sample of non-users.
	People in both samples should be matched on as many *other* factors as possible. For example, each sample should have similar numbers of people of each age.
	Why? The development of brain tumours might be age-related.
Were the numbers in each group (sample) large enough?	With small samples, the results may be strongly affected by chance – who is picked. With larger samples this is less likely. So you get a truer picture of the whole group.

Questions

1 Getting dressed in the morning is an everyday activity. Explain why even this is not 'completely safe'.

2 Explain why your risk is reduced by texting rather making a voice call.

3 How might mobile phones make children safer? How might they make children less safe?

4 a Look at the first row of the table above. What factor and what outcome are being studied?

  b For a fair test, the samples should be matched. Give an example to show what *sample matching* means.

5 One study found that frequent use of mobile phones reduced men's sperm counts. It was based on a sample of 15 men. Why is this study not reliable?

X-ray safety

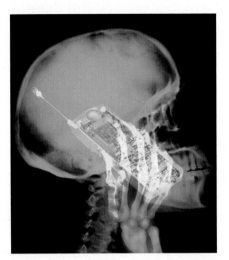

X-rays have saved many thousands of lives. But they are a form of ionizing radiation. X-ray photons can ionize molecules in your body. This can disrupt your body chemistry, and cause cancer. So benefits must be balanced against risks.

Both the health benefits and the risks of X-rays are well known. Using mobile phones has benefits but uncertain risks.

Shoe shops used to check the fit of your shoes using an X-ray machine. By the late 1950s, people realized that this produced an unnecessary exposure to ionizing radiation. And it could be damaging. The machines were banned.

Discovery of a correlation

Alice Stewart (see photo) and George Kneale carried out a survey on a large number of women and their children.

They discovered a correlation between X-ray exposure of mothers during pregnancy and cancers in their children.

This study made doctors more cautious about using X-rays. The risks associated with X-rays for small children and pregnant women usually outweigh any benefit.

Obituaries

Alice Stewart

Alice Stewart was a British doctor. She collected and analysed information from women whose children had died of cancer between 1953 and 1955. Soon the answer was clear. Just one medical X-ray for a pregnant woman was enough to double the risk of early cancer for her child.

How great is the risk?

Generally, health outcomes are reported as relative risks. For example, 'people exposed to high levels of sunlight were four times more likely to develop eye cataracts'. What might this mean?

▶ If your risk was one in a million, it rises to 4 in a million - not a worry!
▶ If your risk was 5 in 100, it rises to 20 in 100 - worth thinking about!

Some people will be at higher risk because of their skin type, their diet, or their personal or family medical history. Your doctor can help you interpret information about health risks.

Questions

6 What does it mean to say X-ray photons are 'ionizing'?

7 Why do doctors still use X-rays, despite the correlation between X-ray exposure and cancer?

Find out about:
▶ records of the Earth's past temperatures
▶ how the atmosphere keeps the Earth warm
▶ why the amount of CO_2 in the atmosphere is changing

Ⓔ Global warming

Are summers now hotter and winters milder than they once were? This is a question about **climate**, or average weather in a place over many years.

You cannot answer it from personal experience, because you can only be in one place at a time. And memory can be unreliable. Instead, you need to collect and analyse lots of data.

Weather stations have been keeping temperature records for over a century. There is a clear pattern. The Earth's average temperature has been increasing since 1800.

Most scientists think that the amount of CO_2 in the atmosphere is causing the Earth's average temperature to rise. Why?

▶ Both global temperatures and the amount of CO_2 have increased recently.
▶ There is evidence from the distant past that CO_2 level and temperature change together.
▶ Scientists can explain how CO_2 in the atmosphere warms the Earth.

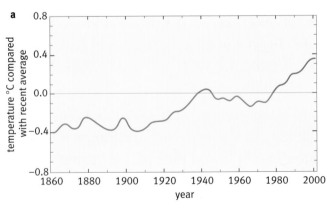

The Earth's surface temperature over the past 140 years (data from thermometers).

Questions

1 Personal experience does not provide reliable evidence of climate change. Why not?

2 All of the statements about CO_2 and the Earth's average temperature describe correlations. Which statement is also about cause and effect?

The greenhouse effect

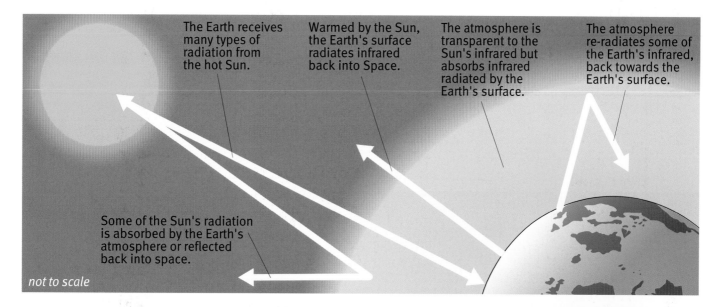

The Earth receives many types of radiation from the hot Sun.

Warmed by the Sun, the Earth's surface radiates infrared back into Space.

The atmosphere is transparent to the Sun's infrared but absorbs infrared radiated by the Earth's surface.

The atmosphere re-radiates some of the Earth's infrared, back towards the Earth's surface.

Some of the Sun's radiation is absorbed by the Earth's atmosphere or reflected back into space.

not to scale

Without its atmosphere, the Earth's average surface temperature would be −18 °C. That's how cold it is on the Moon. In fact the Earth's average temperature is 15 °C. This warming of the Earth by its atmosphere is called the **greenhouse effect**.

Life on Earth depends on the greenhouse effect. Without it, the Earth's water would be frozen. Liquid water is essential to life.

Greenhouse gases

Tiny amounts of a few gases in the atmosphere make all the difference. Carbon dioxide, methane, and water vapour absorb some of the Earth's infrared radiation. They are called **greenhouse gases**.

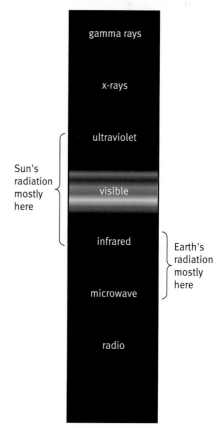

gamma rays

x-rays

ultraviolet

Sun's radiation mostly here

visible

infrared

Earth's radiation mostly here

microwave

radio

Questions

3 a Which of the following gases are found in the Earth's atmosphere: nitrogen, methane, oxygen, carbon dioxide, water vapour, argon?

b Which of them are *not* greenhouse gases?

4 Explain what difference the greenhouse effect makes to life on Earth.

Key words
climate
greenhouse effect
greenhouse gases

145

The carbon cycle

Carbon dioxide is a greenhouse gas that plays a key role in global warming. Industrial societies produce CO_2 as never before.

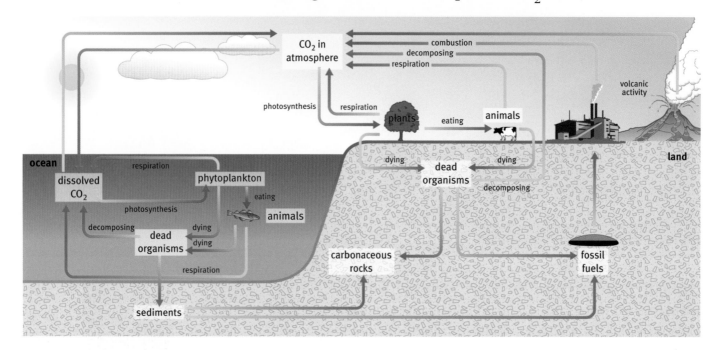

The Earth's crust, oceans, atmosphere, and living organisms all contain carbon. Carbon atoms are used over and over again in natural processes. The **carbon cycle** describes stores of carbon and processes that move carbon.

Hundreds of millions of years ago, the amount of carbon dioxide in the atmosphere was much higher than it is today. Green plants made use of that CO_2 and released oxygen. This made life possible for animals. Eventually, lots of carbon was locked up underground in the form of fossil fuels, as well as rocks such as limestone and chalk.

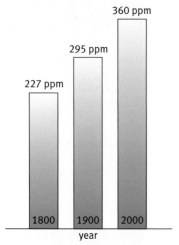

In 1800, the concentration of CO_2 in the atmosphere was only 277 parts per million (ppm).

This means there were 277 molecules of CO_2 for every 1 000 000 molecules that make up dry air.

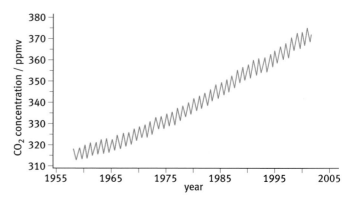

Measurements show that CO_2 levels go up and down each year. The average is rising by 2 ppm every year.

Human activities release carbon

People want to live comfortably. In some parts of the world, many feel they have a right to processed foods, unlimited clean water and electricity, refrigerators and other manufactured goods, bigger houses and flats. All of these things require energy.

But whenever fossil fuels – coal, oil, and gas – are burned, they increase the amount of carbon dioxide in the atmosphere. The amount of CO_2 humans produce is huge – thousands of millions of tonnes each year.

Methane, another greenhouse gas, is produced by grazing animals and from rice paddies.

Key words
carbon cycle
deforestation

Questions

5 Forest land can be cleared for farming by burning the trees. This is called **deforestation**. Why does tree-burning increase the amount of carbon dioxide in the atmosphere? (Hint: Use the diagram of the carbon cycle.)

6 If aviation fuel were heavily taxed, what might happen to the amount of air travel? Explain your answer.

Motor vehicles are a major source of greenhouse gas emissions.

A power station like this supplies enough electricity for a major city. Every day it uses several trainloads of coal and sends thousands of tonnes of carbon dioxide into the atmosphere.

Air transport is a big user of fossil fuels. Aviation fuel is cheap because it is untaxed, unlike petrol for cars.

People in the UK use more energy on keeping buildings warm than on anything else.

Find out about:
▶ records of the Earth's past temperatures
▶ how the atmosphere keeps the Earth warm
▶ why the amount of CO_2 in the atmosphere is changing

(F) Changing climates?

In the 1990s scientists still argued about what was happening to climates. Now almost all agree that the world is warming.

- Never before have temperatures increased so fast as during the last 50 years.
- Human activities are contributing more to climate change than natural factors.
- Future emissions of greenhouse gases are likely to raise global temperatures by between 1.4 and 5.8 °C during your lifetime.

It's Costa Blackpool!

Average temperatures in the UK are set to rise by over 3 °C in the next few decades, according to some scientists. You could enjoy a Mediterranean climate, with vineyards in the north of England.

But scientists also say that global warming may also lead to flooding of low-lying areas and an increase in violent storms. Or temperatures could drop instead, changing the British Isles to another Iceland.

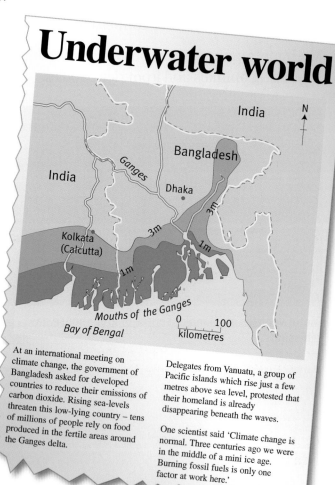

Underwater world

At an international meeting on climate change, the government of Bangladesh asked for developed countries to reduce their emissions of carbon dioxide. Rising sea-levels threaten this low-lying country – tens of millions of people rely on food produced in the fertile areas around the Ganges delta.

Delegates from Vanuatu, a group of Pacific islands which rise just a few metres above sea level, protested that their homeland is already disappearing beneath the waves.

One scientist said 'Climate change is normal. Three centuries ago we were in the middle of a mini ice age. Burning fossil fuels is only one factor at work here.'

What can governments do?

Facing election every few years, democratic governments are sensitive to public opinion. They find it difficult to do what's best for the long term.

To reduce greenhouse gas emissions, the UK government needs to change people's expectations and behaviour. It can do this by spending tax money in different ways. It can also introduce new taxes, laws, and regulations.

In September 2000, protesters opposing higher fuel taxes staged a dramatic series of blockades at petrol depots.

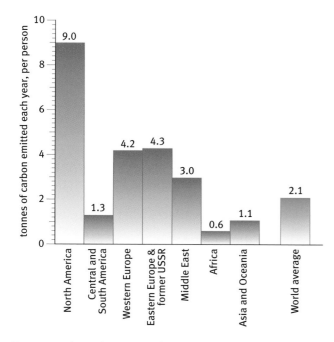

Europe and North America have just one-fifth of the world's population. But they account for more than 60% of carbon emissions.

Nobody can predict climate futures accurately. As a result, some politicians are not convinced of the need for action. Joint international action is very hard to achieve.

What can you do?

Perhaps you will take action yourself, now and in the future. You could:

» turn the heating down
» use a car less
» have fewer holidays involving air travel
» use electricity from non-fossil energy sources

Perhaps you think laws should be passed to encourage or even force others to do the same.

Questions

1 The articles on page 148 include many technical terms relating to climate change. Make a list of them, and try to explain as many of them as you can. One has been done for you.

Term	Meaning
Climate	average weather conditions at a place over many years

2 Scientists cannot be sure of the possible effects of climate change. Which words in the articles suggest that things are uncertain?

3 Describe possible benefits and risks of global warming to people in the UK.

4 Look at the photos on page 147. For each one, suggest what the government could do to reduce carbon emissions.

P2 Radiation and life

Science explanations

This chapter introduces the electromagnetic spectrum.

You should know:

▶ how to think about any form of radiation in terms of its source, its journey path and what happens when it is absorbed

▶ a beam of electromagnetic radiation delivers energy in 'packets' called photons

▶ how to describe the electromagnetic spectrum, with its parts in order of their photon energies

▶ what different parts of the electromagnetic spectrum can be used for

▶ two factors that affect the energy deposited by a beam of electromagnetic radiation

▶ how the intensity of an electromagnetic beam changes with distance.

▶ why ionizing radiation is hazardous

▶ which parts of the electromagnetic spectrum are ionizing

▶ how people can be protected from ionizing radiation

▶ how microwaves heat materials, including living cells

▶ some features of microwave ovens that protect users

▶ sunlight provides the energy for photosynthesis and warms the Earth's surface

▶ how photosynthesis affects what molecules are in the atmosphere

▶ what the greenhouse effect is (and be able to identify greenhouse gases)

▶ how to use the carbon cycle to explain several things about the atmosphere

▶ how the atmosphere's ozone layer protects living organisms

▶ what global warming means

▶ some possible effects of global warming

Ideas about science

To make personal and social decisions about health or global warming, it can be important to assess the risks and benefits. For risks and benefits from different parts of the electromagnetic spectrum

You should be able to:

▶ explain why nothing is completely safe

▶ suggest why people will accept (or reject) the risk of a certain activity, e.g. sunbathing because they want a tan

▶ suggest ways of reducing particular risks

▶ interpret information on the size of risks, presented in different ways

▶ discuss a given risk, taking account of both the chances of it occurring and the consequences if it did

▶ explain that if it is not possible to be sure about the results of doing something, and if serious harm could result, then in makes sense to avoid it (the 'precautionary principle')

▶ explain the ALARA principle and how it applies to an issue

You should also be able to:

▶ correctly use the ideas of correlation and cause when discussing topical issues related to this chapter

▶ suggest factors that might increase the chance of an outcome

▶ explain that individual cases do not provide convincing evidence for or against a correlation

▶ evaluate a health study by commenting on sample size or sample matching

▶ evaluate a claimed causal link by discussing the presence (or absence) of a plausible mechanism

▶ discuss personal and social choices in terms of actual risk and perceived risk

These ideas are illustrated through Case Studies, including: whether sunlight is good for you; UV and the ozone layer; microwave ovens, mobile phones, and X-ray scans; global warming.

Why study life on Earth?

Life on Earth - so many different kinds of living thing it's almost unbelievable. 'How did life begin?', and, 'Where do we come from?' are two of the biggest questions we ask science to answer.

Scientists think life began on Earth 3500 million years ago. Modern humans have only been around for about 40 000 years. And since then many other species have become extinct. We can learn to look after life on Earth better for future generations.

The science

Fossils are evidence for how life on Earth has evolved. Simple organisms have gradually developed and changed, forming new, larger species.

All life forms depend on their environment and on other species for survival. Larger organisms have evolved communication systems (nerves and hormones), that help them to survive.

Ideas about science

Today, most scientists agree that evolution happens. But 200 years ago they didn't. And not all scientists agree about how life on Earth started. Developing new explanations takes a lot of evidence and imagination. Even then, people may have reasons not to accept them.

Life on Earth

Find out about:

- how life on Earth may have begun and is evolving
- how scientists developed an explanation for evolution
- how humans evolved
- why some species become extinct, and whether this matters

Find out about:
- why living things are all different
- what a species is
- evidence for evolution

Ⓐ The variety of life

You can usually see the differences between different kinds of living things on Earth. But there are also a lot of similarities, even between living things that don't look the same. For example, almost all living things use DNA. This is how they pass on information from one generation to the next.

Human skin cells and cells in these butterfly wings use the same chemical reaction to make pigment.

Classification – working out where we belong

Scientists use the similarities and differences between things to put them into groups. You've probably come across this idea before. It's called classification. The biggest group that humans belong to is *Animalia* (animals). The smallest is *Homo sapiens*, or human beings. *Homo sapiens* is our **species** name.

Animals → Vertebrates → Mammals → Primates → *Homo sapiens*

largest group

smallest group

You are most closely related to other members of *Homo sapiens*. But you belong to these other groups as well.

What makes a species?

A species is a group of living things that are so similar that:

- they can breed together
- their offspring can also breed (they are **fertile**)

Horses and donkeys are good examples to explain species. They can breed together and produce offspring called mules. But mules are **infertile**. So horses and donkeys look pretty similar, but they are different species.

Horses and donkeys do look very similar. But their offspring are infertile. So horses and donkeys are different species.

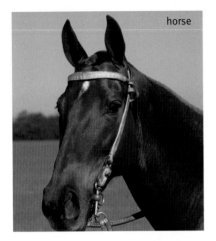

horse

donkey

mule

Are all members of a species the same?

It's easy to see the differences between dogs and people. But all dogs are not identical to each other. Neither are all people.

Members of a species are different from each other. This **variation** is very important in evolution.

What causes variation?

There are different causes of variation.

- The photograph above shows both men and women. This difference is controlled by some of their genes. It is **genetic** variation.
- One of the women in the front has pierced ears. Other people don't. This difference has been caused by something other than genes. It is **environmental** variation.
- People have different skin colours. This is partly genetic variation. But it is also affected by environment – how much sun their skin is exposed to.

Most variation is caused by a mixture of genes and environment.

Key words

species
fertile
infertile
variation
genetic
environmental

Questions

1 What species do you belong to?

2 Horses and donkeys look similar. Explain why they are different species.

3 Explain what the word 'variation' means. Use two examples in your answer.

4 Write down one difference in people that is caused by:

  a genes only

  b genes and environment

  c environment only

Explaining similarities – the evidence for evolution

Most scientists agree that life on Earth started from a few simple living things. This explains why living things have so many similarities.

These simple living things changed over time. Many other species were produced. This is called **evolution**. It is still happening today.

What evidence is there for evolution?

Fossils are made from the dead bodies of living things. They are very important as evidence for evolution. Almost all fossils found are of extinct species. This is more than 99% of all species that have ever lived on Earth.

How reliable is fossil evidence?

There are gaps in the fossil record. Sometimes a new species seems to appear without an in-between link to an earlier species.

But scientists have collected millions of fossils. This huge amount of evidence has helped to build up a picture of evolution.

Why are there gaps in the fossil record?

▶ Conditions have to be just right for fossils to develop.
▶ Evolution doesn't happen at the same speed all the time. It happens in spurts.

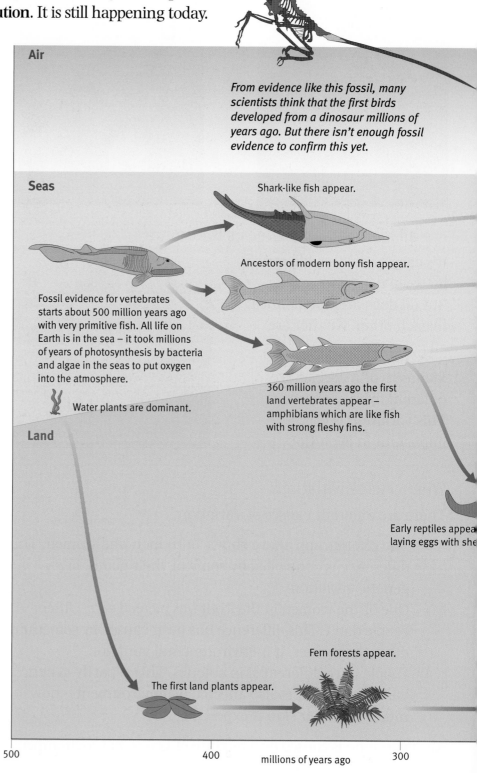

Air

From evidence like this fossil, many scientists think that the first birds developed from a dinosaur millions of years ago. But there isn't enough fossil evidence to confirm this yet.

Seas

Shark-like fish appear.

Ancestors of modern bony fish appear.

Fossil evidence for vertebrates starts about 500 million years ago with very primitive fish. All life on Earth is in the sea – it took millions of years of photosynthesis by bacteria and algae in the seas to put oxygen into the atmosphere.

Water plants are dominant.

360 million years ago the first land vertebrates appear – amphibians which are like fish with strong fleshy fins.

Land

Early reptiles appea[r]
laying eggs with she[ll]

Fern forests appear.

The first land plants appear.

500   400   millions of years ago   300

A 'spurt' of evolution may still take tens of thousands of years. But the right conditions for fossil-making may not happen during that time. So there would be no fossil evidence of these changes.

What other evidence do we have for evolution?

Scientists can also compare the genes from different living things. The more genes two living things share, the more closely related they are. This helps scientists to work out where different species fit on the evolutionary tree.

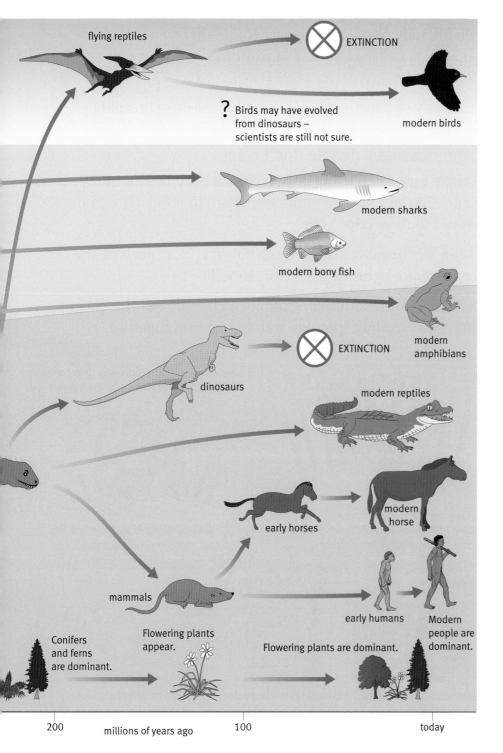

Over 98% of human genes are the same as those of a chimpanzee, but only 85% are the same as those of a mouse.

Questions

5 Most species that have lived on Earth are now extinct. What percentage are living now?

6 Fossils are one type of evidence for evolution. Name another.

Find out about:

▶ how evolution happens – natural selection
▶ how humans have changed some species

B Evidence for change NOW

Evolution did not just happen in the past. Scientists can measure changes in species which are happening now. Humans are causing many of these changes.

Selective breeding

Imagine you are a pig farmer. You notice that your pigs are all different. Some grow bigger than others. So you choose these pigs to breed from. You want more of your pigs to have this feature.

This way of causing change is called **selective breeding**.

Some changes people don't want

People have been using poisons to kill head lice for many years. In the 1980s, doctors were sure that head lice in the UK would soon be wiped out.

But a few headlice survived the poisons. Now parts of the country are fighting groups of 'superlice'.

So headlice are another example of change. But this wasn't selective breeding – no one *wanted* to cause superlice.

Selective breeding has produced tulips with different coloured flowers.

Head lice are quite common. They feed on blood.

For many years people used the same shampoo to kill head lice.

A few head lice in the population were able to survive. Their cells were probably able to break down the poison.

'Superlouse' was more likely to breed than the head lice killed by the poison.

Eggs laid by 'Superlouse' hatched into lice that also survived the poison.

These lice spread to other people and bred.

The number of resistant lice in the population increased. People couldn't get rid of their head lice.

Scientists developed a new poison to kill the head lice.

The cycle began again – and the species changed a little more.

Natural selection

Head lice are changing because of human beings. But humans haven't been around on Earth for very long. Most changes to species happened before human beings arrived. Something else in the environment caused the changes. This is called **natural selection**. Natural selection is how evolution happens.

Steps in natural selection

① *Living things in a species are not identical. They have variation.*

Ancestors of modern giraffes had variation in the length of their necks.

② *They compete for things like food, shelter, and a mate. But what if something in the environment changes?*

Food supply became scarce. The giraffes competed for food.

③ *Some will have features that help them to survive. They are more likely to breed. They pass their genes on to their offspring.*

Taller giraffes were more likely to survive and breed. They passed on their features to the next generation.

④ *More of the next generation have the useful feature. If the environment stays the same, even more of the following generation will have the useful feature.*

Over many generations, more giraffes with longer necks were born.

Questions

1 How does evolution happen?

2 Copy and complete the table to compare selective breeding and natural selection.

Steps in selective breeding	Steps in natural selection
Living things in a species are not all the same.	Living things in a species are not all the same.
Humans choose the individuals with the feature that they want.	
These are the plants or animals that are allowed to breed.	
They pass their genes on to their offspring.	
More of the next generation will have the chosen feature.	
If people keep choosing the same feature, even more of the following generation will have it.	

Find out about:
▶ how Darwin explained evolution
▶ the argument his explanation caused
▶ how explanations get accepted

(c) The story of Charles Darwin

Today most scientists agree that evolution happens. But it wasn't always like this. A very important person in the story of evolution was Charles Darwin.

Darwin's big idea

Darwin worked out how evolution could happen. He explained how natural selection could produce evolution. But he didn't come up with this idea overnight. It took many years.

Charles Darwin was born in 1809. When he was 22, Darwin was given the chance to sail on HMS *Beagle*. The ship was on a round-the-world trip to make maps.

Journey of the *Beagle*

The *Beagle* stopped at lots of places along the way. At each stop, Darwin looked at different types of animals and plants. He collected very many specimens. He made lots of observations about what he saw. He recorded these data in notes and pictures.

One place the *Beagle* stopped at was the Galápagos Islands, near South America. Birds called finches live on these islands. Darwin noticed that different species lived on each island.

Darwin on HMS *Beagle*

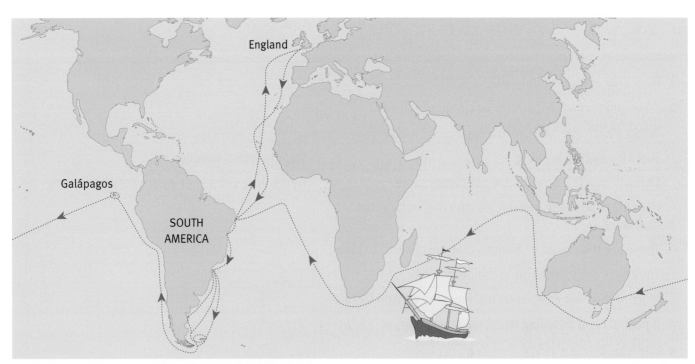

The *Beagle* stopped at different places around the world.

The famous Galápagos finches

Each kind of finch had a different beak. They seemed to be designed for eating different things. For example, one finch had a beak like a parrot for cracking nuts. Another had a very tiny beak for eating seeds.

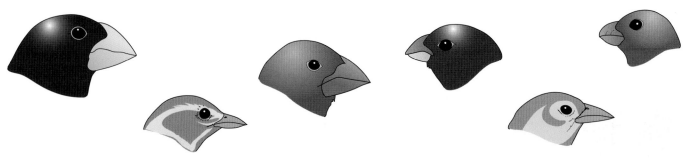

Different species of finch

In his notes, Darwin started to ask himself a question. He wondered if all the different finches could have evolved from just one species.

What was special about Darwin?

Darwin wasn't the first scientist to think that evolution happens. But most people at the time didn't agree with this idea.

Darwin started by looking at many different living things. He made lots of observations. Then:

- He thought about what he had seen. He was creative and imaginative.
- He came up with an idea to explain how evolution could happen.
- His idea was a good one, because it explained all the observations he had made.

Darwin showed his notes to a friend, Thomas Huxley. Huxley was also a scientist. When he read the notes, Huxley said: "How stupid of me not to have thought of this first!"

One might really fancy that from an original paucity of birds in this archipelago one species had been taken and modified for different ends.

Charles Darwin, *The Voyage of the Beagle*, 1839

Questions

1 Darwin made many observations about different species. How did he record his data?

2 What was special about how Darwin thought about his data?

3 Why was Darwin's explanation a good one?

Darwin found more evidence for natural selection at home.

Competition means that many elephants don't survive.

More evidence back home

Back in England, Darwin moved to a new home in Kent. The new house had some pet pigeons. They had many different shapes and colours. But Darwin knew they all belonged to the same species. So he realized that:

> animals or plants from the same species are all different – this is a kind of variation

Too many to survive

Next, Darwin realized that:

> there are always too many of any species to survive

Think about elephants. They usually reproduce from age 30 to 90. Darwin worked out that after 750 years there would be nearly 19 million elephants from just one pair. This doesn't happen, because elephants are all in **competition** for food and space. A lot of them don't survive.

Darwin put these ideas together. He saw that some animals in a population were better suited to survive than others. So natural selection could make a species change over time. Darwin had explained how evolution could happen.

Same data, different explanations

Other scientists also saw that living things were different and they also saw fossils that showed changes in species.

A French scientist called Lamarck had a different explanation to Darwin's. He said that animals changed during their lifetime. Then they passed these changes on to their young. He used the example of a giraffe.

This idea may sound a bit daft now, but Lamarck was a good scientist. He was trying to explain changes in species. But he wanted his explanation to be accepted by other people. He knew that people would be against natural selection.

The giraffe stretches its neck to reach the food.

The neck becomes longer.

MUNCH MUNCH

The giraffe passes its new longer neck on to its offspring.

Giraffe evolution explained by Lamarck

Why were people against natural selection?

Darwin wrote his idea of natural selection into a book. It was published in 1859 and is called *On the Origin of Species*. This book caused one of the biggest arguments in the history of science.

Almost everyone in Victorian society disagreed with the idea of natural selection.

Most people thought that everything in the Bible should be believed just as it was written. The Bible said that all life on Earth was created in six days. There was no natural selection, and no evolution.

What changed people's minds?

The British Association for the Advancement of Science meets every year. Scientists meet to share their ideas. In 1860, many scientists argued against Darwin's idea.

But his two friends, Thomas Huxley and Joseph Hooker, defended it. They were very good scientists. They were also very good at speaking in public. So they helped to change many people's minds about natural selection.

Key words

competition

Questions

4 Do you agree that evolution happens? Explain why you think this.

5 Most people in the 1800s disagreed with natural selection. What evidence did they have against this explanation?

6 Fossil evidence shows that over thousands of years giraffes have evolved longer necks. How did these scientists account for the data:

  a Darwin   **b** Lamarck

It's a disgrace – the thought of us being related to apes!

God made every animal and plant unique. He put fossils on Earth to show us his many designs.

People agreed with Darwin's observations. But they didn't agree with his explanation.

The British Association for the Advancement of Science (BA) meets every year.

Huxley and Hooker argued in favour of Darwin's theory.

Find out about:
▶ what the first life on Earth was like
▶ how scientists think life on Earth began

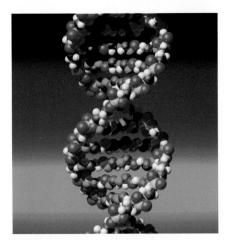

Most cells contain DNA. DNA is copied to pass on information to the next generation. This model is millions of times bigger than the real chemical.

Ⓓ Where did life come from?

Life on Earth began about 3500 million years ago. There are lots of clues to how it started. But scientists don't all agree about what the evidence means.

Living means reproducing

Living things can all reproduce. The first living things were molecules that could copy themselves.

Where did it start?

Scientists have two main ideas about where life on Earth came from.

▶ Life started somewhere else in the Solar System. It was brought to Earth on a comet or a meteorite.
▶ Life started at the bottom of the oceans.

The right conditions

The conditions on Earth 3500 million years ago were very different to now. But they must have been just right for life to grow.

When life began on Earth, the planet was very different. It may have looked like this.

Living things on Earth are suited to survive where they live. If they're not well suited, they die out. This is natural selection.

What if conditions on Earth had been different at *any* time in the last 3500 million years? Life as we know it might not exist. Very different living things might have evolved to suit living on Earth.

Questions

1 How long ago did life begin on Earth?

2 What were the very first living things?

3 Write down the *two* different ideas scientists have for where life began.

4 What could have caused life on Earth to evolve differently?

The oldest evidence for life in Britain

The piece of marble on the right is nearly 3000 million years old. It was made from the bodies of billions of single-celled living things. It is the oldest evidence for life in Britain.

Living things get bigger

The first living organisms were only one cell big. **Multicellular** – many-celled – living things appeared hundreds of millions of years later.

Why did organisms get bigger?

Becoming multicellular had lots of advantages. For example, living things could get bigger. Also, cells could become **specialized**. Different cells changed so they could do one job better. Working together like this is more efficient than each cell trying to do every job.

Was it all good news?

Becoming multicellular also caused one problem. Bigger organisms, like the sea urchin in the photo, need ways for cells to communicate.

This marble comes from the Scottish island of Iona.

This sea anemone is multicellular. It has hundreds of thousands of cells working together.

The sea urchin has special cells to detect food. Different cells move the urchin to the food.

Doctor, will you be operating on my eye?

Well, I usually do feet, but lie down and I'll have a go . . .

Becoming specialized means that you are very good at doing one particular job.

Questions

5 What is meant by multicellular?

6 Write down *two* advantages of being multicellular.

7 What problem did living things have to solve when they became multicellular?

Find out about:
▶ your body's communications systems

E Keep in touch

Sound, sight, cold, and wet. All these things make the woman in the photo jump back from the car. One day this **response** could save her life.

Humans aren't the only animals that can sense something and react to it. All living things must do this to survive.

How does this work? Different parts of the body must be able to communicate with each other.

What are the body's communication systems?

Parts of your body communicate with each other in two ways.

▶ **Nerve cells** (**neurons**) are very long, thin cells. They can link up cells in different parts of the body. They carry **electrical impulses** around the body.

▶ Chemicals called **hormones** are carried in the blood. They are made in one part of the body. They make something happen in a different part of the body.

Why does the body need two communication systems?

Sometimes you need a fast response. Nerve cells carry electrical impulses very quickly. But their effect only lasts a very short time.

Sometimes you need a response that lasts for a longer time. For example, to control changes that take a long time, like growing. Hormones travel much more slowly. But their effects last much longer.

axon

This diagram shows a nerve cell (neuron).

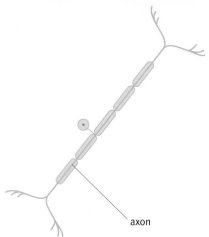

central nervous system (brain and spinal cord)

nerve impulse

nerve impulse

❶ Temperature receptors in the skin detect the stimulus.

❷ The central nervous system coordinates all the information it receives.

❸ The effector – arm muscle contracts.

❹ The response – hand moves away.

How does your nervous system work?

You touch a very hot plate – you move your hand away. This response protects your body from damage.

Let's look at another example.

- ◗ You walk from a dark cinema into a light room.
- ◗ Light receptors in the eyes detect the light.
- ◗ Muscles around your pupils contract.
- ◗ Your pupils get smaller.

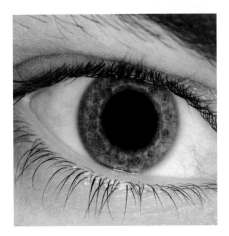 

Hormone responses

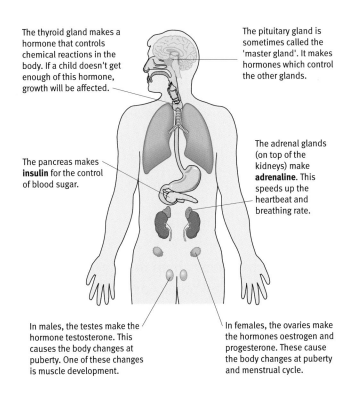

The thyroid gland makes a hormone that controls chemical reactions in the body. If a child doesn't get enough of this hormone, growth will be affected.

The pituitary gland is sometimes called the 'master gland'. It makes hormones which control the other glands.

The pancreas makes **insulin** for the control of blood sugar.

The adrenal glands (on top of the kidneys) make **adrenaline**. This speeds up the heartbeat and breathing rate.

In males, the testes make the hormone testosterone. This causes the body changes at puberty. One of these changes is muscle development.

In females, the ovaries make the hormones oestrogen and progesterone. These cause the body changes at puberty and menstrual cycle.

Hormones are made by parts of the body called glands.

Questions

1 How is information carried by the:

 a nervous system

 b hormonal system

2 Your spinal cord and brain make up your central nervous system. What does this do?

3 Copy and complete the table to show examples of nervous communication.

Stimulus	Receptor	Effector	Response
heat	temperature receptor in skin	muscle in arm	move hand away
bright light			

4 Describe *two* examples of hormone communication.

5 Explain why your body needs two communication systems.

Find out about:

- what we know about human evolution
- how new observations may make scientists change an explanation

(F) Human evolution

Gorillas and chimpanzees are apes. Apes and human beings share many features. For example, human DNA is less than 2% different from chimp DNA.

So does this mean that human beings evolved from apes? No. But apes and humans do share an ancestor.

Gorillas and chimpanzees are our closest living relatives.

Where did the first humans come from?

The photo is a fossil skull of an ape-like animal. It lived in Africa over 20 million years ago.

Modern apes and human beings evolved from an ancestor like this. At some point, they started to develop differently.

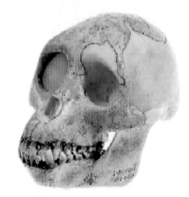

Scientists have dated these ape fossils to over 20 million years old.

Human beings have bigger brains

Human beings have two big differences from apes:

- bigger brains
- walking upright

At first, scientists explained that apes which had developed big brains were able to stand up. So they predicted that big brains evolved before walking upright. But then new evidence was found that disagreed with this idea.

Hominids

In 1924, a skull was dug up in South Africa. It was the first skull found of a **hominid**. Hominids are animals that are more like humans than apes. They lived in Africa between 1.5 and 4 million years ago.

The skull really surprised scientists because the animal:

 ▶ had a small brain, not much different to apes
 ▶ walked upright

These observations disagreed with the scientists' prediction.

A new explanation

Around 7 million years ago, Africa was getting drier. Areas of trees were becoming grass. Apes that could find food in the grasslands wouldn't have to compete with other apes in the trees. An ape that walked upright would be able to see over the tall grass. This would have helped them survive.

Early humans

There were several different species of hominid. They shared a **common ancestor**. Over time, most of these hominids died out. But one species had the largest brains. This helped them to survive. They were early humans. By 150 000 years ago, a small group of them had evolved into modern humans – *Homo sapiens*. They started to leave Africa and explore the rest of the world.

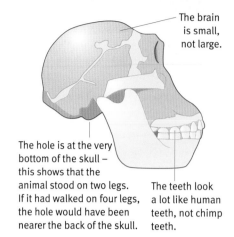

The brain is small, not large.

The hole is at the very bottom of the skull – this shows that the animal stood on two legs. If it had walked on four legs, the hole would have been nearer the back of the skull.

The teeth look a lot like human teeth, not chimp teeth.

Big brains helped early humans learn to use tools, hunt, and make fire.

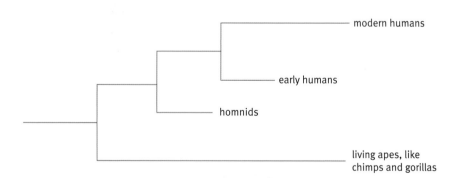

modern humans

early humans

homnids

living apes, like chimps and gorillas

Hominids shared a common ancestor. Only one species survived and evolved into *Homo sapiens*.

Questions

1 What is a hominid?

2 Draw a diagram to show how all hominids had a common ancestor.

3 Give *two* ways that big brains helped some early humans survive.

4 Scientists predicted that hominids had big brains before they started to walk upright. This was proved wrong. Explain how.

Key words

hominid

common ancestor

Find out about:
▶ why some species are under threat
▶ whether it matters if species become extinct

(G) Extinction!

Over the last few million years many species of plants and animals have lived on Earth. Most of these species have died out. They are **extinct**.

Where an animal or plant lives is called its **habitat**. Any quick changes in their habitat can put them at risk of extinction.

Around the world over 12 000 species of plants and animals are today at risk of extinction. They are **endangered**.

Changes in the environment

All living things need factors like water and the right temperature to survive. Rising temperatures are changing many habitats. This global warming is putting many species at risk.

New species

New species moving into the habitat can put another one at risk.

▶ Animals and plants compete with each other for the things they need. Two different species that need exactly the same things cannot live together.

▶ The new species could be a **predator** of the species already living there.
▶ If the new species causes **disease**, it could wipe out the native population.

Wildlife begins to feel the heat of global warming

Six regions were studied, representing 20% of the Earth's land area.

A large international study says that up to a quarter of the species on Earth face extinction from global warming.

Royal Bengal tigers are already endangered. Rising sea levels from global warming may flood their last habitat.

Red squirrels used to live all over the UK. Now the larger American grey squirrels have taken over most of their habitats.

In the 1960s, the virus that causes Dutch Elm disease came to the UK. It destroyed most of the UK elm population.

Going hungry

Plants and animals need other species in their habitat. For example, in this food chain spiders eat caterpillars.

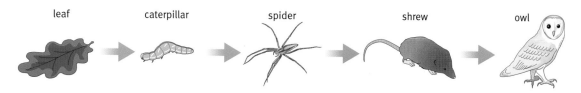

So if the caterpillars all died, the spiders could be at risk. That could also endanger the shrew and the owl.

The food web

Most animals eat more than one thing. Many different food chains contain the same animals. They can be joined together into a **food web**.

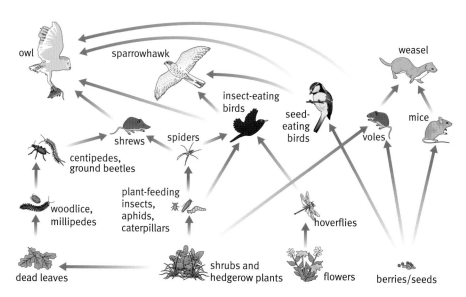

A new animal coming into a food web can affect plants and animals already living there.

Key words

extinct
habitat
endangered
predator
disease
food web

Questions

1 Look at the food web on this page.

  a A disease kills all the flowering plants. Explain what happens to the number of hoverflies.

  b Mink move into the habitat. They eat voles.

    i The number of mice decreases. Explain why.

    ii Explain what would happen to the number of caterpillars.

2 Explain what is meant by **a** extinct **b** endangered.

3 Name *two* things that

  a plant species may compete for

  b animal species may compete for

Dodos were not able to survive the changes in their environment. This is a disaster for any species.

Are humans to blame for some extinctions?

In 1598, Dutch sailors arrived on the island of Mauritius in the Indian Ocean. In the wooded areas along the coast they found fat, flightless birds that they called dodos. By 1700, all the dodos were dead. The species had become extinct.

The popular belief is that sailors ate them all. But this explanation appears too simple. Written reports from the time suggest that dodos were not very nice to eat.

What killed the dodos?

Humans may not have eaten dodos. But did they cause their extinction without meaning to? When the sailors arrived, they brought with them rats, cats, and dogs. These may have attacked the dodos' chicks or eaten their eggs. The sailors also cut down trees to make space for their houses. Maybe this took away the dodos' habitat.

So human beings can cause other species to become extinct:

> ‣ directly, e.g. by hunting
> ‣ **indirectly**, e.g. by taking away their habitat, or bringing other species into the habitat

Pandas are endangered. They eat bamboo but there are only small areas of this left in China.

Isn't extinction just part of life?

Twenty First Century Science put this question to Georgina Mace of the UK Zoological Society.

Georgina Mace

"It is true that species have always gone extinct. This is a natural process. But the pattern of extinction today is different from what has been recorded in the past.

▶ The rate of species extinction today is thousands of times higher than in the past.

▶ Current extinctions are almost all due to humans."

Does extinction matter?

If many species become extinct, there will be less variety on Earth. This variety is very important. For example:

▶ People depend on other species for many things. Food, fuel, and natural fibres (such as cotton and wool) all come from other species.

▶ Many medicines have come from wild plants and animals. There are probably many other medicines in plants that haven't been found yet.

Foxgloves are very poisonous. But they have given us a powerful medicine to treat heart disease.

The variety of life on Earth is called **biodiversity**.

Biodiversity and sustainability

The Earth is 4500 million years old. Human beings have been here for about 160 000 years. If Earth is going to be a good home for future generations, then people today must take care of the planet.

Keeping biodiversity is part of using Earth in a sustainable way. **Sustainability** means meeting the needs of people today without damaging Earth for people of the future.

Key words

indirectly
biodiversity
sustainability

Questions

4 Explain how humans can cause extinction of other species

    a directly **b** indirectly

5 Find out how human beings have caused the extinction of:

    a *Didus ineptus* (the dodo)

    b *Equus quagga*

    c *Ectopistes migratorius*

    d *Achatinella mustelina*

B3 Life on Earth

Science explanations

In this chapter you have learnt how life on Earth has evolved. You have also seen how scientists work out explanations for things they see happening on Earth.

You should know:

▷ all life on Earth has evolved from the first very simple living things

▷ evidence for evolution comes from fossils and by comparing the DNA of different organisms

▷ the first living things appeared on Earth 3500 million years ago and were molecules that could copy themselves

▷ these living things may have developed on Earth, or they may have come to Earth from somewhere else

▷ if conditions on Earth had been different at any time since life first began, then evolution may have happened differently

▷ members of a species are not identical, there is variation between them

▷ variation is caused by the environment or genes, but most features are affected by both

▷ evolution happens by natural selection:

  – members of a species are all different from each other (variation)

  – they compete with each other for different resources

  – some have features that given them a better chance of surviving and reproducing

  – they pass on features through their genes to the next generation

▷ more of the next generation have these useful features

▷ the difference between natural selection and selective breeding

▷ the main parts of the human nervous system

▷ how nervous and hormonal systems communicate information around the body

▷ that the evolution of a larger brain gave some early human a better chance of survival

▷ that many hominid species evolved from a common ancestor, but only one survived and became modern humans

▷ living organisms depend on their environment and each other for survival

▷ animals and plants in the same habitat compete for different resources

▷ how a change in a food web can affect all the species there

▷ species may become extinct if:

  – their environment changes

  – a new species arrives that is a competitor a predator, or causes disease

  – another plant or animal in the food web becomes extinct

▷ two examples of modern extinctions caused:

  – directly by humans, for example, by hunting

  – indirectly by humans, for example, destroying their habitat

▷ why keeping biodiversity is important for us and for future generations

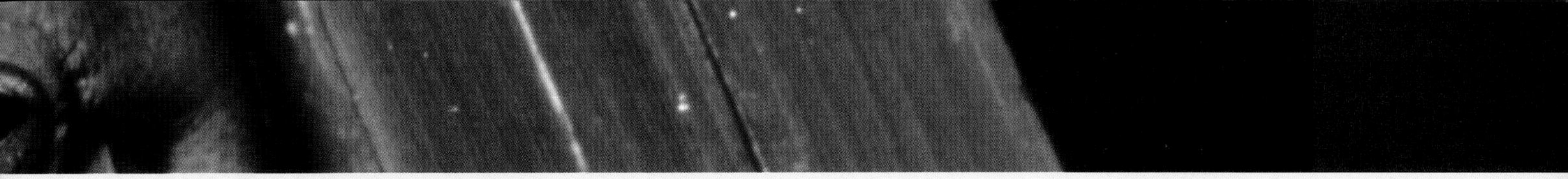

Ideas about science

Working out how something happens – an explanation – takes imagination and creativity. Scientists don't always agree about what the correct explanation for something is.

This Module looks at several explanations, including natural selection and where life on Earth began. From these you should be able to identify:

▶ statements that are data

▶ statements that are all or part of an explanation

▶ data or observations that an explanation can account for

▶ data or observations that don't agree with an explanation

Scientists don't always come to the same conclusion about what some data means. The debate about Darwin's idea of natural selection is one example of this. You should know:

▶ working out an explanation takes creativity and imagination

▶ why Darwin's explanation was a good one

▶ why other scientists disagreed with his ideas at the time

New observations about human evolution are being found. Sometimes scientists use an explanation to predict an observation which hasn't been made yet. For example, scientists predicted that human evolved a big brain before they began to walk upright. Then they found fossils which did not agree with this prediction. You should know:

▶ how observations that agree or disagree with a prediction can make scientists more or less confident about an explanation

Some scientific questions have not been answered yet. You should know:

▶ scientists have two different explanations for how life on Earth began, but there is not enough evidence to decide between them

Why study food?

Today, most of us do not have to spend time growing or catching food. Modern farming needs only a few people to make all our food. It is important that food is safe to eat.
Food safety depends on the care taken at every stage in the food chain; from farm to home.

The science

Science can help to explain how farming affects the natural environment. For example, making and using fertilizers can have a big effect on the 'cycling' of elements such as nitrogen.

Science can also explain the chemical changes that take place in your body when you eat food. Research can tell us about the effects of diet on health, and it helps doctors treat diseases such as diabetes.

Ideas about science

Making the right choices about food and farming can help to make the food chain more sustainable. Governments try to protect consumers by regulating the food chain.
The decisions they make need to use scientific information so that judgements about risk are based on evidence.

Food matters

Find out about:

- the food chain from farm to plate
- farming methods and their effects on the environment
- natural and artificial chemicals in food, including food additives
- the possible links between obesity and diabetes

Find out about:
▶ the food chain from farm to plate

Ⓐ The food chain

Bread, cakes, biscuits, and pasta all begin life on the farm. There is a long **food chain** from farms to your plate.

On the farm

Farmers plant seeds of wheat in the soil. The seeds grow to make new plants. At **harvest** time, the farmers gather the crop. Flour comes from the seeds in the ears of wheat.

Soil must have enough nitrogen compounds and other chemicals for healthy plant growth. Farmers use fertilizers or manures to keep the soil **fertile.**

A combine harvester cuts the crop and gathers it. Then it separates the seeds. The seeds are the wheat grain needed to make flour.

At the mill

A lot of of food looks very different from the raw crop. Wheat grains are broken up by rollers in a mill to turn them into flour.

On the road

Transport of food is an important part of the food chain. More energy is needed if food has to travel many miles to reach your home.

A miller scoops wheat grains before they are milled to make flour.

A baker in a supermarket mixes the ingredients to make bread dough.

Taking bread from an oven in a commercial bakery.

At the bakery

Bakers mix flour with water, fat, and yeast to make bread dough. The yeast grows, in the dough. As it grows, it produces carbon dioxide gas. This makes the dough rise.

Bakers shape the dough to make loaves, rolls, or flat breads. Then they bake the dough in a hot oven to make bread.

In the supermarket

People who buy and eat food have choices to make.

- ▶ Does it taste good?
- ▶ Is it good for you?
- ▶ Is it good for the environment?

When buying bread there are many choices: white or wholemeal? sliced or unsliced? organic or not?

Key words

food chain

harvest

fertile

Questions

1 Make a flow diagram to show the stages of the food chain, from wheat in a farmer's field to a piece of bread on your plate.

2 Some people want us to eat more food that is grown nearer to our homes. Write down two advantages and two disadvantages of choosing to buy food that is grown locally.

Find out about:
- how to keep soils fertile
- ways to protect crops from pests

B Farming challenges

Farmers have to make sure that their crops grow well. This means that they have to keep the soil fertile.

Farmers must also protect their crops from pests and diseases.

The nutrient challenge

Chemicals for plant growth

Plants need to make **sugars**, **proteins**, and other chemicals as they grow. Plants make sugars from carbon dioxide and water. They need energy from light to do this. This is photosynthesis.

Plants take in other elements from the soil. One of these elements is nitrogen, which plants need to make proteins. There are nitrogen compounds in soil water. The roots of growing plants draw in soil water containing the nitrogen compounds.

Cycles of nutrients

Imagine a wild apple tree growing in a hedge. It takes in nitrogen compounds from the soil to make leaves and fruit.

Each autumn, the apples and leaves fall to the ground and rot away. Rotting releases nitrogen compounds from the apples and leaves. Rain washes the nitrogen compounds back into the soil. So each year the nitrogen is recycled.

However, people may pick the apples from the tree. This means that less nitrogen can be recycled back to the soil.

Therefore, farmers use **fertilizers** and **manures**. These put back into the soil the nutrients removed as crops grow and are harvested.

Using animal slurry to fertilize a wheat crop

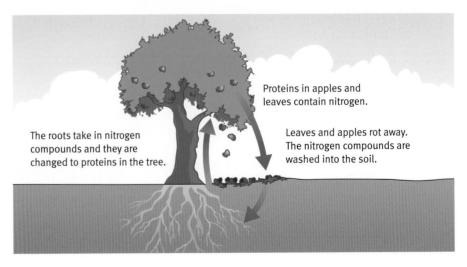

The roots take in nitrogen compounds and they are changed to proteins in the tree.

Proteins in apples and leaves contain nitrogen.

Leaves and apples rot away. The nitrogen compounds are washed into the soil.

The pest challenge

Pests

Farmers try to protect their growing crops from:

▶ insect **pests**
▶ weeds
▶ diseases caused by fungi

A fungus can do a lot of damage to a wheat crop.
The fungus quickly spreads once one plant is infected.

Wheat crops are sprayed with a pesticide to prevent disease.

Controlling the pests

One way of controlling pests is to use chemicals to kill them.
Some **pesticides** are natural chemicals. Other pesticides are manufactured.

Questions

1 a Where does the carbon come from that plants use to make sugars and protein?

b Copy and complete this word equation to show what happens in photosynthesis.

.... + water → sugar + ...

2 a Where do plants get the nitrogen they need for healthy growth?

b Soil gets less fertile if crops are grown and harvested in the same place year after year. Explain why.

3 Some pests harm crops after harvest. Suggest one pest that could damage stored food.

Key words

sugars
protein
fertilizers
manure
pest
pesticide

c Farming for food

Intensive farming

On the farm

Intensive farmers try to get as big a **yield** as possible from their land. Their fields are large, so it is easier to work on them with machinery.

Some intensive farms concentrate on animals. These might be cows for milk or pigs for meat. Other intensive farms mainly grow crops.

Intensive farming on a big scale.

Fertile soils

Intensive farmers use manufactured fertilizers to add nitrogen compounds to the soil. This can make it possible to add just the right amount of fertilizer when it is needed.

Fighting pests and diseases

Insect pests eat crops. Weeds in the crop compete for water, light, and nutrients. Diseases make plants sick, so that they do not grow so well.

Intensive farmers use pesticides. They may spray crops several times:

- to kill weeds
- to kill insects that might carry disease or eat the crop
- to stop the spread of disease

Intensive farming and the environment

Intensive farming means that food can be produced on a smaller area of land. This could mean that more land is free for woods and other areas for wildlife. It could also mean more land for housing and roads.

Weeds compete with the crop for space, light, water, and nutrients.

But growing the same crop in large fields reduces the variety of wildlife. Also, pesticides kill the weeds and insects that are food for other living things.

Using too much fertilizer can also do harm. In wet weather, the nutrients can be washed into streams. Here they cause water weeds to grow very fast. Later, the weeds die and rot. Rotting uses up the oxygen in the water. Fish die if there is not enough oxygen.

Large dairy farms produce a large volume of animal manure. Some of this can be spread on the land but not all. Manures leaking into streams also pollute the water and kill fish.

Chemicals from farmland have been washed into the Kennet and Avon canal. The canal is rich in nutrients. Algae grow fast and choke the waterway.

Farming, food, and the consumer

Intensive farming can keep down the cost of food. Working on a large scale helps to keep down costs.

Using fertilizers and pesticides makes large crops. These have the quality that many people now expect. For example, vegetables and fruit are large. They are all about the same size and free of pests.

But some pesticides soak right into crops to kill from the inside out. Other pesticides are sprayed on the surface. Traces of pesticides may remain in the food. Some people worry about these pesticide residues. Usually the levels are well below the safety margins.

Sustainability

Over half the energy used for agriculture is used to make fertilizers. So intensive farming depends on cheap energy from fossil fuels. This type of farming may do little to recycle nutrients.

Much of the food produced travels large distances before it reaches the public. Nearly 40 per cent of the lorries on our roads carry food. About 12 per cent of the fuel burnt in the UK is for food transport and packaging.

Key words

intensive
yield

Questions

1 Why do plant crops grow less well if there are lots of weeds growing in the field?

2 Make a table with two columns. In one column list the advantages of intensive farming. In the second column list the disadvantages.

③ Give examples of people who

  a benefit from intensive farming

  b may be harmed by intensive farming

Harvesting squash (a variety of marrow) from a field in an organic farm.

Farmer with pigs on an organic farm.

Ladybird eating aphids.

Organic farming

On the farm

On many **organic farms** the farmers keep animals and grow crops.

Fertile soils

Organic farmers use manures instead of fertilizers. So the dung from the animals is used to add nutrients to the soil.

Organic farmers rotate their crops. This also helps to keep soil fertile.

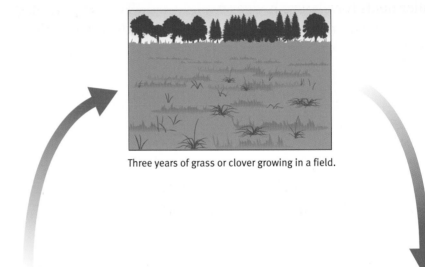

Three years of grass or clover growing in a field.

A year of a root crops such as beet to feed animals.

Two years of a cereal crop such as wheat.

Fighting pests and diseases

Organic farmers use predators to control pests. For example, ladybirds feed on greenfly. Smaller fields mean that there are more hedges and ditches. These are homes for animals that feed on pests.

Crop rotation can also help to prevent disease. The fungi that cause disease on one crop may not survive on the next crop. So the disease can die out when a different crop is growing on the land.

Organic farmers put up with some weeds. After harvest the weeds are ploughed into the soil to make it more fertile.

Organic farmers are allowed to use a very small number of chemical pesticides. But they must get permission to do so.

Organic farming and the environment

Smaller fields have more hedges round them. This helps to stop the wind blowing away soil from ploughed fields. Hedges also offer homes for wildlife. There are no pesticides killing the insects that are food for larger animals.

Manuring and ploughing can lead to nutrients being washed from the soil into streams.

Farming, food, and the consumer

Organic fruit and vegetables may be smaller. They may vary more in size and appearance. Organic food is generally more expensive, because it takes more labour to produce it.

The Soil Association is one of the organizations that sets standards for organic producers. It checks up on organic farms. A farm cannot call itself 'organic' if it does not meet the standards.

Some customers choose organic food because they think that it tastes better. Others think that organic farmers treat their animals better.

The **Food Standards Agency** reports that there is not enough evidence to show that organic food is healthier. However, some people feel that it is safer and worry about the chemical residues from intensive farming.

Sustainability

Organic farmers aim to use sustainable resources. They recycle nutrients and produce less waste. Manures from animals fertilize the soil. Straw from cereal crops provides bedding for animals.

Organic farmers save on the cost of fertilizers and pesticides but they have to pay for more workers.

This logo can only appear on food that has been produced according to strict standards.

Key words

organic farm
Food Standards Agency

Questions

4 Make a table with two columns. In one column list the advantages of organic farming. In the second column list the disadvantages.

5 Give examples of people who

a benefit from organic farming

b may be harmed by organic farming

Find out about:
▶ food additives

Strawberries can quickly turn mouldy. The large quantity of sugar in jam preserves the fruit.

Ⓓ Preserving and processing food

Preserving food

Preservatives

Some foods last a long time in a kitchen cupboard. These foods often contain **preservatives**. Preservatives have been used for hundreds of years. Older preservatives are sugar, salt, and vinegar. These are still used to preserve some foods.

The main purpose of preservatives is to stop mould or bacteria growing in food.

Antioxidants

Antioxidants stop the air making foods go 'off'. Oxygen turns fats and oils rancid. Rancid food tastes horrible. Other foods change colour if they react with oxygen.

Processing foods

Food manufacturers also use **additives** to make products that people want to buy and eat.

Colours

Manufacturers add colours to replace the natural colour lost during food processing or storage. They also add colour to make food products look good.

Food colours brighten the coating of these sweets.

Flavourings

Many processed foods and drinks have flavourings in them. These are usually added in very small amounts. They give a particular taste or smell.

Sweeteners

Sweeteners replace sugar in diet drinks and low-calorie foods. For example, aspartame and saccharin are many times sweeter than sugar. Only very small amounts are used.

Emulsifiers and stabilizers

Emulsifiers help ingredients such as oil and water to mix. **Stabilizers** help to stop these ingredients from separating again.

Emulsifiers and stabilizers also give foods an even texture. Manufacturers need them to make foods such as low-fat spreads and yogurt.

E numbers

An **E number** shows that a food additive has passed safety tests. It is allowed in the European Union. The numbering system is used for additives from natural sources and for artificial additives.

- ▶ E100 series: colours
- ▶ E200 series: preservatives
- ▶ E300 series: antioxidants
- ▶ E400+ series: emulsifiers, stabilizers, and other additives

Flavourings do not have E numbers. They are controlled by different laws.

Manufacturers use emulsifiers to stop food ingredients from separating: for example, ice cream, chocolate, cakes, low-fat spreads, and salad cream.

The law says that anything added to food during processing must be shown on the label. Most companies obey the law. Sometimes labels do not list everything. Very occasionally, illegal ingredients are found in food.

Questions

1 Look at the list of E numbers. Write down the reasons for adding these natural chemicals to food:

   a lactic acid, E270

   b pectin, E440

   c cochineal, E120

   d vitamin C (ascorbic acid), E300

2 Write down the reasons for adding these artificial chemicals to food:

   a methyl cellulose, E461

   b erythrosine, E127

   c BHA (butylated hydroxyanisole), E320

   d sulfur dioxide, E220

③ Some people think that adding colour makes food look more attractive. Other people think there should be no added colours because they are possibly harmful to some people. What do you think? Give your reasons.

Key words

preservatives	emulsifiers
antioxidants	stabilizers
additives	E numbers

Find out about:
- food digestion
- risks from harmful chemicals in food

Key words
cellulose
starch
amino acid
digestion

E Healthy and harmful chemicals

Chemicals in a healthy diet

Food contains the chemicals that people need to stay alive.

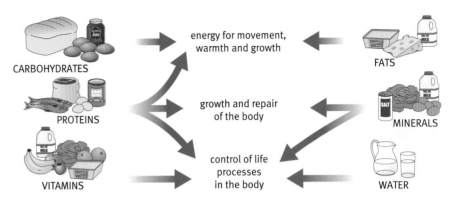

The nutrients in food and what they do.

A healthy diet must also include minerals and vitamins. Water is another vital part of the diet.

What you eat should also include chemicals such as **cellulose**. Cellulose from plants makes up the fibre in the diet. The body cannot digest cellulose.

Natural polymers

Starch and cellulose are natural polymers (see Section E in Module C2 *Material choices*). They are both long chains of glucose molecules. The glucose molecules are joined in a different way in each. This makes starch easy to digest but not cellulose.

Proteins are also natural polymers (see Section D in Module C2 *Material choices*). They are long chains of **amino acids**. There are many types of protein. Each protein has a different number of amino acids in a chain. The amino acids are also in a different order.

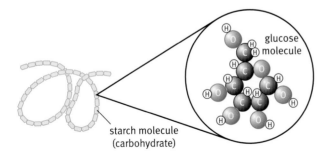

Starch is a polymer made by linking up sugar molecules in a long chain. The sugar is glucose. Glucose is made of carbon, hydrogen, and oxygen atoms.

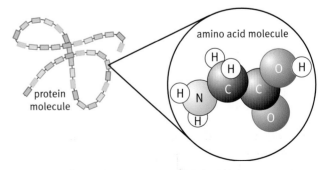

Proteins are polymers with long chains of amino acids. Amino acids are made of carbon, hydrogen, oxygen, and nitrogen atoms. There are sometimes other atoms too.

Digestion

When you swallow, food passes from your mouth to your stomach. Later it moves into your small intestine. Muscles in the gut wall squeeze the food along. They also mix the food with digestive juices. These juices contain enzymes.

The enzymes speed up the chemical reactions of **digestion**. The chemical changes break down the polymers in food into small molecules. This must happen because only small molecules can pass through the wall of the gut into your blood.

The enzymes break down:

- ▶ starch into sugars
- ▶ proteins into amino acids

Enzymes in the human body cannot break down cellulose.

Growth

Cells in the body make new cells all the time. These new cells are needed:

- ▶ for growth
- ▶ to replace worn out cells
- ▶ to replace damaged cells

As cells grow, they take in amino acids from the bloodstream. Cells build up the amino acids to make new proteins.

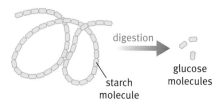

Enzymes in saliva and in the stomach break down starch into the sugar glucose.

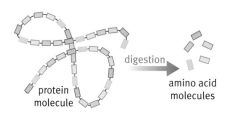

Enzymes in the small intestine break down proteins into amino acids.

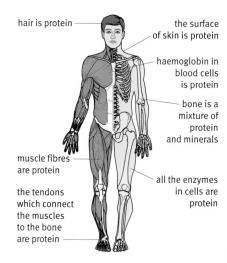

Some proteins in the human body.

> ### Questions
>
> **1 a** Name the three elements found in all carbohydrates.
>
> **b** Name an element found in proteins that is not in carbohydrates.
>
> **2** Potatoes contain starch and cellulose. When you eat potato what happens
>
> **a** to starch?
>
> **b** to cellulose?
>
> **3** Scientists estimate that there are about 100 000 different proteins in a human body. How can so many proteins be made from just 20 amino acids?
>
> **4** Copy and complete this flow diagram:
>
>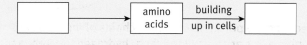

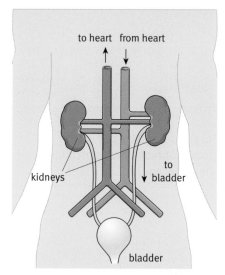

You have two kidneys. They filter your blood to take out waste chemicals, such as urea. The waste chemicals that come from bile are yellow.

Excretion

If you eat a lot of protein, you may have more amino acids in your blood than your body can use. The body cannot store the amino acids. It has to get rid of them if their level in the blood is too high.

The liver breaks down amino acids into **urea**. Urea is a colourless chemical which is very soluble in water. The blood carries urea from the liver to the **kidneys**. The kidneys remove the urea from the blood. It passes out with the urine.

Toxic chemicals in food and drink

Food gives pleasure and is vital for life. But foods can sometimes be dangerous too. Sometimes food can kill.

Moulds growing on nuts and dried fruit can produce aflatoxins. Aflatoxins can cause cancer. In the EU there are legal limits for aflatoxins in foods, to make sure that people take in as little of them as possible.

Most of the people who die by eating mushrooms have eaten Death Cap. **Toxins** in these mushrooms destroy the liver.

Cassava is a root crop. The roots of cassava contain poisonous chemicals. Shredding the roots and squeezing out the juice removes most of the toxins. Heating dries the flour. It also gets rid of the rest of the toxins.

Cooking starchy foods at a high temperature can produce acrylamide. This was discovered in 2002 and scientists are now actively researching the issue. High doses of acrylamide can cause cancer in animals and so it may also harm people's health.

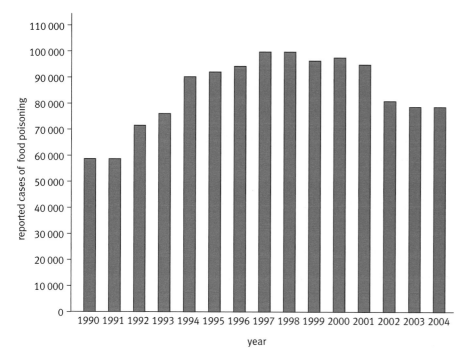

Reported cases of food poisoning in England and Wales. Some bacteria produce toxins when they grow in food. Bacteria on cooked foods can cause food poisoning. Bacteria grow fast at room temperature. They soon produce enough toxin to make people sick.

Food allergies

Some people have an **allergy** to proteins in food. Most allergic reactions to food are mild, but sometimes they can be very serious.

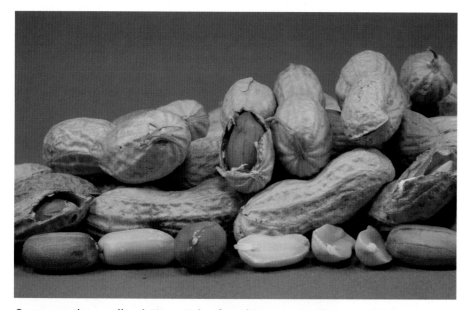

Some people are allergic to proteins found in peanuts. These proteins are not destroyed by cooking. So both fresh and roasted peanuts can cause an allergic reaction.

Key words

urea   toxin
kidney   allergy

Questions

5 Give one example of a toxic chemical present in food because of

   a the type of crop grown

   b the method of farming

   c the way the food is stored

   d the method of cooking

   e what happens to the food after cooking

6 Why must cooked food be kept hot or cold, but never just at room temperature?

7 Suggest three questions that you would like to ask if you met a scientist doing research into the issue of acrylamide in cooked food.

Find out about:
- the risks of being overweight
- the two types of diabetes
- risk factors for diabetes

(F) Diet and diabetes

Healthy eating

What you eat can make a big difference to your health and well-being. As well as the nutrients in a balanced diet, a healthy diet:

- contains lots of fruit and vegetables
- is based on starchy foods, such as wholegrain bread, pasta, rice, and potatoes
- is low in foods with a lot of fat, salt, and sugar, such as salty snacks, soft drinks, and sweets.

More than half your daily energy from food should come from carbohydrates. Many processed foods contain carbohydrates that get into the bloodstream very quickly. They also flow through your body quickly. This means that you soon feel hungry again. It is better to eat foods with carbohydrate that is digested and absorbed more slowly.

Obesity and health risks

Obese people have put on so much weight that it is a danger to their health. **Obesity** is mainly caused by eating too much and not taking enough exercise. By 2020, over half of young people will be obese, if childhood obesity goes on increasing as fast as it is now.

Obesity increases the risk of heart diseases (see Section G in Module B2 *Keeping healthy*). It also increases the risk of other diseases, such as **diabetes**.

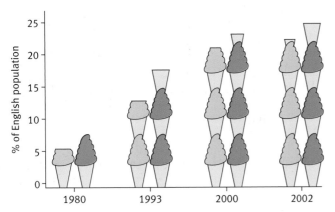

Percentage of males (blue) and females (red) in England who are obese.

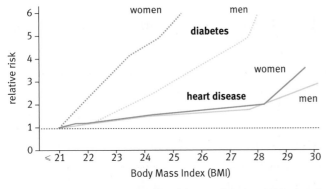

Ranges of body mass index (BMI) by sex in 2001. This data is from the Department of Health Survey for England. BMI is a number that shows a person's body mass adjusted for height.

A person with diabetes checks their blood sugar levels regularly.

Diabetes

Diabetes is the third most common long-term disease in the UK, after heart disease and cancer. People with diabetes have high levels of glucose in their blood, unless they are treated. Their bodies cannot use glucose properly.

There are two types of diabetes: Type 1 and Type 2.

Key words

obesity

diabetes

insulin

hormone

pancreas

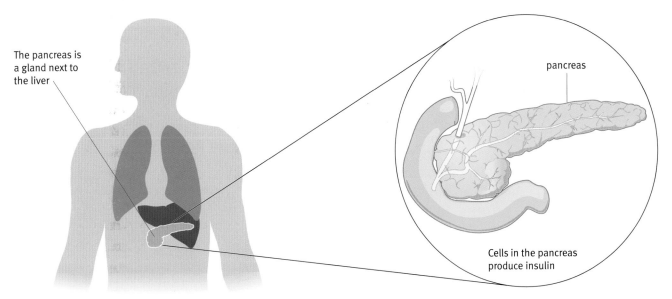

The pancreas is a gland next to the liver

pancreas

Cells in the pancreas produce insulin

Insulin controls the level of sugar in blood. It lets sugar molecules into cells.

When the sugar levels rise the pancreas cells release insulin into the blood.

In type 1 diabetes the special cells in the pancreas are destroyed. The pancreas cannot make insulin.

In type 2 diabetes the pancreas does not make enough insulin or cells do not respond to the insulin there is.

Every cell of the body needs energy to survive. **Insulin** is a **hormone** produced in the **pancreas**. The hormone is critical for cells to take up glucose sugar and use it for energy.

Type 1 diabetes

Type 1 diabetes is more likely to start in younger people, but it can develop at any age. Cells in the pancreas that make insulin are destroyed. Insulin is a hormone that controls the levels of glucose in the blood. This type of diabetes is treated with insulin injections.

A person with type 1 diabetes injects insulin several times a day to keep blood glucose levels normal. The injection includes human insulin produced by bacteria that have been genetically modified.

Questions

1 What kinds of food are most likely to cause obesity if eaten in large quantities?

2 Why can it be unhealthy to be overweight?

Type 2 diabetes

Type 2 diabetes is usually diagnosed in older people. The older you are, the greater the risk. But more young people are now developing type 2 diabetes. This type of diabetes can sometimes be treated with diet and exercise alone. But people with type 2 diabetes often need medicine. They sometimes need insulin too.

A dietician can advise someone with Type 2 diabetes. Choosing a healthy diet can help to control the condition.

People with type 2 diabetes can still make insulin. The problem is that the cells in the body no longer react normally to the hormone. Much more insulin than normal is needed to keep blood glucose levels at the right level.

Who gets type 2 diabetes?

Diabetes is a common health condition. There are 1.8 million people with diabetes in the UK. That is about 3 in every 100 people. There may be a million more people who have diabetes but do not know it. Over three-quarters of all the people with diabetes have type 2 diabetes.

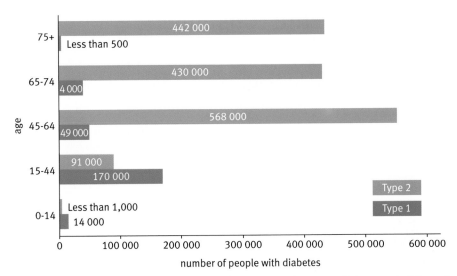

Estimates of the numbers of people with type 1 and type 2 diabetes at different ages in the population of 60 million people in the UK.

Risk factors

Being overweight is a leading **risk factor** for type 2 diabetes. People with a Body Mass Index (BMI) greater than 30 are obese. The risk of developing type 2 diabetes increases by up to ten times in people with a BMI of more than 30.

Taking little exercise is also a risk factor for diabetes. This is not just because people who take little exercise are often overweight. Physical activity helps the body to keep blood glucose levels in check.

Two other risk factors for type 2 diabetes are genetics and age. Type 2 diabetes tends to run in families. Also, members of some minority ethnic communities living in the UK develop type 2 diabetes at a younger age. The risk of developing diabetes is about five times higher in these communities.

> **Key words**
> risk factor

Questions

3 Look at the chart showing how many people have diabetes in different age ranges. Write down two conclusions you can make from the data.

4 The number of people with type 2 diabetes is growing. Suggest a reason for this.

5 Give two ways in which people can change their lifestyle to reduce the risk of getting type 2 diabetes.

6 What evidence is there that genetics may be a risk factor for type 2 diabetes?

7 Why is it sometimes possible to control type 2 diabetes just by careful choice of diet, but not type 1 diabetes?

Find out about:
▶ regulation of the food chain
▶ consumer protection in the food industry

G Food and the consumer

Governments and food safety

The European Union has passed laws on the safety of food. The laws cover the whole of the food chain.

Country flags flying outside the European parliament building in Strasbourg.

It is the job of national and local governments in the EU countries to apply the laws. They have to make sure that farmers, manufacturers, and traders obey the rules.

The Food Standards Agency

The government of the UK set up the Food Standards Agency in 2000.

The Agency aims to:

▶ reduce the amount of illness caused by food
▶ help people to eat more healthily
▶ promote honest and informative **food labelling**
▶ promote best practice in the food industry
▶ make sure that people obey food laws

Research and food

The Food Standards Agency wants its advice to the public to be based on up-to-date food science. It pays for scientists to do research on important issues. It also has expert committees to give advice.

Some food issues are very controversial. Scientists do not always agree about what the evidence means.

Sometimes there is doubt about the size of a risk to health. Then the Agency asks one of its committees of experts for advice.

Key words
food labelling

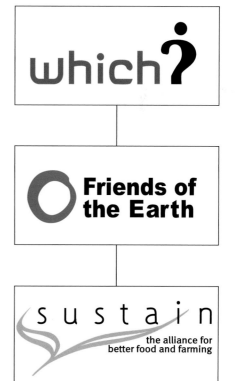

These are some of the many organizations that campaign on behalf of the public. They want farming and food systems that are better for public health, animal welfare, and the environment.

Labelling

Food labels give people information about foods. People can use them to make choices about what they eat.

Food labelling is controlled by law. Manufacturers cannot just print what they like on labels. This protects people from false claims or misleading descriptions.

Speaking up for the consumer

Some of the work of the Food Standards Agency is controversial. Not everyone agrees with its scientific advice. Some people argue against the decisions it makes, based on the complex evidence.

Questions

1 Write down two aims of the Food Standards Agency.

2 Where does the Food Standards Agency get its advice from?

3 Name an organization that campaigns for better food.

4 You meet someone who thinks that food should be 100% safe. How would you explain that this is impossible? Give at least two arguments.

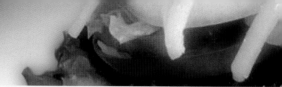

C3 Food matters

Science explanations

Chemicals are all around us. Their interactions govern our lives.

You should know:

▷ all living things are made of chemicals

▷ there is continual cycling of elements in the environment

▷ the nitrogen cycle is an example of a natural cycle

▷ where crops are harvested elements, such as nitrogen, potassium, and phosphorus, are lost from the soil

▷ land becomes less fertile unless these elements are replaced

▷ organic and intensive farmers use different methods to keep soil fertile for growing crops

▷ organic and intensive farmers use different methods to protect crops against pests and diseases

▷ farmers have to follow UK national standards if they want to claim that their products are organic

▷ farming has an impact on the natural environment

▷ some methods of farming are more sustainable than others

▷ some natural chemicals in plants that we eat may be toxic if they are not cooked properly, or they may cause allergies in some people

▷ moulds that contaminate crops during storage (such as aflatoxin in nuts and cereals) may add toxic chemicals to food

▷ chemicals used in farming (such as pesticides and herbicides) may be in the products we eat and be harmful

▷ harmful chemicals may be produced during food processing and cooking

▷ natural and synthetic chemicals may be added to food during processing

  – food colours can be used to make processed food look more attractive

  – flavourings enhance the taste of food

  – artificial sweeteners help to reduce the amount of sugar in processed foods and drinks

– emulsifiers and stabilizers help to mix ingredients together that would normally separate, such as oil and water

– preservatives help to keep food safe for longer by stopping the growth of harmful microbes

– antioxidants are added to foods containing fats or oils to stop them reacting with oxygen in the air

▷ many chemicals in living things are natural polymers (including carbohydrates and proteins)

▷ cellulose, starch and sugars are carbohydrates that are made up of carbon, hydrogen and oxygen

▷ amino acids and proteins consist mainly of carbon, hydrogen, oxygen and nitrogen

▷ digestion breaks down natural polymers to smaller, soluble compounds (for example digestion breaks down starch to glucose, and proteins to amino acids)

▷ these small molecules can be absorbed and transported in the blood

▷ cells grow by building up amino acids from the blood into new proteins

▷ excess amino acids are broken down in the liver to form urea, which is excreted by the kidneys in urine

▷ high levels of sugar, common in some processed foods, are quickly absorbed into the blood stream, causing a rapid rise in the blood sugar level

▷ there are two types of diabetes (type 1 and type 2)

▷ late-onset diabetes (type 2) is more likely to be triggered by a poor diet

▷ obesity is one of the risk factors for type 2 diabetes

▷ In type 1 diabetes the pancreas stops producing enough of the hormone, insulin

▷ In type 2 diabetes the body no longer responds to its own insulin or does not make enough insulin

▷ type 1 diabetes is controlled by insulin injections and type 2 diabetes can be controlled by diet and exercise

Ideas about science

Science-based technology provides people with many things that they value, and which enhance the quality of life. Some applications of science can have unwanted affects on our quality of life or the environment.

For different farming methods you should be able to:

▶ identify the groups affected, and the main costs and benefits of a decision for each group

▶ explain how science helps to find ways of using natural resources in a more sustainable way

▶ show you know that regulations and laws control scientific research and applications

▶ distinguish from what can be done from what should be done

▶ explain why different decisions may be made in different social and economic contexts

New technologies and processes based on scientific advances sometimes introduce new risks. Some people are worried about the health effects arising from the use of some food additives. You should be able to:

▶ explain why nothing is completely safe

▶ suggest ways of reducing some risks

Scientific advisory committees carry out risk assessments to determine the safe levels of chemicals in food. The Food Standards Agency is an independent food safety watchdog set up by an Act of Parliament to protect the public's health and consumer interests in relation to food.

Additives with an E number have passed a safety test and been approved for use in the UK and the rest of the EU. Food labelling can help consumers decide which products to buy. You should be able to:

▶ interpret information on the size of risks

▶ show you know that regulations and laws control scientific research and applications

▶ explain that if it is not possible to be sure about the results of doing something, and if serious harm could result, then it makes sense to avoid it (the 'precautionary principle')

People's perception of the size of a risk is often very different from the actual measured risk. People tend to over-estimate the risk of unfamiliar things (like chemicals with strange names added to food compared with overeating and obesity), and things whose effect is invisible (like pesticides residues). You should be able to:

▶ discuss a particular risk, taking account both of the chance of it happening and the consequences if it did

▶ suggest why people will accept (or reject) the risk of a certain activity, for example, eating a diet rich in sugar and fat because they enjoy this food

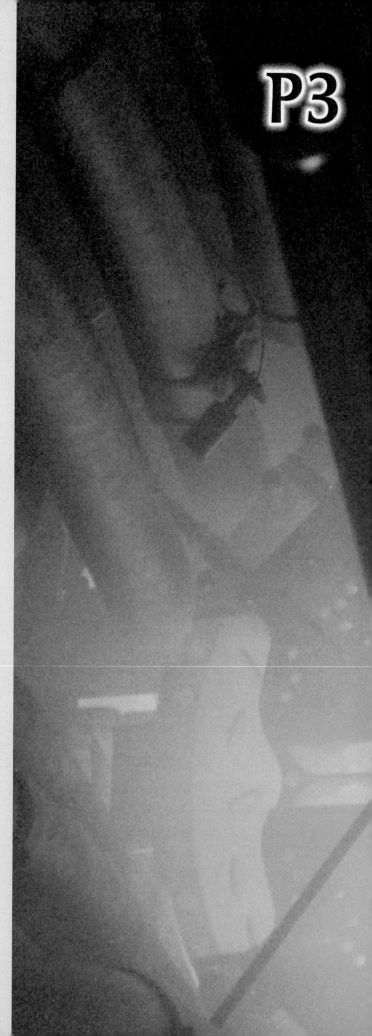

Why study radioactive materials?

People make jokes about radioactivity. If you visit a nuclear power station, or if you have hospital treatment with radiation, they may say you will 'glow in the dark'. People may worry about radioactivity when they don't need to.

Most of us take electricity for granted. But today's power stations are becoming old and soon will need replacement. Should nuclear power stations be built as replacements?

The science

Radiation from radioactive materials comes from deep inside their atoms. To use radioactive materials safely you need to know about the different types of radiation.

Nuclear power stations produce nuclear waste. This waste can be dangerous for tens of thousands of years.

Ideas about science

Nothing can be completely safe. Before any medical procedure uses radioactive materials, doctors and their patients carefully weigh up the benefits against the risks.

Soon, decisions about getting rid of nuclear waste, or building new power stations will be made. Who will decide, and how can you have your say?

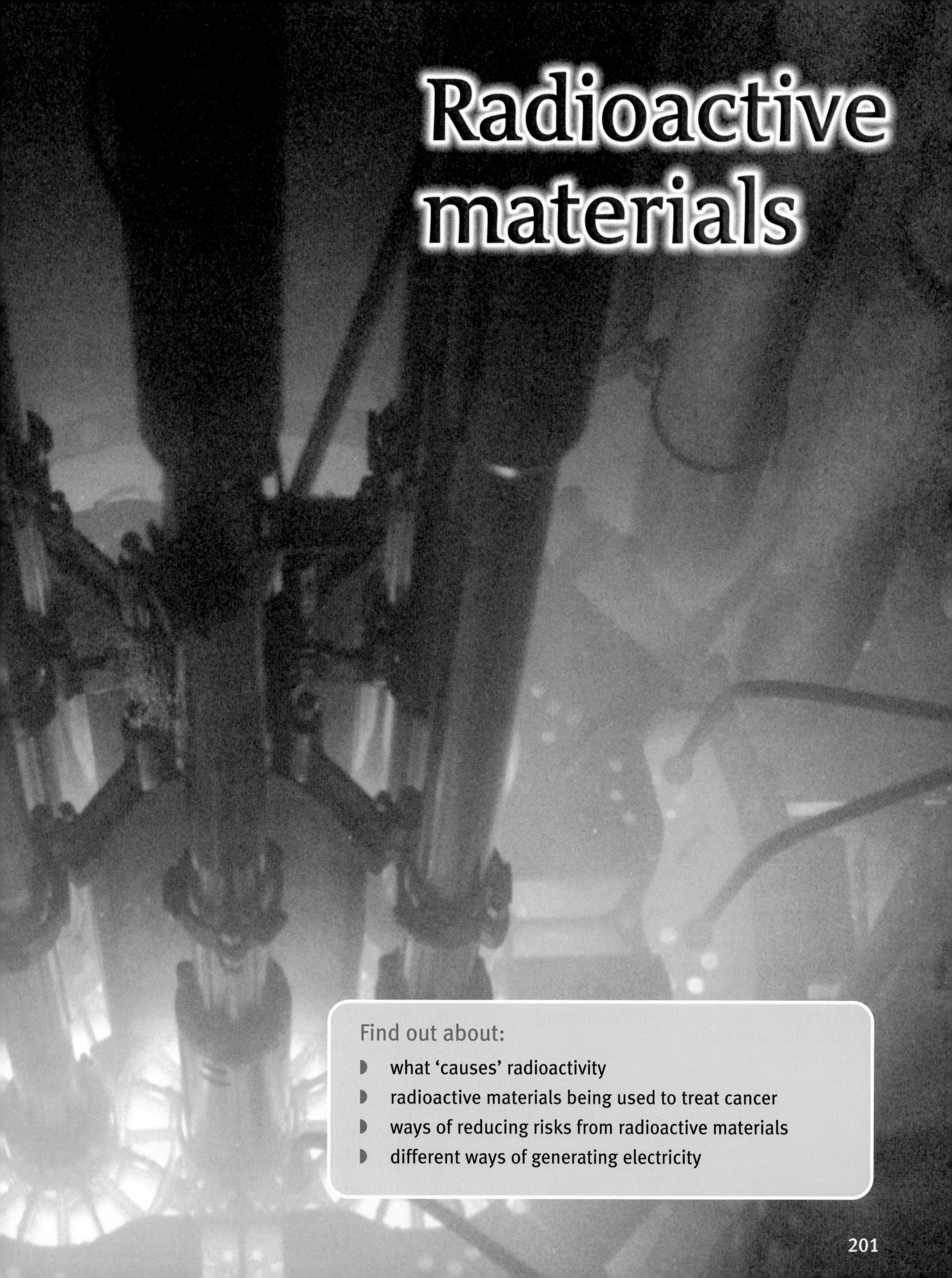

Radioactive materials

Find out about:

- what 'causes' radioactivity
- radioactive materials being used to treat cancer
- ways of reducing risks from radioactive materials
- different ways of generating electricity

High voltage cables carry electricity from power stations to the National Grid.

A Energy patterns

Energy consumer

Every day you use energy sources. You blow dry your hair, listen to some music, or use a computer. In winter the heating goes on. The heating system may use natural gas; the other three rely on electricity. Natural gas is a **primary energy source**. Electricity is called a **secondary energy source** because it is generated from primary sources.

Easy electricity

Electricity is convenient and clean. You just flick a switch. There are no flames and no fumes in your home. But there are flames and fumes hundreds of miles away – in a power station.

About a hundred power stations in the UK supply electricity to consumers through a network called the National Grid.

Electricity demand changes

Boiling a kettle makes a demand on the National Grid. A typical kettle demands a power of 1 kW. Every other mains electrical device makes a demand too, whenever it is switched on.

The total demand varies through the day and over the year. It rises to a peak at teatime on a winter's day. When demand rises, more power stations are brought 'on stream'.

The peak demand is 60 gigawatts (GW). This is equivalent to each of the 60 million people in the UK switching on a kettle, all at the same time.

Meeting demand

Minute by minute, the National Grid must be able to meet demand. Otherwise there will be a power blackout. The knock-on effects can be serious.

One evening in August 2003, south London was without power for just 40 minutes. But 250 000 people were affected. Buildings along the Thames were in darkness. Hundreds of traffic lights failed. Tens of thousands of commuters were stuck in tunnels on London's underground, for several hours.

Is electricity efficient?

Electricity is convenient. But it is also wasteful – especially when used for heating. A gas-fired power station wastes nearly half of the primary energy source. More energy is wasted in the cables and transformers of the National Grid. By contrast, a domestic gas water boiler is about 80% efficient.

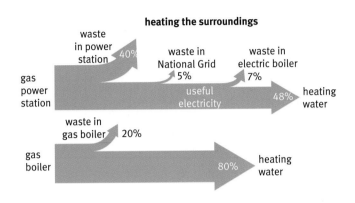

Using a primary source to heat water directly is much more efficient than using electricity.

Is electricity clean?

In 2005, three quarters of the UK's electricity came from fossil fuels, like coal and natural gas. Burning fossil fuels releases carbon dioxide (CO_2) into the atmosphere. This contributes to climate change (see Module P2 *Radiation and life*).

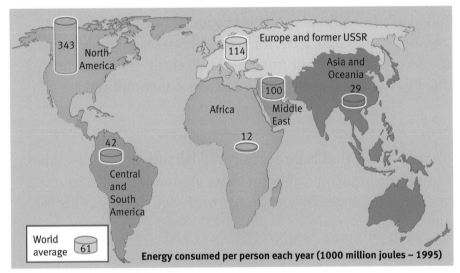

Energy consumed per person each year (1000 million joules – 1995)

As countries become industrialized, living standards rise and energy use increases.

Limiting climate change

The UK must reduce its carbon emissions to limit climate change. Some people think building new nuclear power stations could help. When operating, these power stations produce practically no CO_2. But nuclear power causes problems as well.

Key words

primary energy source
secondary energy source

Questions

1 Write down three things you do during a day that directly use:

 a a primary energy source

 b a secondary energy source

2 Look at the graph of changing electricity demand.

 a i When is the highest demand?
  ii Explain why.

 b When would a blackout be
  i most likely
  ii least likely?

3 Has electricity reduced or increased the pollution in

 a towns

 b the world?

 Explain your answers.

Find out about:
- background radiation
- a radioactive gas called radon
- radiation dose and risk

B Radiation all around

Radiation sources

If you switch on a Geiger counter, you will hear it click. It is picking up **background radiation**, which is all around you. Most background radiation comes from natural sources.

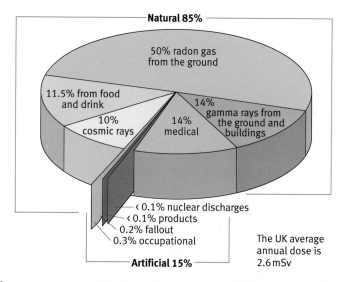

How different sources contribute to the average **radiation dose** in the UK.

Silver mines were contaminated with radon gas. The miners breathed it in and suffered.

Radon

Radon is a hazardous gas. It is produced naturally in rocks. Over 400 years ago, a doctor wrote about the high death rate amongst German silver miners. He thought they were being killed by dust, and called their disease 'consumption'.

Radioactive gas

We now know that radon is harmful because it is **radioactive**. It produces **ionizing radiation** that can damage cells. In some cases, cell damage triggers an uncontrolled growth. This is cancer.

Radiation dose

The risk to miners was high for two reasons:

- Radon can build up in enclosed spaces, such as mines. In the atmosphere, what little radon there is spreads out. In mines, the rocks keep producing it and it cannot escape. So the radon concentration is 30 000 times higher than in the atmosphere.

The miners breathed in the radon.
The miners became ill because the radon gave off its harmful radiation *inside their lungs*. Lung tissue is easily damaged.

Both of these reasons led to the miners getting a large radiation dose.

Measuring dose

Radiation dose is measured in millisieverts (mSv). The UK average dose is 2.6 mSv a year.

▸ For comparison, with a dose of 1000 mSv (400 times larger) three out of a hundred people, on average, develop a cancer.

Radiation from flying

Ionizing radiation from outer space is called cosmic radiation.

▸ Flying to Australia gives you a dose of 0.1 mSv, from cosmic rays. That's not much if you go on holiday, but it soon adds up for flight crews.

Is there a safe dose?

There is no such thing as a safe dose. Just one radon atom might cause a cancer.

This is like a person being knocked down by a bus the first time they cross a road. The chance of it happening is low, but it still exists. The lower the dose, the lower the risk. But the risk is never zero.

Dose summary (1)
Radiation dose is affected by
▸ amount of radiation
▸ type of exposed tissue

It is difficult to be sure about the harm that low doses of radiation can cause. Alice Stewart was a British doctor who studied the health of people working in the American nuclear industry. Her early results suggested that radiation is more harmful to children and to elderly people. She was attacked for her ideas, and the employers prevented any further access to medical records.

Questions

1 **a** In what units is radiation dose measured?

b What is the average annual radiation dose in the UK?

c What two factors increased the dose for a silver miner?

2 Imagine you are so small that you can follow a radon atom. Write an account of its journey from the rocks into a miner's lungs.

3 On what two factors does radiation dose depend?

Key words
background radiation
radiation dose
radioactive
ionizing radiation

A hazard at home

Radon gas builds up in enclosed spaces. In some parts of the UK, it seeps into houses.

Living with radon

Government Information Leaflet

There is radon all around you. It is radioactive and can be hazardous – especially in high doses.

Radon gives out a type of ionizing radiation called **alpha radiation**. Like all ionizing radiations, alpha radiation can damage cells and might start a cancerous growth.

> Radon is a gas that can build up in enclosed spaces. Some homes are more likely to be contaminated with radon.

What about my home?

You and your family are at risk if you inhale radon-contaminated air. The map shows the areas where there is most contamination.

> If you live in one of these areas, get your house tested for radon gas.

What if the test shows radon?

Radon comes from the rocks underneath some buildings. It seeps into unprotected houses through the floorboards. If your house *is* contaminated, get it protected. An approved builder will put in

- a concrete seal to keep the radon under your floorboards and
- a pump to remove it safely

> The risk is real: put in a seal.

Radon gas can build up inside your home. Sealing the floor and pumping out the gas is an effective cure.

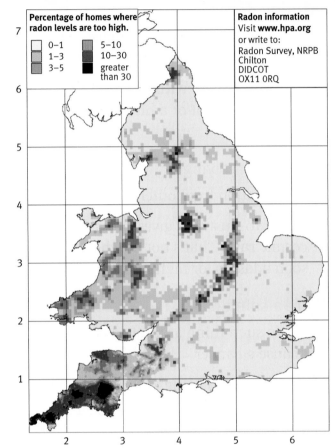

Percentage of homes where radon levels are too high.

0–1	5–10
1–3	10–30
3–5	greater than 30

Radon information
Visit **www.hpa.org**
or write to:
Radon Survey, NRPB
Chilton
DIDCOT
OX11 0RQ

Radon-affected areas in England and Wales. Based on measurements made in over 400 000 homes.

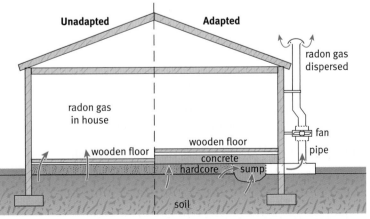

Unadapted   Adapted

radon gas in house

radon gas dispersed

wooden floor

wooden floor

fan

pipe

concrete

hardcore   sump

soil

Irradiation and contamination

Radon in the air exposes you to alpha radiation. Exposure to a radiation source outside your body is called **irradiation**. Radon irradiation presents a very low risk because alpha radiation:

- only travels a few centimetres in air
- is easily absorbed

Your clothes will stop alpha radiation. So will the outer layer of dead cells on your skin.

But if a radiation source enters your body, or gets on your skin or clothes, it is called **contamination**. You become contaminated. If you swallow or breathe in any radioactive material, your vital organs have no protection. They will absorb its radiation. Breathing in radon gas is dangerous.

Cause of death	Average number of deaths per year
cancer caused by radon	2500
cancer among workers caused by asbestos	3000
skin cancer caused by ultraviolet radiation	1500
road deaths	3400
cancer caused by smoking	40 000
CJD	82
House fire	570
All causes	500 000

Estimated deaths per year in the UK population of 60 million (2002)

Radon and risk

On average, radon makes up half the UK annual radiation dose. About 2500 people die each year from its effects (1 in every 20 000 people). Radon is only one hazard. There are risks with driving to school, sunbathing, swimming, and even eating. Many risky activities have a benefit. You need to decide whether to take the risk.

Alpha radiation
- highly ionizing
- short range in air
- easily absorbed (e.g. by paper, clothes or dead skin cells)

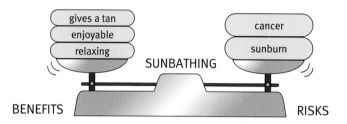

Many people sunbathe. They reckon the benefits outweigh the risks.

Key words
alpha radiation
irradiation
contamination

Questions

4 Explain the difference between irradiation and contamination.

5 a How big a dose of radiation do you get by taking a flight to Australia?

   b Where do cosmic rays come from?

   c Is this irradiation or contamination?

6 Look at the table of deaths on the left.

   a Are you more likely to die from a car crash or from radon?

   b Which causes more cancer deaths, radon or asbestos?

⑦ There is a risk from radon gas building up in houses. Which of these are good ways to reduce the risk?
- stop breathing
- move house
- wear a special gas mask
- adapt the house

⑧ Choose three causes of death from the table.

Write down two ways of reducing the risk from each chosen cause (e.g. walk to school).

C Radiation and health

Radioactive materials can cause cancer. But they can also be used to diagnose and cure many health problems.

Medical imaging

Jo has been feeling unusually tired for some time. Her doctors decide to investigate whether an infection may have damaged her kidneys when she was younger.

They plan to give her an injection of DMSA. This is a chemical that is taken up by normal kidney cells. Before doing this, they need to be sure that she is not pregnant.

The DMSA has been labelled as radioactive. This means its molecules contain an atom of technetium-99m (Tc-99m), which is radioactive.

The Tc-99m gives out its **gamma radiation** from within the kidneys. Gamma is very penetrating. So nearly all of it escapes from Jo's body and is picked up by a special gamma camera.

Jo's scan shows that she has only a small area of damage. The doctors will take no further action.

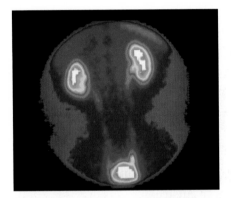

This gamma scan shows correctly functioning kidneys – the top two white areas.

Glowing in the dark

Jo was temporarily contaminated by the radioactive technetium. For the next few hours, until her body got rid of the technetium, she was told to:

▶ flush the toilet a few times after using it
▶ wash her hands thoroughly
▶ avoid close physical contact with friends and family

Is it worth it?

There was a small chance that some gamma radiation would damage Jo's healthy cells. Before the treatment, her mum had to sign a consent form.

Jo's mum said 'We felt the risk was very small. And it was worth it to find out what was wrong. Even with ordinary medicines, there can be risks. You have to weigh these things up. Nothing is completely safe.'

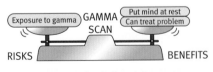

Jo's mum weighed the risk against the benefit and felt the investigation was worth it.

Treatment for thyroid cancer

Alf has thyroid cancer. First he will have surgery, to remove the tumour. Then he must have **radiotherapy**, to kill any cancer cells that may remain.

A hospital leaflet describes what will happen.

Radioiodine treatment

You will have to come in to hospital for a few days. You will stay in a single room.

You will be given a capsule to swallow, which contains iodine-131. This form of iodine is radioactive. You cannot eat or drink anything else for a couple of hours.

- The radioiodine is absorbed in your body.

- Radioiodine naturally collects in your thyroid, because this gland uses iodine to make its hormone.

- The radioiodine gives out **beta radiation**, which is absorbed in the thyroid.

- Any remaining cancer cells should be killed by the radiation.

You will have to stay in your room and take some precautions for the safety of visitors and staff. You will remain in hospital for a few days, until the amount of radioactivity in your body has fallen sufficiently.

Many other conditions can be treated with radiation too.

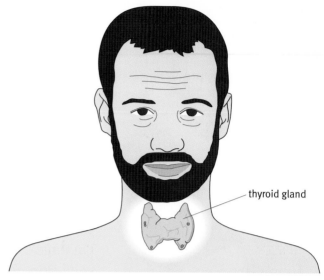

The thyroid gland is located in the front of the neck, below the voice box.

Diagnosis using radioactive materials takes place in the nuclear medicine department of a hospital.

Questions

1 Look at the paragraph headed 'Medical imaging'. Write out the key steps as a flow diagram or bullet points.

2 Look at the precautions that Jo has to take after the scan. Write a few sentences explaining to Jo why she has to do each of them.

3 It would be safe to stand next to Jo but not to kiss her. Use the words 'irradiation' and 'contamination' to explain why.

Key words

gamma radiation
radiotherapy
beta radiation

Hospital radiologists wear badges to monitor their radiation dose.

Regulating radiation dose

Patients exposed to radiation think the benefits are worth the risk. Doctors, nurses, and radiologists are also exposed. And they don't get any benefit. To reduce their radiation dose, medical staff take a number of precautions. They:

- use protective clothing and screens to reduce irradiation
- wear gloves and aprons to reduce risk of contamination
- wear special badges to monitor their dose

What affects radiation dose?

The dose measures the potential harm done by the radiation. On page 205, you saw that it depends on the amount of radiation and the type of tissue that is exposed. It also depends on the type of radiation.

Alpha is the most ionizing of the three radiations. It can cause the most damage to a cell. The same amount of alpha radiation gives a bigger dose than beta or gamma radiation.

Properties of three types of radiation

Radiation	Range in air	Stopped by	Ionizing power
alpha	a few cm	paper/dead skin cells	strong
beta	10 to 15 cm	thin aluminium	weak
gamma	metres	thick lead	very weak

Dose summary (2)

Radiation dose is affected by
- amount of radiation
- type of exposed tissue
- type of radiation

Amount of radiation

Radiation is all around you. At any time, there is a tiny chance that it might collide with something crucial within one of your cells. It's a bit like a game of dodge ball, with tennis balls bouncing around a court. The more moving tennis balls there are, the higher the risk of being hit.

A gamma scan is similar. Increasing the intensity of gamma radiation increases the dose. Exposure time, too, is important.

The chance of being hit goes up with the number of tennis balls in play.

Sterilization

Ionizing radiations can harm your cells. But they can *kill* bacteria. Gamma radiation is used for sterilizing surgical instruments and some hygiene products, such as tampons. The products are first sealed from the air and then exposed to the radiation. This passes through the sealed packet and kills the bacteria inside.

Gamma rays kill the bacteria on and inside these test tubes.

Food can be treated in the same way. Irradiating food kills bacteria and prevents spoilage. Bacteria can quickly spoil herbs and spices. As of 2005, irradiation is permitted in the UK only for herbs and spices. But the food label must tell you.

Ingredients: Ground Ginger (irradiated).

Ideal to flavour curries, casseroles, traditional breads and desserts.

Keep away from direct sunlight.

Replace cap tightly after use to prevent loss of flavour and aroma.

PRODUCT OF SOUTH AFRICA

Irradiation does not make food radioactive.

Questions

4 Look at these events: X-ray scan, gamma scan, inhaling radon, sunbathing, sterilizing strawberries. Which ones are examples of irradiation and which are contamination?

5 Which type of radiation is

   a most penetrating

   b most ionizing

   c most harmful to tissue?

6 Write down three uses of radioactive materials mentioned in this section. Choose one of these and write the key points on how radiation is used.

7 Look at the paragraph headed 'Regulating radiation dose'. For each of the bullets, describe in detail how the precaution prevents contamination and irradiation.

Find out about:
▶ radioactive decay
▶ what makes an atom radioactive

D Changes inside the atom

Making gold

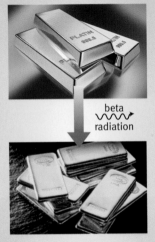

beta radiation

When platinum-197 decays, it turns into a new element – gold. A good way to make money? No. The price of gold is only half the price of platinum.

A cut diamond sitting on a lump of coal. Each of these is made of carbon atoms. Some of the atoms will be radioactive.

Many elements have more than one type of atom. For example, there are carbon-12 and carbon-11 atoms. In most ways they are identical. They can all:

▶ be part of coal, diamond, or graphite
▶ burn to form carbon dioxide
▶ be a part of complex molecules

Radioactive decay

The main difference is that carbon-12 atoms do not change. They are stable.

But carbon-11 atoms are radioactive. Randomly, these atoms give out energetic radiation. Each carbon-11 atom does it only once. And what is left afterwards is not carbon, but a different element – boron. The process is called **radioactive decay**. It is not a chemical change; it is a change *inside* the atom.

Inside the atom

Atoms are small – about a ten millionth of a millimetre across. Their outer layer is made of electrons. Most of their mass is concentrated in a tiny core, called a **nucleus**.

Compared to the whole atom, the tiny nucleus is like a pinhead in a stadium.

The nucleus itself contains two types of particle: **protons** and **neutrons**. All atoms of any element have the same number of protons. For example, carbon atoms always have six protons. But they can have different numbers of neutrons and still be carbon. Carbon-11 and carbon-12 are called isotopes of carbon. The word isotope is used to describe different atoms of the same element.

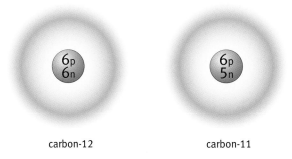

carbon-12   carbon-11

Carbon-11 has 11 particles in its nucleus: 6 protons and 5 neutrons. The nucleus of carbon-12 has 6 protons and 6 neutrons.

What makes an atom radioactive?

Some atoms, with particular combinations of protons and neutrons in the nucleus, are unstable. The atom decays to become more stable. It emits energetic radiation and the nucleus changes. This is why the word 'nuclear' appears in *nuclear reactor*, *nuclear medicine* and *nuclear weapon*.

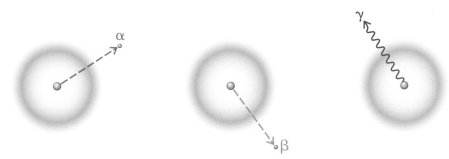

It is the nucleus of an atom that makes it radioactive and emits the radiation.

Medical isotopes

Carbon-11 atoms can be put into molecules of carbon methionine. Doctors use this chemical to produce brain scans.

Radioactive isotopes are quite rare in Nature – because most of them have decayed. But hospitals need a regular supply of several isotopes to use for diagnosis and treatment. These are made in nuclear reactors, and prepared in laboratories around the country.

Key words

radioactive decay
nucleus
protons
neutron

Questions

1 Which of these will test whether something is radioactive?

  A look at it just with your eye
  B burn it
  C put it in acid
  D put it by a Geiger counter;
  E look at it through a microscope

2 Put these in order of size with the biggest first: proton, atom, nucleus, molecule, pinhead.

213

Find out about:
▶ energy from nuclear fission
▶ nuclear power stations

Ⓔ Nuclear power

Nuclear fission

Radioactive atoms have an unstable nucleus. Other nuclei can be made so unstable that they split in two. This process is called **nuclear fission**.

For example, the nucleus of a uranium-235 atom breaks apart when it absorbs a neutron. And the products of nuclear fission all have kinetic energy.

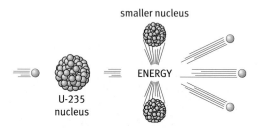

Splitting the nucleus of an atom

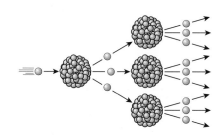

A chain reaction

The fission of one atom can set off several more, because each fission reaction releases a few neutrons. If there are enough U-235 atoms close together, there will be a chain reaction, involving more and more atoms. This can release huge amounts of energy.

Nuclear power stations

In the 1950s, many countries started building nuclear reactors. They hoped that nuclear power would:

▶ produce cheap electricity
▶ reduce the need to import fossil fuels

But the building of nuclear power stations in Europe and North America stopped in 1986.

The devastating power of a nuclear weapon.

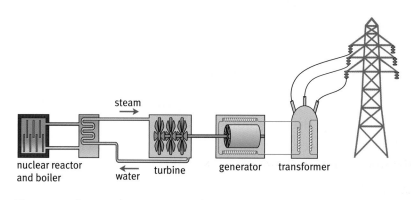

The stages in a nuclear power station.

Controlling the chain

A nuclear reactor is a controlled chain reaction. The fission takes place in fuel rods that contain uranium-235. This makes them extremely hot.

Generating electricity

A fluid, called a coolant, is pumped through the nuclear reactor. The hot fuel rods heat the coolant to around 500 °C. It then flows through a heat exchanger in the boiler, turning water into steam. The steam drives turbines that, in turn, drive generators.

The Chernobyl disaster

Chernobyl is a small town in the Ukraine. It is now deserted: a ghost town. In 1986, its nuclear reactor overheated. This produced too much steam, and the reactor's top blew off – like steam lifting a saucepan lid. Winds carried radioactive dust as far as Wales, where some fields are still contaminated.

Fortunately, major accidents at nuclear power stations are rare.

The fuel rods are not radioactive until they are put into a reactor. As fission products build up, the rods become radioactive.

The reactor core is sealed and shielded. Very little radiation gets out.

> **Key words**
> nuclear fission

Questions

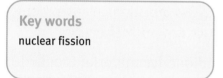
(a)   (b)   →(c)

1 A rumour is a bit like a chain reaction. Alex tells a story to three friends. Each of them tells three friends and so on. How many people have heard the story when it is told:

  a the first time (from Alex)

  b the second time (from three friends)

  c the third time?

2 Explain how the rumour in question **1** is like a chain reaction.

3 Which part of a nuclear power station

  a produces steam

  b produces electricity

  c contains the energy source

  d uses the steam to turn a shaft?

4 Look at the box called 'In the news'. Explain what each bullet point means and why it is important.

Nuclear waste

The National Grid got its first nuclear power station in 1956. For many years, nuclear power stations have produced over 20% of the UK's electricity. Along with medicine, industry and scientific research, they also produce radioactive waste. The waste is called the UK's 'nuclear legacy'.

The waste problem

Radioactive waste has very little effect on the background radiation level. But it is still hazardous. This is because of contamination. Imagine some waste leaks into the water supply. This could be taken up by a carrot, which you eat. The radioactive material is now in your stomach, where it can irradiate your internal organs. This is dangerous – it is like the radon and the silver miners on page 204.

Contamination of the water supply would affect many generations. This is because some radioactive materials last for thousands of years.

The pattern of radioactive decay

The amount of radiation from a radioactive material is called its **activity**. This decreases with time.

▶ At first there are a lot of radioactive atoms.
▶ Each atom gives out radiation as it decays to become more stable.
▶ The activity of the material falls because fewer and fewer radioactive atoms remain.

The graph below shows the pattern of radioactive decay for radon.

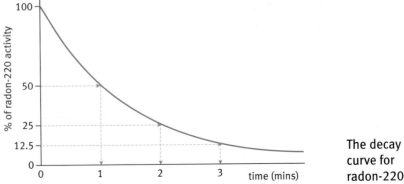

The decay curve for radon-220

Notice that the amount of radiation halves every minute. This is the half-life of radon-220. The **half-life** is the time it takes for the activity to drop by half.

All radioactive materials follow the same pattern of decay. But they can have different half-lives. For example

- iridium-192 has a half-life of 74 days
- strontium-81 has a half-life of 22 minutes

The shorter the half-life, the greater the activity for the same amount of material. Of these three materials, radon-220 is the most active.

Types of waste
The nuclear industry deals with three types of nuclear waste.

- **High Level Waste** (HLW). This is 'spent' fuel rods. HLW gets hot because it is so radioactive. It has to be stored carefully but it doesn't last long. And there isn't very much of it: all the UK's HLW is kept in a pool of water at Sellafield.
- **Intermediate Level Waste** (ILW). This is less radioactive than HLW. But the amount of ILW is increasing, as HLW decays to become ILW.
- **Low Level Waste** (LLW). Protective clothing and medical equipment can be slightly radioactive. It is packed in drums and dumped in a landfill site that has been lined to prevent leaks.

High level radioactive waste is hot, so it is stored underwater.

The control room at a nuclear waste storage plant enables people to monitor the waste continuously.

Questions

1 What does the term 'nuclear legacy' refer to?

2 Iodine-132 is used to investigate problems with the thyroid gland, which absorbs iodine. It is a gamma emitter.

 a Explain why it is useful that iodine-132 gives out gamma radiation.

 b Iodine-132 has a half-life of 13 hours. Why would it be a problem if the half-life was:

  i a lot shorter
  ii a lot longer?

Key words

activity	Intermediate Level Waste
half-life	Low Level Waste
High Level Waste	

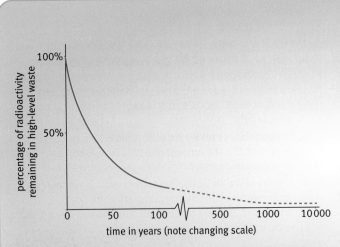

High Level Waste decays quickly at first. When its activity falls, it becomes Intermediate Level Waste. ILW stays radioactive for thousands of years.

Dealing with ILW

Intermediate Level Waste presents the biggest problem, because it is very long-lived. Currently, it is chopped up, mixed with concrete, and stored in large stainless-steel containers. This is secure but not permanent. The long-term solution has to be secure *and* permanent.

Years ago the UK dumped nuclear waste at sea, to be dispersed. Later, people suggested burying it in Arctic ice, or firing it into Space. But these options are too risky.

Current possibilities include

▶ keeping it on the surface, in storage containers
▶ burying it deep in rock

Decisions, decisions

In 2004, the government set up the Nuclear Decommissioning Authority to deal with the legacy of existing waste. It will spend £1 000 million every year, or about £50 000 million in total.

But before it can start work, the government needs to find a method of disposing of nuclear waste that is acceptable to the public.

Questions

3 Choose one of the views expressed by the people on the right. Write a letter to that person trying to change their view.

4 a Imagine you *have* to choose one method of disposal for ILW. Which would you choose? Explain why.

b Explain why you *do* have to choose.

Energy futures

Find out about:
▶ different ways of generating electricity
▶ their benefits and risks
▶ how to make your choices known

Who decides?

Electricity is a secondary energy source. Energy companies, operating under government regulation, generate and distribute it.

Energy companies also make decisions on your behalf. When you boil a kettle, the electricity may have come from any type of primary source.

Primary sources of energy

Fossil fuels like coal, oil, and gas are finite (they will run out in the end). Power stations burn them and release waste, including carbon dioxide, into the atmosphere.

Nuclear fuel comes from uranium mines. There are large but finite reserves. It produces solid radioactive waste that has to be handled carefully.

Renewable energy sources like wind, geothermal, and solar power produce very little waste. They are sustainable primary sources, because they should last forever.

Oil and gas are fossil fuels that formed over millions of years. They are extracted from underground reserves through wells like this.

Primary source	Estimated generating cost in 2020 (pence per unit)	CO$_2$ produced (tonnes per 1000 units)	Typical power output (MW)	Other issues
coal	3.0–3.5	40	1000	CO$_2$
gas	2.0–2.5	20	600	CO$_2$
nuclear	3.4–8.3	0.1	1000	radioactive waste long build
wind	1.5–2.5 onshore 2.0–3.0 offshore	0.01	2 (per turbine)	not constant
solar	15–20 ? (70 in 2005)	0	peak 1 kW per m^2	small scale only

Different ways of generating electricity

Generating electricity

Fossil and nuclear fuels are used to boil water and make steam. The high-pressure steam passes through a steam turbine.

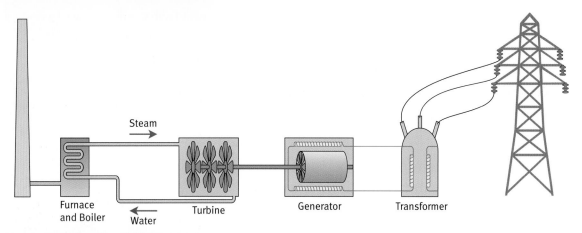

How a power station works

This turbine has lots of small blades that drive it round.

Regular maintainance keeps the generators running smoothly.

Power stations burning natural gas have an extra turbine that harnesses the flow of hot exhaust gases. This makes them the most efficient type of power station.

Reducing CO_2 emissions

Using more-efficient gas-fired power stations is one way of reducing the amount of CO_2 produced. Others include:

◗ using nuclear power
◗ using renewable energy sources
◗ reducing total electricity consumption

None of these is the perfect answer. Each one presents challenges.

And you have to assess the whole life of the power station to get the full story. At the end of their lifetime, power stations must be dismantled. This is called **decommissioning**.

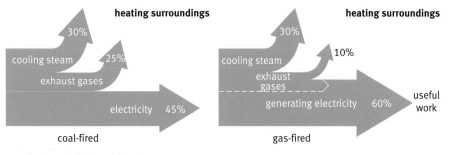

The Sankey diagrams show where the energy goes. Less is wasted in a gas-fired power station.

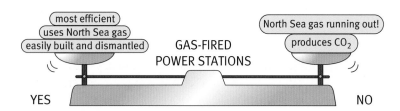

Build gas-fired power stations?

Nuclear challenges

Nuclear power stations release no carbon dioxide. But building them uses materials and energy and releases some CO_2. Decommissioning them also releases CO_2. And they produce radioactive waste.

Can renewables make a real difference?

A life cycle assessment shows that power generation from the Sun and winds releases little CO_2. Of course output depends on the weather.

- Less solar power can be generated when it is cloudy.
- Wind power generation stops if the air is still.

But recent studies suggest that renewable energy sources could provide the UK with a reliable supply of electricity. It needs a variety of generator types, at sites all around the country. You may soon see micro-generators on the roofs of many offices and homes.

Use less energy?

Energy consumption rises year by year. In your lifetime, you are likely to use as much energy as all four of your grandparents put together. Every energy saving you can make will help.

Making decisions

Energy companies will continue to use a variety of primary energy sources. You can influence the amount of each type that they use. Make your views heard. One thing is certain: there is no easy answer.

The cost of nuclear power has to take in the whole life of the power station.

Key words

fossil fuels

renewable energy sources

nuclear fuel

decommissioning

Questions

1 Choose one example of a power station that uses a fossil fuel and one example that uses a renewable energy source. For each one, describe its advantages and disadvantages.

2 a What are the two biggest objections to nuclear power?

 b Why do some people now think it is a 'green' source of energy?

 c Draw a set of scales for nuclear power. Put all the arguments in favour on the right and those against on the left.

 d Put ticks against each argument. More ticks show a stronger argument.

 e Which side has more ticks?

3 Write a letter to your Member of Parliament expressing your views about nuclear power. Use your answer to question **2** to make your letter persuasive and show that you have considered the issues.

Year	Percentage of electricity generated				
	gas	coal	renewables	nuclear	other
2002	38	32	3	23	4
2010	56	16	10	16	2
2020	?	?	?20	?8	?

Future power sources. These figures show that many decisions have yet to be made.

Science explanations

This Module is about radioactive materials and how electricity is generated.

You should know:

▶ radioactive materials randomly emit ionizing radiation all the time

▶ three kinds of radiation and their different properties

▶ the difference between contamination and irradiation

▶ what radiation dose measures, and what factors affect it

▶ how ionizing radiation can damage living cells

▶ atoms have an outer shell of electrons and a nucleus, made of protons and neutrons

▶ all atoms of any element have the same number of protons, but they can have different numbers of neutrons

▶ the activity of radioactive sources decreases over time

▶ radioactive elements have a wide range of half-life values

▶ some uses of ionizing radiation from radioactive materials

▶ there are three categories of radioactive waste, each with different methods of disposal

▶ why electricity is called a secondary energy source

▶ what renewable energy sources are used for generating electricity

▶ burning carbon fuels in power stations produces carbon dioxide

▶ what nuclear fission means

▶ how nuclear power stations work and what waste they produce

▶ how to label a block diagram showing the main parts of a power station

▶ how to interpret a Sankey diagram

▶ how to evaluate information about different types of power station

Ideas about science

To make personal and social decisions about health, it can be important to assess the risks and benefits.

For risks and benefits about the use of radioactive materials you should be able to:

▶ explain why nothing is completely safe

▶ suggest ways of reducing some risks

▶ interpret information on the size of risks

▶ suggest why people will accept (or reject) the risk of a certain activity

Where there are health risks associated with radioactive materials, you should be able to:

▶ identify the groups affected, and the main benefits and costs of a course of action for each group

▶ explain and use the idea of sustainable development

▶ show you know that regulations and laws control scientific research and applications

These ideas are illustrated by: radon in homes; medical imaging and treatment; debates about the disposal of nuclear waste; and possible energy futures.

Glossary

23 pairs Human body cells have 23 pairs of chromosomes in the nucleus.

absorb (radiation) Radiation is absorbed when its energy is used up inside a material, for example, blank paper absorbs light.

accuracy How close a measurement is to the true value.

activity The rate at which nuclei in a sample of radioactive material decay and give out alpha, beta, or gamma radiation.

additive (food) A chemical that is added to food, for example, to improve its appearance or to make it keep longer.

adrenaline A hormone which has many effects on the body. For example, increasing heart rate, increasing breathing rate.

allele Different versions of the same gene.

allergy People with an allergy suffer symptoms when they eat some foods which most people find harmless. Symptoms can include itchy skin, shortness of breath or an upset stomach.

alpha radiation The least penetrating type of ionising radiation, produced by the nucleus of an atom in radioactive decay.

amino acid Small molecules made when proteins are digested.

antibiotic Drugs that kill or stop the growth of bacteria and fungi.

antibody Chemicals made by white blood cells to help destroy microorganisms.

antioxidant A chemical added to food to stop it 'going off' in the air.

artery Blood vessel which carries blood away from the heart.

asexual reproduction When an organism has offspring without a mate. The offspring have just one parent.

asteroid A dwarf rocky planet, generally orbiting the Sun between the orbits of Mars and Jupiter.

atom The smallest particle of an element. The atoms of each element are the same but they are different from the atoms of other elements.

background radiation The low-level radiation, mostly from natural sources, that everyone is exposed to all the time, everywhere.

bacteria One type of single-celled microorganism. They do not have a nucleus. Some bacteria may cause disease.

best estimate When you are measuring a quantity, this is the value in which you have most confidence.

beta radiation One of several types of ionising radiation, produced by the nucleus of an atom in radioactive decay. More penetrating than gamma radiation but less penetrating than gamma radiation.

big bang An explosion of a single mass of material. This is an explanation about the start of the Universe.

biodiversity The great variety of living things, both within a species and between different species.

carbon cycle Carbon and carbon compounds are always moving between the Earth, oceans, atmosphere, and living things. This happens because of human and natural processes.

carrier Someone who has the recessive allele for a characteristic or disease but who does not have the characteristic or disease itself.

catalyst Speeds up a chemical reaction without being used up itself.

cause When there is evidence that changes in a factor produce an outcome, then the factor causes the outcome. For example, increases in the pollen count cause increases in the number of cases of of hay fever.

cellulose The chemical which makes up most of the fibre in food. The human body cannot digest cellulose.

chain Many atoms joined together in a line. Polymers are long-chain molecules.

chemical change/reaction A change that forms a new chemical.

chemical synthesis Making a new chemical.

chromosome Threads of genes found in the nucleus of a cell.

climate The average weather in a region over many years.

clinical trial When a new drug is tested on humans to find out whether it is safe and whether it works.

clone Organisms genetically identical to another.

combustion When a chemical reacts rapidly with oxygen, releasing energy.

comet A rocky lump, held together by frozen gases and water, that orbits the Sun.

common ancestor A species which two or more other species both evolved from.

competition Living things need some of the same resources, for example, food, water, light, or shelter.

compression A material is in compression when forces are trying to push it together and make it smaller.

concentration The amount of a chemical in a particular mass or volume of material. For example, the amount of pollutant in a certain volume of air.

conservation of atoms All the atoms present at the beginning of a chemical reaction are still there at the end. No new atoms are created and no atoms are destroyed during a chemical reaction.

contamination Having a radioactive material inside the body, or having it on the skin or clothes.

continental drift The movement of continents, attached to tectonic plates, at an average rate of just 10 cm each year. It produces significant changes over geological timescales.

core The Earth's core is made mostly from iron, solid at the centre and liquid above.

coronary artery Arteries that supply the heart muscle with blood. This provides oxygen and nutrients for the muscle cells.

correlation A link between two things. For example, if an outcome happens when a factor is present, but not when it is absent. Or if an outcome increases or decreases when a factor increases. For example, when pollen count increases hayfever cases also increase.

cross-link Links between polymer chains.

crude oil A dark, oily liquid found in the Earth, which is a mixture of hydrocarbons.

crust A rocky layer at the surface of the Earth, 10–40 km deep.

cystic fibrosis An inherited disorder. The disorder is caused by recessive alleles.

decommissioning Dismantling and removing a power station at the end of its useful life so that it is safe.

deforestation Cutting down forests and burning the trees, to make more land available for farming.

diabetes An early sign of diabetes is high levels of sugar in a person's blood. In type 1 diabetes the pancreas cannot make the insulin that helps to control sugar levels in blood. In type 2 diabetes the pancreas does not make enough insulin, or body cells do not respond normally to insulin.

digestion Breaking down large food molecules into smaller ones. This is needed so that they can pass into your blood.

dominant Describes an allele that will show up in an organism even if a different allele of the gene is present. You only need to have one copy of a dominant allele to have the feature it produces.

E numbers Every food additive has an E number. E numbers show that the additive has passed safety tests and been approved for use throughout the European Union.

electron A negatively charged particle found in atoms, which orbits the nucleus.

earthquake Event in which rocks break to allow plate movement, causing the ground to shake.

embryo selection A process where an embryo's genes are checked before the embryo is put into the mother's womb. Only healthy embryos are chosen.

emit Give off.

emulsifier Emulsifiers are chemicals which help to mix together two liquids that would normally separate such as an oil and water. In an emulsion one liquid is spread through the other in tiny droplets.

endangered Species which are at risk of becoming extinct.

environment Everything that surrounds you. This is factors like the air, the Earth, water, as well as other living things.

environmental Things in your environment that affect the way you develop.

erosion The movement of solids at the Earth's surface (e.g. soil, mud, rock) caused by wind, water, ice, and gravity.

ethics A set of principles which may show how to behave in a situation.

evolution The gradual changing of populations over time.

exoplanet The planet of any star other than the Sun.

extinct A species is extinct when all the members of the species have died out.

false negative A wrong test result. The test result says that a person does not have a medical condition when he or she does.

false positive A wrong test result. The test result says that a person has a medical condition when he or she does not.

fertile Soil that is fertile contains all the chemicals plants need to grow.

fertilizer A chemical or mixture of chemicals that is mixed with the soil to help plants grow better.

financial incentive Money which is received by (or not taken away from) a person or organization to encourage them to behave in a certain way. For example, higher car tax duty on large cars is aimed at encouraging people to buy small cars that use less petrol.

flexible A flexible material that bends easily without breaking.

food additive A chemical that is added to food, for example, to improve its appearance or to make it keep longer.

food chain In the food industry this covers all the stages from where food grows, through harvesting, processing, preservation and cooking to being eaten.

food labelling Food labelling on packages gives people information to help them decide what to buy. Labels list the ingredients. They may give a summary of the nutritional value of the food. Sometimes they include advice about allergies.

Food Standards Agency The Food Standards Agency is an independent food safety watchdog set up by an Act of Parliament to protect the public's health and consumer interests in relation to food.

food web A series of linked food chains showing the feeding relationships in a habitat - 'what eats what'.

fossil The stony remains of an animal or plant that lived millions of years ago.

fossil fuel Natural gas, oil, or coal.

fungi A group of living things, including some microorganisms, that cannot make their own food.

galaxy A collection of thousands of millions of stars held together by gravity.

gamma radiation The most penetrating type of ionizing radiation, produced by the nucleus of an atom in radioactive decay.

gene The material in the nuclei of cells which controls what an organism is like.

gene therapy Replacing faulty alleles with normal alleles. The aim is to cure genetic disorders.

genetic Factors that are affected by an organism's genes.

greenhouse effect The atmosphere absorbs infrared radiation from the Earth's surface and radiates some of it back to the surface, making it warmer than it would otherwise be.

greenhouse gas Gases that contribute to the greenhouse effect. Includes carbon dioxide, methane and water vapour.

habitat The place where an organism lives.

half-life The time taken for the amount of a radioactive element in a sample to fall to half its original value.

hard A hard material is difficult to dent or scratch.

harvest Farmers harvest their ripe crops. What they gather in is their harvest.

heart attack The coronary arteries become blocked and the supply of blood to the heart muscle is interrupted, damaging the heart muscle.

high level waste A category of nuclear waste that is highly radioactive and hot. Produced in nuclear reactors and nuclear weapons processing.

hominid Animals more like humans than apes that lived in Africa millions of years ago.

hormone A chemical messenger secreted by specialized cells in animals and plants. Hormones bring about changes in cells or tissues in different parts of the animal or plant.

human trial Another name for clinical trials.

Huntington's disorder An inherited disease of the nervous system. The symptoms do not show up until middle age.

hydrocarbon A chemical made of carbon and hydrogen only.

immune Able to react to an infection quickly, stopping the microorganisms before they can make you ill, usually because you've been exposed to them before.

immune system A group of organs and tissues in the body that fight infections.

incinerator A factory for burning rubbish and generating electricity.

indirectly When something humans do affects another species, but this wasn't the reason for the action. For example, a species habitat is destroyed when land is cleared for farming.

infectious A disease which can be caught. The microorganism which casues it is passed from one person to another through the air, through water, or by touch.

infertile Cannot produce offspring.

inherited A feature that is passed from parents to offspring by their genes.

insulin A hormone produced by the pancreas. It is a chemical which helps to control the level of sugar (glucose) in the blood.

intensity The intensity of radiation is a measure of the energy arriving at a unit of surface each second.

intensive Modern farming methods that try to grow the maximum crop or maximum numbers of animals per area of land.

intermediate level waste A category of nuclear waste that is generally short-lived but requires some shielding to protect living organisms. For example, contaminated materials that result from decommissioning a nuclear reactor.

ion A bit of a molecule, broken off by ionizing radiation.

ionization The process in which radiation with sufficient energy breaks a bit off of a molecule. This can damage living cells.

ionizing radiation Radiation that is high in energy and can damage living cells. Includes parts of the electromagnetic spectrum (ultraviolet radiation, X-rays, and gamma rays), also radiation produced by radioactive materials (alpha and beta radiation).

irradiation Being exposed to radiation from an external source.

kidney Organs that remove waste chemicals from the blood and excrete them in the urine.

landfill Dumping rubbish in holes in the ground.

life cycle assessment A way of analysing the production, use, and disposal of a material or product to add up the total energy and water used and the effects on the environment.

life cycle (star) All stars have a beginning and an end. Physical processes in a star and its appearance change throughout its life.

lifestyle (diseases) Diseases which are not caused by microorganisms. They are triggered by other factors. For example, smoking diet, lack of exercise.

light pollution Light created by humans, for example, street lighting, that prevents city dwellers from seeing more than a few bright stars. It also causes problems for astronomers.

light-year The distance travelled by light in a year.

low level waste A category of nuclear waste that contains small amounts of short-lived radioactivity. For example, paper, rags, tools, clothing, and filters from hospitals and industry.

mantle A thick layer of rock beneath the Earth's crust, which extends about halfway down to the Earth's centre.

manure Animal or plant material used to fertilize soil. Farmyard manure is a mixture of dung and straw.

mass extinction Event in the history of the Earth when many species became extinct at the same time.

match Some studies into diseases compare two groups of people. People in each group are chosen to be as similar as possible (matched) so that the results can be fairly compared.

material The polymers, metals, glasses, and ceramics that we use to make all sorts of objects and structures.

mean value A type of average, found by adding up a set of measurements and then dividing by the number of measurements. You can have more confidence in the mean of a set of measurements than in a single measurement.

microorganisms Living organisms that can only be seen by looking at them through a microscope. They include bacteria, viruses, and fungi.

Milky Way The galaxy in which the Sun and its planets, including Earth, are located.

model Scientists use models to help picture what their explanations mean. Chemists model molecules by linking coloured balls to represent atoms.

molecule Some chemicals exist as groups of atoms joined together. For example, oxygen exists as O_2 molecules and water exists as H_2O molecules.

multicellular An organism made up of many cells.

natural A material that occurs naturally but may need processing to make it useful, such as silk, cotton, leather, and asbestos.

natural resource Resources which exist naturally. They are not artificial. Examples are air, water, wood, crude oil and metal ores.

natural selection When some animals or plants are better suited to their environment they are more likely to survive and breed. These animals or plants then pass on their features to the next generation.

nerve cell A cell in the nervous system that transmits electrical signals to allow communication within the body.

neuron Nerve cell.

neutron An uncharged particle found in the nucleus of atoms. The relative mass of a neutron is 1.

non-ionizing radiation Radiation with photons that do not have enough energy to ionize molecules.

nuclear fission The process in which a nucleus of uranium-235 breaks apart, releasing energy, when it absorbs a neutron.

nuclear fuel In a nuclear reactor, each uranium-235 nucleus in a fuel rod undergoes fission and releases energy when hit by a neutron.

nuclear fusion The process in which atoms of hydrogen combine to form helium, releasing energy. This happens in stars, including the Sun.

nucleus The part of a cell containing genetic material.

nucleus (plural nuclei) The tiny central part of an atom (made up of protons and neutrons). Most of the mass of an atom is concentrated in its nucleus.

obesity People are obese if they have put on so much weight that their health is in danger.

oceanic ridge A line of underwater mountains in an ocean, where new seafloor constantly forms.

organic farm A farm which avoids the use of synthetic chemicals. Organic farms use manures and crop rotation to keep soil fertile.

outcome The health effect resulting from some cause.

outlier A measured result that seems very different from other repeat measurements, or from the value you would expect, which you therefore strongly suspect is wrong.

ozone layer A thin layer in the atmosphere, about 30 km up, where oxygen is in the form of ozone molecules. The ozone layer absorbs ultraviolet radiation from sunlight.

pancreas An organ in the body which produces some hormones and digestive enzymes. The hormone insulin is made here.

parallax The apparent shift of an object against a more distant background, as the position of the observer changes. The further away an object is, the less it appears to shift. This can be used to measure how far away an object is, for example, to measure the distance to stars.

penicillin An antibiotic made by one type of fungus.

pest Any living thing that damages crops or animals that are grown for food or other human needs.

pesticide Any chemical used to kill or control pests.

photon A packet of electromagnetic radiation with a particular amount of energy, emitted by a source or absorbed by a detector.

photosynthesis A chemical reaction that happens in green plants using the energy in sunlight. The plant takes in water and carbon dioxide, and uses sunlight to convert them to glucose (a nutrient) and oxygen.

plastic Plastics are polymers. They are solid when cold but can be moulded under pressure when hot. Polythene, PVC, and polystyrene are plastics.

plasticizer A chemical added to a polymer to make it more flexible.

polymer A material made up of very long molecules. The molecules are long chains of smaller molecules.

polymerize The joining of lots of small molecules into a long chain for form a polymer.

predator An animal that kills other animals (its prey) for food.

preservative Chemicals added to food to stop it going bad.

primary energy source A source of energy not derived from other energy source. For example, fossil fuels or uranium.

primary pollutant A harmful chemical that human activity adds directly to the atmosphere.

product (chemical) The new chemicals formed during a chemical reaction.

property/properties Physical or chemical characteristics of a chemical or material. The properties of a chemical, or material, are what make it different from other chemicals.

protein Nutrients that your body needs to make new cells. Protein molecules consist of long chains of amino acids.

proton A positively charged particle found in the nucleus of atoms. The relative mass of a proton is 1.

radiation dose A measure, in millisieverts, of the possible harm done to your body, which takes into account both the amount and type of radiation you have been exposed to.

radioactive Used to describe a material, atom, or element, that produces alpha, beta, or gamma radiation.

radioactive dating Estimating the age of an object such as a rock by measuring its radioactivity. Activity falls with time, in a way that is well understood.

radioactive decay The spontaneous change in an unstable element, giving out alpha, beta, or gamma radiation and changing to a different element that is more stable.

radiotherapy Using radiation to treat a patient.

range The difference between the highest and the lowest of a set of repeat measurements.

ray A line used to represent the path of light, or other radiation.

reactant The chemicals that react together in a chemical reaction.

recessive An allele that will only show up in an organism when a dominant allele of the gene is not present. You must have two copies of a recessive allele to have the feature it produces.

recycling A range of methods for making new materials from materials that have already been used.

reflect Radiation reflects when it bounces off a surface. For example, light is reflected by a mirror.

regulation Rules that can be enforced by an authority such as the government. For example, the law says that all vehicles that are three years or more old must have an annual exhaust emission test is a regulation that helps to reduce atmospheric pollution.

renewable energy sources Resources that can be used to generate electricity without being used up, such as the wind, tides, and sunlight.

resistant Microorganisms that are not killed by antibiotics.

respiration A reaction that happens in the cells of all living things. It converts glucose and oxygen to carbon dioxide and water, and releases energy.

response Action or behaviour that is caused by a stimulus.

risk factor A variable linked to an increased risk of disease. Risk factors are linked to disease but may not be the cause of the disease.

rubber A material that springs back into shape if bent or stretched.

seafloor spreading The process of forming new ocean floor at oceanic ridges.

secondary energy source Energy in a form that can be distributed easily but is manufactured by using an energy resource such as a fossil fuel or wind. Examples of secondary energy sources are electricity, hot water used in heating systems, and steam.

secondary pollutant A harmful chemical formed in a atmosphere by reactions involving other pollutants.

selective breeding Choosing parent organisms with certain characteristics and mating them to try to produce offspring that have these characteristics.

sex cell Cells produced by males and females for reproduction – egg cells and sperm cells. Sex cells carry a copy of the parent's genetic information. They join together at fertilisation.

soft A soft material is easy to dent or scratch.

Solar System The Sun and objects which orbit around it - planets and their moons, comets, and asteroids.

source An object that produces radiation.

specialized Cells that have developed into one particular type. For example, skin cells, nerve cells, root cells.

species A group of organisms that can breed to produce fertile offspring.

stabilizer A food additive which helps to keep ingredients evenly and smoothly mixed.

star life cycle All stars have a beginning and an end. Physical processes in a star and its appearance change throughout its life.

starch A type of carbohydrate found in bread, potatoes, and rice. Plants produce starch to store the energy food they make by photosynthesis. Starch molecules are a long chain of glucose molecules.

stem cell Unspecialized animal cells which can develop into different types of cells.

stiff A stiff material is difficult to bend or stretch.

strong A strong material is hard to pull apart or crush.

sugar A carbohydrate that tastes sweet and is soluble in water. Common sugars are table sugar (sucrose), milk sugar (lactose) and the sugar made by photosynthesis (glucose).

Sun The star nearest Earth. Fusion of hydrogen in the Sun releases energy which makes life on Earth possible.

sustainability/sustainable (development) Using the Earth's resources in a way that can continue in future. Sustainable development meets the needs of today without stopping people meeting their needs in future.

symptom What a person has when they have a particular illness. For example, a rash, high temperature, or sore throat.

synthetic A material made by a chemical process, not naturally occurring.

tectonic plate Giant slabs of rock (about 12, comprising crust and upper mantle) which make up the Earth's outer layer.

tension A material is in tension when forces are trying to stretch it or pull it apart.

toxin A poisonous chemical produced by a microorganism, plant or animal.

transmit Radiation is transmitted when it travels right through something and continues on. For example, light is transmitted by glass.

ultraviolet radiation (UV) Radiation that we cannot see, which blackens film. It is beyond the violet end of the visible spectrum.

Universe All things (including the Earth and everything else in space).

urea A chemical made in the liver when amino acids are broken down. Urea is excreted in the kidneys.

vaccination Introducing to the body a chemical (a vaccine) used to make a person immune to a disease. A vaccine contains weakened or dead microorganisms, or parts of the microorganism, so that the body makes antibodies to the disease without being ill.

vaccine Weakened or dead microorganisms, or parts of a disease microorganism. They cause the body to make antibodies to the disease without being ill.

value The size of a measured property. For example the value of the density of water is 1 g/cm^3.

variation Differences between living organisms. This could be differences between species. There are also differences between members of a population from the same species.

vein Blood vessels which carry blood towards the heart.

virus Microorganisms that can only live and reproduce inside living cells.

volcano A vent in the Earth's surface that erupts magma, gases, and solids.

white blood cell Cells in the blood that fight microorganisms. Some white blood cells digest invading microorganisms. Others produce antibodies.

word equation A summary in words of a chemical reaction.

XX The pair of sex chromosomes found in women's body cells.

XY The pair of sex chromosomes found in men's body cells.

yield The crop yield is the amount of crop that can be grown per area of land.

Index

Publisher's acknowledgements

The publisher would like to thank the following for their kind permission to reproduce copyright material:

P8 ANNABELLA BLUESKY/SCIENCE PHOTO LIBRARY; p10 l Liam Bailey/Photofusion Picture Library/Alamy; p10 r Portrait of sisters hugging/Alamy; p11 DR PAUL ANDREWS, UNIVERSITY OF DUNDEE SCIENCE PHOTO LIBRARY/Science Photo Library; p14 David Crausby/Alamy; p15 b Zooid Pictures; p15 t Dan Sinclair/Zooid Pictures; p17 MAURO FERMARIELLO/Science Photo Library; p18 l DOPAMINE/Science Photo Library; p18r CNRI/Science Photo Library; p19 Oxford University Press; p20 Ian Miles-Flashpoint Pictures/Alamy; p21 b Ariel Skelley/Corbis UK Ltd.; p21 t BSIP, LAURENT/Science Photo Library; p22 b Pascal Goetgheluck/Science Photo Library; p22 c Bsip, Laurent H.Americain/Science Photo Library; p22 t Corbis UK Ltd.; p23 ANDREW PARSONS/PA/Empics; p24 l plainpicture/Alamy; p24 r Mark Clarke/Science Photo Library; p25 l MICHAEL STEPHENS/PA/Empics; p25 r AP Photo; p26 bl Holt Studios International; p26 br Claude Nuridsany & Marie Perennou/Science Photo Library; p26 t David Scharf/Science Photo Library; p27 Ph. Plailly/Eurelios/Science Photo Library; p28 b Dr Yorgos Nikas/Science Photo Library; p28 t Leo Mason/Corbis UK Ltd.; p29 Yoav Levy/PHOTOTAKE Inc/Alamy; P32 JOE PASIEKA/SCIENCE PHOTO LIBRARY; p34 ESA/ PLI/Corbis UK Ltd.; p36 l Harvey Pincis/Science Photo Library; p36 r John Wilkinson/Ecoscene/Corbis UK Ltd.; p38 NETCEN; p42 tl Tek Image/Science Photo Library; p42 tr Raoux John/Orlando Sentinel/Sygma/Corbis UK Ltd.; p44 Nick Hawkes; Ecoscene/Corbis UK Ltd.; p45 Charles D. Winters/Science Photo Library; p48 bl Burkard Manufacturing Co. Limited; p48 br Wellcome Trust; p48 t Dr Jeremy Burgess/Science Photo Library; p49 Sipa Press (SIPA)/Rex Features; p50 Caroline Penn/Corbis UK Ltd.; p51 l Martin Bond/Science Photo Library; p51r Jim Winkley/Corbis UK Ltd.; p52 b NASA/Zooid Pictures; p52 t Hulton-Deutsch Collection/Corbis UK Ltd.; p53 David Townend/Photofusion Picture Library/Alamy; P56 NASA/SCIENCE PHOTO LIBRARY; p60c Enzo & Paolo Ragazzini/Corbis UK Ltd.; p60 l Jack Sullivan/Alamy; p60 r Sinclair Stammers/Science Photo Library; p62 b Bettmann//Corbis UK Ltd.; p62 t Theowulf Mähl/Photolibrary.com; p64 Dr Ken MacDonald/Science Photo Library; p68l Eckhard Slawik/Science Photo Library; p68r Charles O'Rear/Corbis UK Ltd.; p69 b David Brodie; p69 t Pierre Thomas/Laboratoire de Sciences de la Terre - ENS de Lyon; p71 Mike Widdowson; p72l N.A.Sharp, NOAO/AURA/NSF/National Optical Astronomy Observatories; p72 r N.A.Sharp/NSO/Kitt Peak FTS/AURA/NSF/National Optical Astronomy Observatories; p73 b David Malin/Anglo-Australia Observatory; p73 t NASA/Zooid Pictures; p74 Jerry Lodriguss/Science Photo Library; p75 b NACO/VLT/ESO/European Southern Observatory HQ; p75 t Zooid Pictures; p76 b Data courtesy Marc Imhoff of NASA GSFC and Christopher Elvidge of NOAA NGDC. Image by Craig Mayhew and Robert Simmon, NASA GSFC./NASA; p76 t Two Micron All Sky Survey (2MASS); p77 b Science Photo Library; p77 t NASA/Zooid Pictures; P80 G. BRAD LEWIS/SCIENCE PHOTO LIBRARY; p82 b Guzelian Photographers; p82 t Science Photo Library; p83 Sipa Press/Rex Features; p84 Guzelian Photographers; p85 David Scharf/Science Photo Library; p86 Guzelian Photographers; p88 Jose Luis Pelaez, Inc./Corbis UK Ltd.; p89 Guzelian Photographers; p90 Jose Luis Pelaez, Inc./Corbis UK Ltd.; p90 b Neal and Molly Jansen/Alamy ; p90 t John Dee/Rex Features ; p91 Detail Parenting/Alamy; p92 b W. Eugene Smith/Time Life Pictures/Getty Images; Robert Pickett/Corbis UK Ltd.; Paul A. Souders/Corbis UK Ltd.; p94 b Simon Fraser/MRC Unit, Newcastle General Hospital/Science Photo Library; p94 c Dr P. Marazzi/Science Photo Library; p94 t Erich Schrempp//Science Photo Library; p95 b Humphrey Evans/Cordaiy Photo Library Ltd./Corbis UK Ltd.; p95 t Ed Kashi/Corbis UK Ltd.; p96 b Science Photo Library; p96 t Guzelian Photographers; p97 Biophoto Associates/Science Photo Library; p98 c Bettmann/Corbis UK Ltd.; p98 l MATT MEADOWS, PETER ARNOLD INC./Science Photo Library; p98 r Sipa Press/Rex Features; p100 Janine Wiedel Photolibrary/Alamy; p104 OUP/ Digital Vision; p106 Oxford University Press; p107 b Neil Rabinowitz/Corbis UK Ltd.; p107 t David Muscroft/Superstock Ltd.; p108 bl Taryn Cass/Zooid Pictures; p108 br FORESTIER YVES SYGMA/Corbis UK Ltd.; p108 tc David Constantine/Science Photo Library; p108 tl PhotoCuisine/Corbis UK Ltd.; p108 tr Empics; p109 bc Alexis Rosenfeld/Science Photo Library; p109 bl K.M. Westermann/Corbis UK Ltd.; p109 br Bernardo Bucci/Corbis UK Ltd.; p109 tc Dennis Gilbert/VIEW Pictures Ltd/Alamy; p109 tl David Keith Jones/Images of Africa Photobank/Alamy; p109 tr Tom Tracy Photography/Alamy; p110 b Instron® Corporation; p110 t Janine Wiedel Photolibrary/Alamy; p111 b J & P Coats Ltd; p111 t John Cleare Mountain Camera; p112 l Steve Prezant/Corbis UK Ltd.; p112 cl Andrew Syred/Science Photo Library; p112 cr Eye Of Science/Science Photo Library; p114 b Weston Haynes/Keystone/Hulton Archive/Getty Images; p114 t Bettmann/Corbis UK Ltd.; p115 Bettmann/Corbis UK Ltd.; p116 b Taryn Cass/Zooid Pictures; p116 t Dan Sinclair/Zooid Pictures; p119 l Zooid Pictures; p119 r ABACA/Empics; p120 b Corbis UK Ltd.; p120 t James L. Amos/Corbis UK Ltd.; p122 Elizabeth Whiting & Associates/Corbis UK Ltd.; p123 b David Hoffman Photo Library/Alamy; p123 t Ken Hawkins/Focus Group, LLC/Alamy; p124 l Pictor International/ImageState/Alamy; p124 r Geoff Tompkinson/Science Photo Library; p125 Peter Ryan/Science Photo Library; P128 TONY MCCONNELL/SCIENCE PHOTO LIBRARY; p130 TREVOR WORDEN/ Photolibrary.com; p131 l Gildo Nicolo Spadoni/Images.Com/ Photolibrary.com; p131 r Stephanie Sinclair/Corbis UK Ltd.; p132 b Pictor International/ImageState/Alamy; p132 t Ralph A. Clevenger/Corbis UK Ltd.; p133 l Solent News and Photos/Rex Features; p133 r NASA/Science Photo Library; p134 Gideon Mendel/Corbis UK Ltd.; p135 David Wrench/Leslie Garland Picture Library/Alamy; p136 b CNRI/Science Photo Library; p136 bc Philipp Mohr/Alamy; p136 t Simon Belcher/Alamy; p136 tc David Turnley/Corbis UK Ltd.; p137 Mike Hill/Alamy; p139 John Nordell/Index Stock Imagery/Photolibrary.com; p140 Janine Wiedel/Janine Wiedel Photolibrary/Alamy; p141 Martyn F. Chillmaid; p142 t Image Source/Alamy; p143 University of Oxford- Division of Public Health and Primary Health Care; p147 bl KJ Pictures/The Flight Collection/Alamy; p147 br Martin Bond/Photofusion Picture Library/Alamy; p147 tl Yves Forestier/Sygma/Corbis UK Ltd.; p147 tr Oxford University Press; p148 Patrick Ward/Corbis UK Ltd.; p149 David Marsden/Rex Features; P152 B. G THOMSON/SCIENCE PHOTO LIBRARY; p154 l Michael Prince/Corbis UK Ltd.; p154 r Wayne Bennett/Corbis UK Ltd.; p155 b Ray Tang/Rex Features; p155 tc /Corbis UK Ltd.; p155 tl Kit Houghton/Corbis UK Ltd.; p155 tr Will & Deni McIntyre/Corbis UK Ltd.; p157 b Jeff Lepore/Science Photo Library; p157 c Tom Brakefield/Corbis UK Ltd.; p157 t Oxford University Press; p158 b VVG/Science Photo Library; p158 t Holt Studios International; p162 Mary Evans Picture Library; p163 British Association for the Advancement of Science; p164 Digital Art/Corbis UK Ltd.; p165 b Jeffrey L. Rotman/Corbis UK Ltd.; p165 c Robert Lee/Science Photo Library; p165 t Geoscience Features Picture Library; p166 Arend/Smith/Robert Harding Picture Library; p167 l Bsip, Chassenet/Science Photo Library; p167 r Bsip, Chassenet/Science Photo Library; p168 Daniel Cox /Photolibrary.com; p169 Christian Jegou/Publiphoto Diffusion/Science Photo Library; p170 c Niall Benvie/Corbis UK Ltd.; p170 l W. Perry Conway/Corbis UK Ltd.; p170 r Alex Bartel/Science Photo Library; p172 Tim Davis/Science Photo Library; p173 Julia Hancock/Science Photo Library; p178 r Richard Morrell/Corbis UK Ltd.; p178 bl Jason Ingram/Alamy; p178 tl John James/Alamy; p179 b gkphotography/Alamy; p179 tl Gideon Mendel/Corbis UK Ltd.; p179 tr Corbis UK Ltd.; p180 Peter Dean/Agripicture Images/Alamy; p181 l Nigel Cattlin/Holt Studios International Ltd/Alamy; p181 r Peter Dean/Agripicture Images/Alamy; p182 b Nigel Cattlin/Holt Studios International Ltd/Alamy; p182 t Ed Bock/Corbis UK Ltd.; p183 geogphotos/Alamy; p184 b Nic Hamilton/Alamy; p184 c John Garrett/Corbis UK Ltd.; p184 t Paul Glendell/Alamy; p185 Soil Association; p186 b foodfolio/Alamy; p186 t Zooid Pictures; p187 b Zooid Pictures; p187 t Adrienne Hart-Davis/Science Photo Library; p190 bl Nigel Cattlin/Holt Studios International Ltd/Alamy; p190 br Taryn Cass/Zooid Pictures; p190 tl F. Waliyar/International Crops Research Institute for the Semi-Arid Tropics; p190 tr George McCarthy/INTERFOTO Pressebildagentur/Alamy; p191 Lavendelfoto/imagebroker/Alamy; p192 Niehoff/imagebroker/Alamy; p193 Mark Harmel/Alamy; p194 Richard Eaton/Photofusion Picture Library/Alamy; p196 Vincent Kessler/Reuters/Corbis UK Ltd.; p202 Derek Croucher/Corbis UK Ltd.; P204 VICTOR HABBICK VISIONS/SCIENCE PHOTO LIBRARY; p205 Julia Hedgecoe; p208 Photolibrary.com; p209 Prof. Richard Lawson/Central Manchester and Manchester Children's University Hospitals NHS Trust; p210 Mike Derer/AP Photo; p211 l Geoff Tompkinson/Science Photo Library; p211 r Tracy Pompe; p212r Davies & Starr/The Image Bank/Getty Images; p212 bl PETER THORNE, JOHNSON MATTHEY/Science Photo Library; p212 tl Matthias Kulka/Corbis UK Ltd.; p214 US Department Of Energy/Science Photo Library; p215 b Jerry Mason/Science Photo Library; p215 t Keith Beardmore/The Point/British Nuclear Fuels Limited; p217 l STEVE ALLEN/Science Photo Library; p217r Keith Beardmore/The Point/British Nuclear Fuels Limited; p219 Richard Folwell/Science Photo Library; p220 l Peter Bowater/Alamy; p220 r Peter Bowater/Science Photo Library; p221 British Nuclear Fuels Limited

Illustrations by IFA Design, Plymouth, UK and Clive Goodyer

OXFORD
UNIVERSITY PRESS

Great Clarendon Street, Oxford OX2 6DP

Oxford University Press is a department of the University of Oxford.
It furthers the University's objective of excellence in research, scholarship,
and education by publishing worldwide in

Oxford   New York

Auckland   Cape Town   Dar es Salaam   Hong Kong   Karachi
Kuala Lumpur   Madrid   Melbourne   Mexico City   Nairobi
New Delhi   Shanghai   Taipei   Toronto

With offices in

Argentina   Austria   Brazil   Chile   Czech Republic   France   Greece
Guatemala   Hungary   Italy   Japan   Poland   Portugal   Singapore
South Korea   Switzerland   Thailand   Turkey   Ukraine   Vietnam

British Library Cataloguing in Publication Data

Data available

ISBN-13: 978-0-19-915022-9
ISBN-10: 0-19-915022-2

10 9 8 7 6 5 4

Design by IFA Design, Plymouth, UK

Printed in Italy by Rotolito Lombarda

Project Team acknowledgements

These resources have been developed to support teachers and students undertaking the new OCR suite of
GCSE Science Specifications, *Twenty First Century Science*.

Many people from schools, colleges, universities, industry, and the professions have contributed to the production of these resources.
The feedback from over 75 Pilot Centres has been invaluable. It led to significant changes to the course Specifications, and to the
supporting resources for teaching and learning.

We are very grateful to the teachers and students in Pilot Centres for their detailed and constructive recommendations for the
revisions to this course.

The University of York Science Education Group (UYSEG) and Nuffield Curriculum Centre worked in partnership with an OCR team
led by Mary Whitehouse, Elizabeth Herbert, and Emily Clare to create the Specifications, which have their origins in the *Beyond 2000*
report (Millar & Osborne, 1998) and subsequent Key Stage 4 development work undertaken by UYSEG and the Nuffield Curriculum
Centre for QCA. Bryan Milner and Michael Reiss also contributed to this work, which is reported in:
21st Century Science GCSE Pilot Development: Final Report (UYSEG, March 2002).

We would also like to thank Mary Whitehouse and the examining team that developed the Specification for this course.

Sponsors

The development of *Twenty First Century Science*
was made possible by generous support from:

- The Nuffield Foundation
- The Salters' Institute
- The Wellcome Trust